Adirondack Explorations

*Verplanck Colvin*

# Adirondack Explorations

NATURE WRITINGS OF VERPLANCK COLVIN

Compiled and Edited by
PAUL SCHAEFER

With Introductions to Selected Articles by
NORMAN J. VAN VALKENBURGH

Syracuse University Press

First Paperback Edition

00  01  02  03  04  05      6  5  4  3  2  1

Winner of the 1997 John Ben Snow Prize.

This book is published with the assistance of a grant
from the John Ben Snow Foundation.

The paper used in this publication meets the minimum requirements of
American National Standard for Information Sciences—Permanence of Paper
for Printed Library Materials, ANSI Z39.48-1984. ♾™

**Library of Congress Cataloging-in-Publication Data**
Colvin, Verplanck, 1847–1920.
Adirondack explorations : nature writings of Verplanck Colvin /
compiled and edited by Paul Schaefer ; with introductions to
selected articles by Norman J. Van Valkenburgh. — 1st ed.
p.    cm.
ISBN 0-8156-2732-7 (cloth : alk. paper)/ISBN 0-8156-0631-1 (pbk. : alk. paper)
1. Natural history—New York (State)—Adirondack Mountains Region.
2. Surveying—New York (State)—Adirondack Mountains Region.
3. Adirondack Mountains Region (N.Y.)   I. Schaefer, Paul.
II. Title.
QH105.N7C56   1997
508.744′5—dc20      96-43781

*Manufactured in the United States of America*

As a matter of technical geographical interest, the discovery of the true highest pond-source of the Hudson river is, perhaps, more interesting. Far above the chilly waters of Lake Avalanche, at an elevation of 4,293 feet, is *Summit Water*, a minute, unpretending tear of the clouds—as it were—a lonely pool, shivering in the breezes of the mountains, and sending its limpid surplus through Feldspar brook to the Opalescent river, the well-spring of the Hudson.

—VERPLANCK COLVIN
Report on a Topographical Survey
of the Adirondack Wilderness
of New York for 1872

**Paul Schaefer** (1908–96) was a visionary leader of the New York State conservation movement from his early twenties. During his long career, he has served on countless advisory committees for state and private agencies. His numerous awards and honors include the Governor's Award from the New York State Conservation Council (1966), the Conservationist of the Year Award from International Safari (1969), the Governor Mario Cuomo Conservation Award (1985), Chevron USA Conservation Award (1986), the Alexander Calder Conservation Award (1990), and the Governor Mario Cuomo Enviromental Achievement Award (1994). He was involved with the passage of the National Wilderness Act of 1964 and for eleven years was the editor of *The Forest Preserve*. In 1979, Union College recognized his outstanding contributions to conservation by awarding him an honorary doctor of science degree. His first book, *Defending the Wilderness: The Adirondack Writings of Paul Schaefer* (Syracuse University Press, 1989), documents the campaign of more than half a century to preserve the wilderness in the Adirondacks. His *Adirondack Cabin Country* (Syracuse University Press, 1993) is a poignant memoir of his life in the wilderness.

**Norman J. Van Valkenburgh** is a native of the Catskill Mountains. He retired in 1986 from the New York State Department of Environmental Conservation and the former New York State Conservation Department, after a career of thirty-two years. During his tenure he served as Superintendent of the Bureau of Land Acquisition (1973–1976); Director of the department's Region 3, comprising seven counties from the southern Catskills to New York City (1976–1977); and was the State Forester and Director of the Division of Lands and Forests (1977–1986). He is a licensed Land Surveyor in New York and South Carolina and practices as a private consultant.

Van Valkenburgh has authored six books and numerous articles, relating to the history of the Adirondack and Catskill mountains. Some of his books include: *The Adirondack Forest Preserve: A Chronology*, 1979, and *Land Acquisition for New York State: A Historical Perspective*, 1985. He edited Verplanck Colvin's 1898 report after he discovered the original manuscript filed in the archives of the New York State Department of Environmental Conservation. The report was published in 1989 by the Adirondack Research Center of the Association for the Protection of the Adirondacks. Recently, he has turned to writing fictional murder mysteries, including *Murder in the Catskills*, 1992, and *Mayhem in the Catskills*, 1994. He lives in Saugerties, New York.

# Contents

PART FOUR **Albany Institute Lectures**

# Illustrations

# Preface

By the time I was fifteen, I had spent several summers with my family in the east-central Adirondack Mountains. I decided to begin a library about that fascinating country of mountains, rivers, and lakes. My father indicated that there were bookstores in Albany that handled old books and that most likely I could find something over there.

Albany, the capital city of New York, was about twenty miles southwesterly from our home in Schenectady. In those days, a trip of that length by trolley car was usually quite an adventure. I had a considerable walk from our home to the trolley, which took me to downtown Schenectady; there, I transferred to another one that would take me the fifteen miles to Albany.

When the open-sided electric car bound for Albany started to move, it was apparent that the motorman did not want to "spare the horses." He began in a burst of speed that he kept up for most of the trip. There were very few people on the car, and they seemed to relish the ride. When the motorman approached a stop on his route and saw that no one was there to be picked up, he stamped on something on the floor, rang a bell, and increased the speed of the car. At some places, the trolley seemed to weave one way or the other. I hung on for dear life.

Eventually, we reached Albany, and I was glad to find myself on *terra firma* again. I inquired of several pedestrians for directions to bookstores and eventually found myself walking down a narrow street with tall buildings on either side, not far from the capitol. At the foot of the hill, I found a building with a sign on the front: "Scopes' Books." Many books were visible in the store window. After some trepidation, I finally walked in.

Mr. Scopes was standing there, a distinguished-looking old gentleman, bent with age, with white curly hair. When he heard me enter the store, he looked up from what he was doing, peered over the rims of his glasses, and asked, "What can I do for you, son?" I told him that I had come to find books on the Adirondacks, that I wanted to start a library on the region, and I hoped that I could find some old books here that might make a good beginning for such a library.

He looked at me and said, "I think you mean that, don't you, son? You really want to start a library?" "That's right," I said. With that he turned and went to a tall ladder on wheels that was leaning against the bookshelves. He pushed to a specific place; apparently, he had something in mind. He climbed the ladder, reached to the top shelf, and came down with a small thin hardcover book. He handed it to me, and said, "This, son, is the kind of a book you need to start a library. And look, here is the signature of the man who wrote it." The name was Verplanck Colvin.

I was disappointed in the size of the book, but when I opened it and saw a picture of surveyors on a mountain, it looked to me as if it would be a worthwhile beginning. I finally told Mr. Scopes that I wanted it and asked how much would it cost. "Well, that's an expensive one," he said, "But it's worth it. Five dollars."

By no means did I have that much money on me. I told him that I would get the money to him as soon as I could, hoping he would let me take the book. He must have read my thoughts, for he told me I could have the book when I had paid for it in full. To me five dollars was an astounding amount to pay for an old book. He said that he would hold it for me and keep his eye open for other books that might be of interest. These he would have when I came back.

More than a month later, I returned. Waiting for me was the thin volume, *A Report on a Topographical Survey of the Adirondack Wilderness*, and other books that looked interesting and were of considerably more substance.

Not long afterwards, I found another bookstore in Albany, on Spring Street, owned by Harmon Lockrow. Mr. Lockrow also seemed to understand my interest in acquiring more books, and I indicated to him, as I had to Mr. Scopes, that I ultimately wanted to procure a *complete* collection of books—I thought, as many as forty or fifty books—on this wonderful Adirondack country.

I found myself fascinated by this Mr. Colvin, an articulate adventurer, who published essays with accountings of his explorations. As a youth, he had accompanied his father on trips to the nearby Helderbergs to settle property disputes. His father, Andrew Colvin, was a lawyer, deeply involved in defending the tenants in the Rent Wars in the nearby mountains that form the westerly skyline of Albany, arising about fifteen miles from the city. A chain of cliffs near the crest of the range, up to two hundred feet in height, stretches north toward the Adirondacks and south toward the Catskills. Forest heavily covers the talus slope that extends from the base of the cliffs to the level of the relatively open plains a thousand feet below. From any point on the escarpment, it is possible to look out upon this undulating plain nearly fifty miles in diameter, bounded on the north by the Mohawk River and on the east by the sea-level Hudson River and the city of Albany. To reach the Helderbergs in those days, the Colvins traveled by horse and buggy. The long trip across the plains to the mile-long cliffs gave father and son a chance to think about and discuss the origin and uniqueness of the mountain range. There is little doubt that these trips were instrumental in the direction that Colvin's life would take.

His early writings included an illustrated article on those mountains entitled, "The Helderbergs" as well as "Narrative of a Bear Hunt"; "Ascent of Mt. Seward and Its Barometrical Measurement"; an article about an Adirondack mountain; and "The Dome of the Continent," an article on the Rocky Mountains. He completed his early work entirely on his own initiative, as a volunteer who had become enamored by what he saw in these mountain systems. All of these lesser-known works were written before he published *A Report on a Topographical Survey of the Adirondack Wilderness*, which was the first of a long series of documents relating the New York State Land Survey and before he was on the payroll of New York State.

In 1865, four years before "The Helderbergs" appeared in *Harper's New Monthly Magazine*, the eighteen year-old Colvin had explored the upper reaches of the Sacandaga River near Speculator and was talking about the possibility of a park in the Adirondacks. The remote and secluded atmosphere of the whole region undoubtedly attracted him to explore it. By this time destructive lumbering practices were exposing critically important areas of the watershed forest to the incredibly large consuming forest fires that were soon to follow. By 1872 Colvin decided to dedicate his life to the preservation of the Adirondack forest. He was appointed secretary of the New York State Park Commission and became superintendent of the Topographical Survey of the Adirondack Mountains, a job that lasted some twenty-eight years. It was during these years that Verplanck Colvin completed his most important Adirondack writing that appeared in various reports to the New York State Legislature. As the scope of his writing becomes better known, it is crystal clear that no individual in the history of New York State has contributed more to the preservation of the Adirondacks than Verplanck Colvin.

As a youth, I visited the Helderbergs frequently, going sometimes by "shank's mare" and more often by bicycle. The Indian Ladder region, now known as John Boyd Thacher Park, fascinated me with its deep caves, high waterfalls, imposing cliffs, and the exhilaration I found just walking along the escarpment and looking east and north to mountain country that I knew very little about at that time.

One cold winter day while exploring the Helderbergs, I came to a cave known as the Tory Cave. During the Revolutionary War, Tory spies were supposed to have made their headquarters here. From this cave, one could look southeasterly toward Albany, where one of the headquarters of the Revolution existed for some time. The day that I came to that cave, which is high up near the top of the escarpment, I was amazed to find that the weather had caused seepage or dripping from the high limestone ceiling to the floor of the cave. As a result of the constant dripping of water, ice stalagmites had formed, many of them five and six feet in height, with wide variations in diameter from the bottom to the top, sensitively recording the variations in temperature and weather during their formation. At some early time, a large chunk of the escarpment above the cave had fallen so as to block the cave's entrance from winds, which would surely have destroyed the very fragile ice formations. I was excited by my find, photographed what I saw, and mailed the photograph to *Nature Magazine* in Washington. The magazine printed the picture.

Not long after that (1931), I met John S. Apperson, one of the most important conservationists in New York State. He lived in Schenectady and was in the middle of two battles to defeat amendments to the New York State Constitution: the first one would permit the state to reforest and commercially lumber its lands outside the boundaries of the Adirondack and Catskill parks, and the second would permit the building of closed cabins on state lands in the Adirondacks and would threaten the wild forest character of the mountains. While the reforestation amendment passed, it was only after more than 1.5 million acres of land had been added to the Adirondack Park; the closed-cabin amendment was defeated. It was during these battles that I came under Apperson's tutelage and became immersed totally in fighting to keep the Adirondack forests wild. I found that my connection with *Nature Magazine* proved to be a vital factor in the defeat of the closed-cabin amendment because of the number of articles that it published on our behalf. Thus, as it turned out, the Helderbergs, the fascinating mountains that first attracted Colvin's explorations, also encouraged my own interest in mountains and wilderness.

Colvin's *Report on a Topographical Survey of the Adirondack Wilderness* started my own Adirondack library. The library has grown, not to forty or fifty books, but to hundreds of books, letters, documents, maps, and other material so essential for a balanced library on the Adirondacks.

Both Mr. Scopes and Mr. Lockrow, over a long period of years, were extremely helpful to me. I found to my surprise in later years that they had included books that I had not had time to read. Searching for information on the early history of the Adirondacks, I recently found on my bookshelves the volumes of Francis Parkman's *Pioneers of France in the New York: France and England in North America,* which Mr. Scopes obtained for me fifty years ago. The first volume records that Jacques Cartier, the French pioneer, reaching the site of present-day Montreal in 1535, was the first European to see the Adirondack Mountains. Parkman writes that Cartier looked out from a mountaintop across the St. Lawrence and saw "east, west, and south, the mantling forest was over all, and the broad blue ribbon of the great river glistened amid a realm of verdure."

Also in my collection is a map made by the British War Office in London for the invasion armies in North America in 1776, over two centuries after Cartier's time. In the location of the present-day Adirondacks on a large blank area appear the words: "This vast Tract of Land which is the ancient Couchsachrage, one of the four Beaver Hunting Countries of the Six Nations, is not yet Surveyed." Almost another century would pass before Verplanck Colvin set out to fill that void on the old maps.

Central to everything that I was able to acquire on the Adirondacks, from bookstores in Albany and elsewhere, have been the many volumes of Colvin's reports from 1872 to 1898, detailing his explorations of the Adirondacks, the mapping of them, and the political ramifications in which he found himself involved. He was the leading light of the forces that began the struggle in 1865 to save the Adirondacks and finally made significant strides in 1885 with the passage of the "Forever Wild" statute by the New York State Legislature under Governor David B. Hill. Colvin's work and writings played a critical role in the establishment of the Adirondack Park in 1892 and in the passage of the "Forever Wild" constitutional amendment by the 1894 New York State Constitutional Convention that was approved by the people in referendum the same year.

Nineteen ninety-four marked the hundredth anniversary of the passage of that wonderful amendment that gives constitutional protection to millions of acres of wild forest in the Adirondack Park. Looking back over history, there seem to be no comparable activities by other states or nations on this planet Earth that equals the combination of actions by the New York State Legislature and the Constitutional Convention that passed the "Forever Wild" amendment.

Over the years, I have read extensively, many books by many authors. None surpass Colvin's vision and his manner of expression. His earlier writings—unhindered by the technical details required in his later work—show the full-flowering of his ability to describe nature and the world as he saw it. He was able to convey vast amounts of information to many people when there were no conservation organizations or "environmentalists." He was able to create an awareness of the importance of our natural heritage. His writings provided the solid foundation for the "Forever Wild" amendment, which has withstood a hundred years of challenge.

Verplanck Colvin has given me the key that unlocks the richness of the hundreds of books that have been written about the Adirondack country. Through the years, because of his knowledge and activities, the devastated woodlands have changed to marvelous lands healed by nature; great forest and watershed values have recovered; and as time goes on, rivers and lakes will continue to benefit from the original ideas that he proposed that would maintain forever the wild forest character of the Adirondack region.

I have compiled Colvin's writings, the most important and the most beautifully written, in this volume to let you read his words firsthand. With the exception of *Seventh Report on the Survey of the Adirondack Region of New York 1875–1879*, from which I have selected excerpts, the text of each article is in its entirety. I have not included numerous tables and many of Colvin's fine drawings, sketches, maps, and photographs; these are available in the original publications.

PAUL SCHAEFER

Schenectady
Spring 1995

# Acknowledgments

David Greene, my grandson, has spent countless hours helping me select the material to include in this publication and then typing it into the computer. He has spent most of his life in the Adirondacks, either at the old Putnam Farm at the base of Crane Mountain or in North Creek, and has a deep appreciation for Colvin's work. A graduate of Deep Springs College and Cornell University, he has been my eyes and ears during the last couple of years, helping me to organize and catalogue my library. David forwarded the disks to Noel Riedinger-Johnson. Noel prepared the manuscript for publication and worked with the publishers throughout the publishing process.

# A Note on the Text

For the convenience of the reader, capitalization, hyphenation, and punctuation have been made consistent throughout the text.

PART ONE

# Adirondack Surveyor

In 1865 the writer of this paper became desirous of exploring the interior of this vast portion of New York, of which so little could be learned from books and maps. Collecting from the old survey notes all the data that could be made available, he compiled a map of the interior, and traced upon it a route for exploration. Accompanied by a friend, the author entered the wilderness, traversing, by trail or river, with guide and canoe, this strange region of evergreen-clad mountains, where rivers rise from mountain springs, and where deer and panther, bear and wolf roam through the forest solitude. Alas, the old field notes, so carefully collated, were found to be of little service. The guides laughed the old compass maps to scorn.

A score of beauteous lakes were shown to me that were unknown to the old surveyors; the old land-lines passed them by, either on the one side or the other. Where the old Colonial surveyors had incorrectly sketched rivers or lakes on their maps, mountain peaks and rocky ranges loomed upward amid the clouds. A vast semi-Alpine region was revealed, some of whose gray granite peaks rose far above the timber-line into an icy atmosphere.

Astonished, awed, yet delighted at the grandeur and vastness of the region thus spread before me, I resolved to correct the sketch that I had compiled, and prepare a new map of the region, which could not fail to be a valued contribution to the Geography of my native State. Resuming, therefore, in subsequent years the explorations begun in 1865, I searched the wilderness, ascended mountains, traced rivers to their sources, measured with mercurial barometer and hand level the heights of peaks and ridges, and, unaware, at that time, of the singular difficulties caused by magnetic iron and local attraction, endeavored to locate lakes and ponds from mountain tops, by compass bearings.

— VERPLANCK COLVIN
The Adirondack Survey, 1882

# Verplanck Colvin

SUPERINTENDENT OF THE ADIRONDACK SURVEY

*Today, the so-called Legislative Manual serves as the reference for short pro-files of legislators and high-ranking officials in state government, a summary of the organization of the government, and a general description of the var-ious functions and purposes of each department and unit thereof. However, it's all ultra-official and pretty bland stuff when compared to the flowery prose and detailed narratives found in earlier governmental handbooks.*

*The following short biography of Verplanck Colvin is taken from volume 2 of a three-volume set entitled (in the usual all-encompassing and lengthy title particular to the times),* The Public Service of the State of New York During the Administration of Alonzo B. Cornell, Governor, Historical, Descriptive and Biographical Sketches by Various Authors, Illustrated with Views and Portraits, *published in 1882. In the case of this sketch, the "various" author is Colvin himself, so it really is autobiographical. As a bonus, a "portrait" of the subject is included.*

*The writing is characteristically Colvin's. He is not at all reticent about embellishing his own image. On the other hand, he was a remarkable man, capable of moving the mountains of state government and, as stated in the closing words, he was "indomitable . . . in spirit and determination."*

*He mentions two other essays that are included in this book — an 1869* Harper's *article about the Helderbergs and a later article in the same maga-zine about the Rocky Mountains. Sadly, he doesn't mention an earlier com-position; at the age of ten, he wrote and illustrated a book that was never published. The manuscript is lost to history, its subject unknown. Also, he doesn't relate the final chapter to the "private laboratory which he had built near his home." One experiment went awry, and he blew it up.*

— NJVV

Verplanck Colvin was born in the city of Albany, New York, January 4, 1847. His name represents two old families, the one of ancient British, the other of Dutch descent. His paternal great-grandfather, John Colvin, was born in Scotland in 1752, and came to this country twenty years later, settling first at Nine Partners, Dutchess county, where he married Sarah Fuller, of Connecticut, a lineal descendant of the "Mayflower" Fullers. He subsequently removed to Coeymans, Albany county, where he remained upon his farm until his death, having been a Member of Assembly in 1810. Johannes Verplanck, his maternal great-grandfather, was born in Coeymans and was a descendant of the Verplancks from Holland, who settled at Verplancks' Point, on the Hudson river. The father of Johannes Verplanck, by his marriage with Ariantje Verplanck, inherited a great portion of the old Coeymans patent adjoining the Van Rensselaer patent on the south. James Colvin, eldest son of John Colvin and Sarah Fuller Colvin, married Catherine Verplanck, daughter of Johannes and Catherine Huyck Verplanck. The father of Verplanck Colvin is Hon. Andrew J. Colvin, son of James Colvin and Catherine Verplanck Colvin. His mother is Margaret Crane Alling Colvin, a daughter of Prudden Alling, of Newark, New Jersey, and Maria Halsey. The Allings are descendants of the first settlers of that name of New Haven, who settled in Newark, New Jersey, in 1698. The father of Verplanck Colvin, Hon. Andrew J. Colvin, is an eminent practicing lawyer of Albany, who has been City Attorney, District Attorney, and State Senator.

Educated at the Albany Academy and at home, and subsequently by private instructors, Verplanck Colvin, though destined by his father for the law, gave all his leisure time to scientific study, being specially interested in mathematics, geography, chemistry, and natural history. During the war the interest of the boy was excited by the great utility of the war maps prepared by the topographical engineers of the United States army; and in the way of study and practice he made maps and sketches of the topography and scenery of the mountain region around his country residence in Rensselaer county, acquiring health by his tramps across the mountains and artistic skill in map-drafting and sketching of scenery from nature. He continued his study of chemistry in a private laboratory which he had built near his home, even after entering upon the study of the law. The study of

Reprinted from *The Public Service of the State of New York,* 1882, vol. 2.

Geology also greatly interested him and occupied much of his time during leisure hours, and his geological and mineralogical cabinet contains a large collection of most rare specimens of fossils and minerals, collected by himself in the different mountain ranges of the eastern states and in the Rocky Mountains. His legal studies were continued several years in the office of his father and the Hon. Anson Bingham, but his tastes led him in other directions, and he soon acquired celebrity as a writer, his articles, illustrated by his own pencil, and published in *Harper's Magazine*, attracting wide attention. In 1865 he commenced those Adirondack explorations with which his name has since been associated. His account of the Helderberg Mountains first drew public attention to his abilities as an artist and literary man, and his description of the crest of the Snowy Range of the Rocky Mountains—which he named the Dome of the Continent—obtained for him election to honorary membership of the Rocky Mountain Club, of Denver, Colorado. In 1872 he was elected by the Legislature of the State a member of the Commission to which ex-Governor Seymour, ex-Vice-President Wheeler, and others were also appointed, to consider the feasibility of reserving the great forests of Northern New York—the entire Adirondack region—as a State forest preserve. By another act he was placed in charge of the State Survey of this great region, and thus came to make the first triangulation of any portion of the State under legislative authority. He has now been Superintendent of the State Adirondack Survey (covering the whole of this northern district) for ten years, and his reports on the progress of the work of exploration and survey have been eagerly sought and highly valued. His rule prohibiting the use of spirituous liquor of any kind by any of the men in his employ, while engaged upon the work of the Survey, is famous, and has proved, in the face of the most severe exposure—in the wilderness, in storm, in ice, in camps in the deep snows of winter at temperatures below zero—to have been beneficial to the health of the men and essential to the success of the service. He has personally measured and climbed all the highest mountains of the State, hundreds in number; has found in his explorations a great number of lakes unknown to geographers, and was the first to reach and discover Lake "Tear of the Clouds," the highest lake-source of the Hudson river, four thousand three hundred feet above the sea. His explorations and valuable topographical works are known in every portion of the civilized world, even as far as India, whence most complimentary acknowledgments have been sent by the Imperial Government, with a collection of most valuable scientific works presented to Mr. Colvin by direction of the Viceroy.

Mr. Colvin is a member of many scientific societies and associations; is a life member of the American Institute of Mining Engineers; has been for many years one of the Secretaries of the Albany Institute; and has delivered with great success, at Hamilton College, professional lectures on his favorite topics. He is a young man of thirty-five years of age, and unmarried; is nearly six feet in height, muscular, and erect; in manner quiet, but in spirit and determination indomitable.

# The Adirondack Survey

BY VERPLANCK COLVIN, SUPERINTENDENT

*Great Wilderness of New York. — Historical Facts. — Public Domain — Erroneous*
*Colonial Surveys — Origin of the Present Work — New Methods of Survey —*
*Utility of the Work — Topographical Maps — Land-Lines and Monuments*

The Adirondack Survey was first authorized by an 1872 appropriation law,
the text of which left no doubt who was the impelling force behind it. "For
Verplanck Colvin, of Albany, N.Y., ten hundred dollars, to aid in completing
a survey of the Adirondack wilderness of New York, and a map thereof."

The designation of the survey changes from time to time depending on the
wording of the annual funding bills. It was known variously as the "The
Adirondack Survey," "The Adirondack State Land Survey," and "The State
Land Survey." Under whatever name, it continued under Colvin's direction
until April 1900, when another law consigned it to oblivion by declaring "The
office of the Superintendent of the state land survey is hereby abolished."

The fortunes of the survey rose and fell with money to carry on from one
year to the next always in doubt. That $1,000 may have seemed sufficient in
the beginning; however, even Colvin probably missed the significance of the
bill language specifying it was to be used to "aid" in the survey. Indeed,
Colvin made up for almost annual shortfalls from his small inheritance and
provided his own surveying instruments when the state did not. He was
continually vexed over the shortage of funds and often stated (as he does
here), "The appropriations so far granted had been altogether inadequate."

The following article describes the 1881 organization of the survey and is
taken from the same volume of Public Service as the preceding autobiographical sketch. The article is enhanced by Colvin's concise history of the
discovery of the Adirondacks and early surveys of the interior. His description of "new methods of survey" he practiced will be of interest to present-
day surveyors and laymen alike.

7

*Only one person — other than Colvin — lasted the entire span of the survey. Mills Blake was Colvin's boyhood chum and lifelong friend and is listed on the 1881 roster as "assistant in charge Division of Levels." In other writings, Colvin often referred to Blake as "my trusted assistant." He was that; whatever misfortunes Colvin faced, Blake stood by his side throughout.*

*— NJVV*

In the year 1609, two venturous explorers, dreaming of India and the Northwest Passage—first of white men—entered the rivers whose springs are in the heart of the Adirondack Wilderness—the one in his fantastic ship the "Half Moon," the other in the more humble birch canoe of the savage.

Hudson and Champlain—names thus indissolubly linked with the first discovery of the territory of New York—beheld an apparently illimitable wilderness, with broad undulating forests of rich verdure, stretching away to the base of the dark blue mountains or rugged cliffs—all reflected in the gleaming waters that rippled before the keels of their boats.

Then for the first time those shores echoed to words and phrases—English, French and Dutch—which the stern and rigid rocks, unmoved, threw back as freely as they had for centuries the shouts of pagan savages.

But here and there along the shores of the "River of the Mohicans" or the Lac du Iroquois were sunshiny clearings and waving fields of maize, while the smoke from Indian wigwams gave evidence of habitation. Wild fowl flew up from the sedgy marshes at the rattle of the row-locks of the white men's boats; fish chased by fish leaped from the placid surface, and the elk drank under the forest shade at the shore.

The canoes of the wild hunters and fishermen clustered around the boats of the whites, and the eager gesticulations of sign language told Hudson's men that India was not to be reached from here. What then? The stream freshened. The river of the Mohawks poured in milky foam over the rocks of *Ka-hoos.* "What was the region northward still?" the white men asked the Indians. It was the *Cough-sa-gra-ga,* the fearful unexplored wilderness barrier between Algonquin and Iroquois.

Reprinted from *The Public Service of the State of New York,* 1882, vol. 2.

*Edmonds' Ponds, Adirondacks*

Under the Indian name of *Cough-sa-gra-ga*, the mountainous forest of the north was known even a century and a half later, after Dutch and French and English had each in turn made settlements around its borders; the Indian savage, driven backward by the tide of European life, sought in its wild shade the safety no longer given him among the maize fields, and with knife and tomahawk sprinkled the margins of the vast evergreen forest with evidences of bloodthirsty revenge.

But now the wilderness, hitherto deemed barren, began to attract attention. Its forests filled with game, its lakes alive with trout, afforded subsistence to hardy hunters who brought strange and wonderful accounts of mines and minerals; of loadstone beds that turned the compass needle round and round; of silver ore and lead; and of those vast forests of majestic pine and spruce, which, towering against the skies, were to be the wealth of future lumbermen. Quick-witted traders, traversing the wilderness to buy the rich beaver and otter peltry from the trappers, resolved to obtain possession of these lands. In the wild rage of speculation, ignorant of the topographical features of the region, they believed this vast forest to be a land fit for richly productive agriculture, and bit by bit small patents or tracts were located around the margin of *Cough-sa-gra-ga*, until in 1772 Totten and Crossfield, ship carpenters of New York, obtained title, by purchase from the Indians, confirmed by Royal Grant, to what they

claimed covered eight hundred thousand acres, but what was in reality a tract covering about one million acres of this northern forest.

This was in 1772, and it was not until after the purchase had been
made that Totten and Crossfield began to know what they had got. In
this year Ebenezer Jessup set out with an exploring party up the
Hudson River to reach the limit of previous explorations, near where
the railroad station of Thurman now perpetuates the name of a subsequent settler. By batteaux and canoes, by wearisome portages around
falls and rapids, the voyagers reached at length the last available still
water of the Hudson, where they built a log hut called by them the
"Landing House," in which their supplies might be defended from
bears, catamounts, and savages.

Equipped with rude magnetic compasses and clumsy chains;
burdened with weighty packs of provender; and armed with axes,
knives, and rifles, we see the first surveyors in the wilderness. And
now behold these worthy servants of King George the Third, having
left behind them the navigable waters, scrambling on hands and
knees up ledges and the steep sides of nameless mountains, struggling under packs more heavy than those of any pilgrim; dragging
the chains up slopes, reckless of horizontal distances; for, "hungry
and thirsty, their souls fainted within them," and home and civilization were far away indeed.

Slowly, they searched their way back into the forest, following the
indications of the magnetic needle until they unconsciously entered
the region of magnetic iron ore—now the location of great mines—
when the needle, as though bewitched, turned every way under the
influence of the strong polarity of the loadstone rock existing beneath
the moss and wooded soil covering the ledges. Here in places the
distressed surveyors saw the sun rise in the magnetic north and set in
the magnetic south, or rise in the south and set in the north, to their
great discomfiture and chagrin.

However, as there was no help for it, they marked these compass
lines upon the trees, showing the outline of the great purchase, and of
many of the huge townships within it. Yet, they knew so little of the
region they had traversed that, when they had completed their compass routes, and had retraced their way wearily along the lonesome
lines of marked trees, they did not know which way the streams ran
that they had crossed in their long journeyings; and in attempting to
make some sort of map to show where they had been, they exhibited

on the chart of their survey the Raquette river and tributaries to the outlets of Long lake, flowing to the Hudson; whereas, as everyone now knows, they flow to the great River St. Lawrence. Thus, these lines of marked trees, like all other compass surveys, might better never have been made at all. They added little or nothing to the world's knowledge of the topography or actual geography of the region, and left a vast and intricate magnetic line puzzle to be disentangled by future surveyors, who, with transit and theodolite, depend on the polar star for the true meridians, those immovable astronomical lines, whose monuments—the bright scintillating, fixed stars in heaven—man is powerless to change.

The Revolutionary war following closely upon 1772, the colony of New York became one of the thirteen United States. The Crown lands of Great Britain and a vast portion of Totten and Crossfield's purchase, confiscated by the provisional government, were now the property of the people of the State of New York.

Impoverished by the war, the infant State endeavored, by sales of these wild lands, to relieve itself of some portion of the burdens which seven years of exhausting conflict had imposed. But the State was too poor to make proper surveys, and the magnetic needle was once again made use of to mark the outlines of other vast tracts, among which the immense area known as Macomb's purchase, consisting of nearly four millions of acres of land, was the most important, being the greatest grant of lands ever made by the State of New York.

Other grants were also made at different periods; one to the soldiers in payment of arrears, and one to refugees from Canada, etc.; and thus, little by little, the State parted with its title to the greater portion of the public domain.

The theory was that the State received no benefit from these lands as long as they remained public domain, but that when sold they immediately became productive to the public as tax-paying property. This, like some other theories, was found in practice somewhat imperfect. Under this theory the great Macomb purchase was sold for the mere bagatelle of eight pence an acre, and other lands at equally low rates.

There was nothing to prevent lumbermen from purchasing such lands at a few cents per acre, and, after cutting forty, fifty, sixty, or seventy dollars' worth of pine timber from each acre, allowing them

*Cascade House, at Edmonds' Ponds, Adirondacks*

to revert to the State for unpaid taxes. This was selling a forest for a life mortgage of six pence per acre annually and getting but one installment of interest; timber, in the meantime, to the extent of fifty dollars in value, having been taken off from each acre. Such a sale would be considered a remarkably poor business transaction as between individuals; it was mistaken policy on the part of the State.

In this and similar ways, the State has had returned to it, in numerous scattered parcels, after the cutting of the pine trees, a vast portion of these wild lands, where the soil is too rocky and barren to be utilized for farms. The rich, alluvial lands of the St. Lawrence valley, and the lowland intervales of the smaller rivers, which were found rich and productive, became valuable farms, and, as such, productive tax-paying property. But the high, mountainous lands were, in great part, returned to the State in small lots, bit by bit, or at times by townships, generally after being stripped of lumber, if in any way accessible.

Often, in the border regions, the recklessness of lumbermen allowed fire to spread into the great accumulations of brush and boughs cut from the trees in preparing them for lumber, leaving the State little more than arid rock after the fierce forest fires had died away.

The State valued these lands little, cared for them less, and for a hundred years the old irregular compass surveys were allowed to remain as the sole boundaries between lands often extremely valuable for lumbering, and until even these crooked lines of marked trees were in many places chopped or burnt away forever. The increase in the value of lumber in the New York market in recent years, with the accessibility of these forests, gave great and growing value to these pine lands.

About the year 1840, the region came to be named the "Adirondack Mountains," after the tribe of Indians last dwelling among its rocky ranges. This name was given by Professor Ebenezer Emmons while engaged in the first geological survey of the State. He found the region so wild and unexplored that he could do little geological work in the interior, where tree roots and deep moss covered the rocks. He, therefore, confined his geological work principally to the settlements in the margin, and says, in his final report, after climbing two of the mountains in Warren county: "Should the State, therefore, ever enter upon the work of an accurate survey of its territory, Harrington's Hill, in Warrensburgh, and Crain's Mountain, in Athol or Johnsburgh, will form two of the most important points for carrying on a triangulation."

From the time of Professor Emmons to the beginning of the Rebellion, there was no attempt on the part of the State to correct the grave errors of the old compass surveys; and lumbermen and geographers alike remained dependent upon the hasty memoranda of the Colonial explorers. How hasty and imperfect these memoranda were can easily be seen by a reference to Sauthier's map of the Province of New York, or to the subsequent maps of the Totten and Crossfield's Purchase. Within the whole of this last-mentioned tract, the old map showed but one mountain,—that now known as Gore Mountain, in Warren county—and scarcely a score of lakes, instead of the multitude of lofty peaks and chains of glittering ponds which make the Adirondacks the glory of New York. Such compass notes served as the basis for State maps published by private parties, and led to a dissemination of erroneous ideas in regard to the real topography of the region.

The use of topographical maps for the purpose of illustrating in detail all the natural features of a country is, however, of comparatively recent growth. Indeed, it will not be unjust to say that many are unable, without special explanation and instruction, to understand a map prepared on scientific principles, where the elevated ground is

*Saranac River, near lower lake*

shown by exact contour lines and all the inequalities of the surface depicted. If forest, rock, meadow, stream, and lake were always represented in maps in exactly natural colors; if all men were accustomed to birds-eye views of scenery from high elevations, we might expect all of them to readily comprehend such pictorial representations of the world's surface in miniature.

It follows, inasmuch as this is not the case, that a full appreciation of the truths shown by an exact topographical map can only be had by the carefully educated, or by those happy minds to which Providence has given a natural aptitude for such pursuits. The great governing minority are those who understand and make ready use of such maps. Yet, all men can to a greater or less degree enjoy the fruits of such exact knowledge.

Singular as it may seem, it is probable that our great Civil War was the first cause of the awakening of public interest, in this country, in topographical science. The great extent of unmapped, or wrongly mapped country in the south, necessitated constant exertions on the part of the corps of topographical engineers of our army. Military maps of the disputed territory were made by skillful engineers, and on these maps, or "reconnaissances," as they were called, were founded the plans, campaigns, and battles now gone down to history.

From 1861 to 1865, when each wind brought from the south the rumble of cannon and the rumors of death; when the fate of the republic hung trembling in the balance, the people, hungering for news and a clear understanding of the truth, found in the crude battle maps of the New York press, the topographical knowledge necessary to an understanding of the dread events of the war. Day by day the hastily carved plates of lead showed where rivers, forests, mountain ranges, or passes guarded the flanks of armies, or laid them open to their enemies. The importance of exact topographical knowledge was each day better understood.

## Origin of the Present Work

At the close of the war, while the remote wilds of the south had been more or less carefully mapped, the vast *Cough-sa-gra-ga* still remained topographically unmeasured and unknown.

In 1865 the writer of this paper became desirous of exploring the interior of this vast portion of New York, of which so little could be learned from books and maps. Collecting from the old survey notes all the data that could be made available, he compiled a map of the interior, and traced upon it a route for exploration. Accompanied by a friend, the author entered the wilderness, traversing, by trail or river, with guide and canoe, this strange region of evergreen-clad mountains, where rivers rise from mountain springs, and where deer and panther, bear and wolf roam through the forest solitude. Alas, the old field notes, so carefully collated, were found to be of little service. The guides laughed the old compass maps to scorn.

A score of beauteous lakes were shown to me that were unknown to the old surveyors; the old land-lines passed them by, either on the one side or the other. Where the old Colonial surveyors had incorrectly sketched rivers or lakes on their maps, mountain peaks and rocky ranges loomed upward amid the clouds. A vast semi-Alpine region was revealed, some of whose gray granite peaks rose far above the timber-line into an icy atmosphere.

Astonished, awed, yet delighted at the grandeur and vastness of the region thus spread before me, I resolved to correct the sketch that I had compiled and prepare a new map of the region, which could not fail to be a valued contribution to the Geography of my native State. Resuming, therefore, in subsequent years the explorations begun in 1865, I searched the wilderness, ascended mountains, traced rivers to their sources, measured with mercurial barometer and hand

*Haystack Mountain from Upper Ausable Pond*

level the heights of peaks and ridges, and, unaware, at that time, of the singular difficulties caused by magnetic iron and local attraction, endeavored to locate lakes and ponds from mountain tops by compass bearings.

Traversing the wilderness alone, careless of wolves or panthers, sleeping at night upon the river bank, beneath the upturned canoe, and only half wakening at the tramping of a bear; guided by deer paths or the cry of the loon to lakes unknown to maps, I became at length so accustomed to the wilderness, that even the guides deferred to, what they deemed, my superior knowledge of the wilderness. By the year 1870, so much information had been accumulated in regard to lakes and mountains, their approximate locations and elevations, that I resolved to prepare the draft of the new map of the region. Indeed, the longer I continued my investigations, the broader grew the field, until the vastness of the work that opened up before me became astonishing. Thousands upon thousands of square miles of forest stretched from the affluents of the Hudson to the rivulets of the St. Lawrence, over a multitude of mountains nameless and unmeasured. It seemed possible only to locate those prominent points, to which guides and travelers had already given names, and to fill in from my sketches as far as practicable the details of the remainder.

It was at this time that I first became fully aware of the great and irregular changes of variation which the magnetic needle underwent in this region, even in short distances. On high peaks the electricity of the clouds occasionally added its influence to further complicate the phenomena, and it soon became apparent to me that any compass bearings were almost worthless. To this discouraging state of affairs, I could see but one solution, viz.: a triangulation of the entire region, based on carefully measured lines, with the horizontal directions of all stations determined from the true astronomical meridians of circumpolar stars. As this would involve a great expenditure of means, and years of time, which would be ruinous to a private fortune, my friends urgently insisted that it was the duty of the State Government to do the work or to undertake the expense of it. Acting under this advice I appeared before a committee of the Legislature, and explained the great need of such a triangulation; and in 1872, just one hundred years after the compass surveys of Totten and Crossfield, the State of New York made its first appropriation for the Adirondack Survey.

From 1872 to 1877, the Survey was continued under the authority of the Legislature. Light portable theodolites and temporary signals were used, and valuable work was completed each season in different portions of the wilderness. Each season, however, made only more apparent the fearfully involved condition, not only of the land-lines in the wilderness, but of all the old patent lines, even far out into the settlements, throughout the whole of northern New York. The appropriations so far granted had been altogether inadequate. To attempt even a partial disentanglement of the lines of the ancient patents, and the measurement of location of the great rivers traversing the region; to ascertain the actual declination of the magnetic needle from the true meridian at numerous points; to triangulate to these lands lines, corners of tracts; to make river surveys and construct signals, would be a stupendous undertaking and would require far greater means than had been given.

The act of 1878 therefore fixed the expenditure for the Survey at the sum of $10,000 annually, for six years, and afforded the first adequate means for the determination, by trigonometrical measurements, of the true location of the ancient compass lines at the most important points.

## New Methods of Survey

The errors which characterized the Colonial and other old land surveys have been sufficiently explained. They were simply compass surveys, made hurriedly, without any attempt at correct topographi-

*Giant, from Beede House, Adirondacks*

cal work. These compass surveys left nothing more than a few lines of axe-marked trees, which might serve as a guide to keep the sable hunter from being lost in the wilderness while following his traps.

The only authorized maps used by the officials of the tax department of the State Government, in arranging and settling the assessment of lumber lands and settled sections in this vast territory, were known to be so greatly in error that constant trouble and vexation were caused, no means being provided for correcting these errors or for ascertaining the true relative location of land-lines and corners. Equitable assessments and a just and equal taxation of property became difficult, and even the ownership of large areas was involved in doubt.

But to travelers and geographers, the prominent feature of this peculiar state of affairs was that no general information could be had of the interior of the region. It was startling to find that while our Geographical Societies were laboring with enthusiastic energy to learn the secrets of Polar seas, or of the lakes and rivers of the broad "Dark Continent," we had, in our own great State of New York, a vast territory, of the topography of which we knew proportionately as little as of the heart of Equatorial Africa!

To find the errors of the surveys, to show what the true air-line distances were, instead of the guess-work of chained lines, was the first problem. This could only be done where the old lines could be readily re-discovered and measured to by triangulation. An extended triangulation, carried on in connection with a search for corners available as signal stations, was the only correct way in which to execute this portion of the work. This is the measurement of exact horizontal distances.

To find the character of the ground, its relative roughness, the height of passes suitable for railroads, stage or team-roads, or engineering works, it is necessary to know the true height of all these points and of the slope or "gradiant" approach to them. Without this data it would be impossible to represent upon the maps of the Survey the natural features of the ground, the heights of lakes or mountains, or mountain ranges raising themselves as obstacles to human progress. The exact distances of triangulation give a just idea of space and area; the heights and depths and roughness of the region show its actual value. This measurement of exact heights is called leveling.

To place upon paper a miniature representation of all the mountains, passes, rivers, lakes, and settlements which are visible from the triangulation stations, or can be located from them, is the final work. This has to be done upon a blank map in the field; all the features of the country being reproduced by skillful draughting on one uniform scale, so as to represent, as nearly as practicable, the appearance of the region within the limits fixed by the trigonometrical measurements and leveling, as seen from the mountain-tops. This is termed the plane-table mapping, and is the final work, or pictorial map representation, of all the labors and research of the Survey.

In addition to these regular departments of work, the location of important rivers, the forms of large lakes, and the re-location of certain land-lines and corners, call for special subordinate work. This work is divided into river surveys, lake surveys, land-line surveys, and special surveys.

## Triangulation

To secure the desired accuracy in measurement of air-line distances, superb theodolites, of the largest size now in use for such Geodetic work, were introduced upon the Adirondack Survey. These instruments—whose horizontal circles, delicately graduated on silver, read to the tenth of a second of arc—are set up on stands firmly leaded into the solid rock. With these instruments the angles between signals on commanding points—mountain-tops, hills, open spaces, or at lake shores—are read, repeated, and recorded.

Starting from base-lines measured with extreme precision, a series of triangles are thus measured over the whole region, by methods insuring the greatest possible accuracy; so that the trigonometrical computation of the air-line distances between the signal stations, being carried into the wilderness, then around out and back to the base-line from which the measurements started, gives the same value for that base-line by computation, which was first secured by actual measurement. Thus gradually the region is covered with a net-work of triangles, great and small, the sides of these triangles being exact distances, as accurately known as though they were nicely graduated ribbons of steel, stretched taut. These triangle sides have also, in every instance, their true astronomical bearings determined from observations of circumpolar stars; and the termini under the signals being marked by indestructible monuments of stone, each triangle side stands as a new base-line for any special or local surveying which may be needed. By means of this triangulation the actual position, length, and breadth of the ancient land patents, and the true places of lakes, mountains, or passes, are exactly determined, so that the actual areas are known. Should all the old land-lines marked on trees be destroyed by fire, they could be replaced and restored by reference to the monuments marking the triangulation.

### Leveling

Hardly any measurements of true heights above sea-level had been made in the Adirondacks, except with barometer, until the initiation of this Survey. At the commencement of the Survey the barometer was largely used in the preliminary or "flying levels," by which was developed what mountains could be used as primary stations. The element of height was a serious one, among so many mountain ranges, where peaks affording the best conditioned triangles are frequently partly hidden by some slight projection of an intervening ridge. When the careful Geodetic work of the Adirondack Survey was fairly under way, it soon became evident that a substantial basis would have to be given for the trigonometrical leveling, as the determination of differences of height by vertical angles (elevations or depressions) is termed. All altitudes are measured above the mean or

*Upper Ausable Pond, Adirondacks*

average level of the sea, theoretically extended as a spheroid of revolution, as though its glassy surface swept uniformly along below the
hills, plains, or mountains, forming a uniform surface of reference, to
which—were it not for the interposing rock—we might lower a
plumb line from a mountain peak and thus measure the height directly. But it is not possible to make any such measurement of height
directly.

The heart of the Adirondack region is more than two hundred and
fifty miles from the sea-coast at the mouth of the Hudson. Tidal action
is visible at Albany, one hundred and fifty miles above the river's
mouth. But, affected as the waters of a river are by its confined and
winding channel, the current and the winds, it is improper to assume
the mean tide at Albany to be the true mean-tide level of the ocean.
Indeed, we know that there is a slope or fall in the river of four or
five feet in that one hundred and fifty miles. We are, therefore, compelled to go to New York harbor to find the best available mean-tide
level datum on which to base all measurements of altitudes throughout the State. At Governor's Island, in New York harbor, a continuous
study of the fluctuations of the tides has been made for many years
by delicate and repeated measurements, and a careful record of them
kept. From this datum two independent lines of levels have been run
to monuments in Albany. One of these lines was run by the United
States Coast and Geodetic Survey, and the other by the United States

Army Engineer Corps. These two lines of levels terminate at Albany in two independent bench-marks or datums, which may be called in common parlance "height monuments," being centers of stone, whose exact height above the level of the sea is known to the decimal of a foot. On these stone datums at Albany, the height measurements of the Adirondack Survey are now based. No longer dependent upon uncertain data for the altitude of initial points of the Survey, the trigonometrical leveling, thus fixed by exact determination with spirit level and graduated rod, has now been carried by this Survey from tide level into the heart of the wilderness, up great mountain peaks, through wild passes and precipice-hung gorges, along rivers, between lake and lake, between settlement and settlement; and thousands of stations and bench-marks on stone have been left along the routes of the Survey, on which future public works in engineering can be based, and exact heights above tide be instantly obtained at any time. This work is now done, upon the Adirondack Survey, with engineer's levels and graduated rods of the most perfect description. Each level carries a telescope of very high power, provided with a telemetrical attachment for measuring distances by merely sighting over the rough ground to be traversed in leveling. By a device invented by the Superintendent, the cross wires and telemetrical wires are so placed as not to be visible at the same time, so that all error in observing is prevented; and, by means of a horizontal graduated arc, the angles at the instrument stations are observed back and fore between the rods in leveling. The level tube itself is constructed so as to be exceedingly sensitive, and, all the distances on the principal lines being selected so as to be equalized, the best conditions for leveling are maintained. An important feature of the leveling is the care which is used to insure correct height readings on the graduated rods. Two rods are used— both of standard graduations—one being divided according to the French metric system and the other according to the English or foot system. By means of verniers, the one is read to one-fifth of a mile-metre, the other to the thousandth part of a foot. These rods are not held vertical by rodsmen; but are placed in peculiar rod-holders, having double levels and leveling plates (quite as formidable in appearance as the large leveling instrument itself), with heavy tripod support. By means of this contrivance, absolute verticality is secured for the rod, and exact measurements of heights to a thousandth of a foot rendered possible.

*Adirondack Survey — Signal Station, Black Mountain*

## Plane-Table Work

For the final field mapping, the instrument called the Plane-table is used, and consists of a firm and perfectly smooth table mounted on a heavy tripod. The table has the usual contrivances for leveling and adjusting it, and has a very true surface. The blank sheets, carrying only the lines of latitude and longitude and the triangulation stations, are placed on this table and secured to its surface. An instrument termed an Alhidade is then placed upon the table. This Alhidade is a heavy and extremely true ruler of brass, carrying a vertical standard or axis, on which is mounted a powerful telescope and sensitive levels. By means of this Alhidade, the meridian line of the station occupied by the topographer—as shown on the blank map—is then made to correspond with the true astronomical meridian, and sights are taken to numerous stations with the Alhidade telescope, and lines drawn along the ruler edge toward those stations. These lines point to the outlines or foot of a mountain, the edge of a pond, the projection of a point into the waters of a lake—and the intersections of such lines from different stations show the true position of the mountain foot or pond or point. These outlines having been thus located, the topographer, with the aid of the Alhidade—which has a vertical limb attached—works in the details—slopes of ground, ledges, cliffs or peaks, and ravines; sights to each one in turn, and sketches in the minor details that, from his station on some high mountain top, he sees spread out like a gigantic map before him.

## Utility of the Work

The usefulness of the work and the necessity for its completion have been already pretty well shown by the account of the erroneous methods previously used, in which the magnetic compass was employed to subdivide vast areas.

The science of Forestry, as yet hardly studied in this country as a governmental problem, is now growing in importance with us. It may be regarded as an established fact that if the great forests of this state were managed with even a tithe of the care and science which the German Government devotes to its forests, the income of the State from these wild and, at present, unproductive lands would be sufficient each year to pay the whole of the State tax, and relieve the people of that great burden forever. The Prussian Government is said to obtain from a less area of forest a net annual income of $4,000,000. If our State could secure annually one-half of such a sum, the amount of State taxation would soon be inconsiderable. Before this can be done in our country, exact topographical references—similar to those of European countries—must be made, in order to render it possible for the political economist to form practicable plans to utilize our latent forest wealth so as to make it of public benefit. But it is in the correct and equitable taxation of the private lumber lands of this vast district that the absolute necessity for this Survey is shown. At present it is impossible to obtain an accurate land-map of northern New York, which shall show any owner just what he owns, or the Assessors the real location or value of property. It has frequently become necessary for the Comptroller to order hasty compass surveys to be made, to determine little questions of location of lines or the ownership of tracts, or sections, or lots. In such hurried and partial surveys there has been no attempt at permanency, or topographical mapping, or location of monuments; so that, for lack of system and connection, these surveys give no permanent information in shape suitable for the use of the assessors and tax officers. Geographers, travelers, and landowners, or investers in lands, all require well-made, accurate plans of the country in order to understand its capabilities, and to enable them to ascertain how its mineral wealth, its vast water power, and its forests can be best made to serve the uses of mankind.

## Topographical Maps

To enable all these great brain workers to understand our Adirondack region and devise means by which its latent wealth may be made to add to the comfort of our people, the topographical maps, now being prepared, will furnish in clear form the actual position and relation of mountains and lakes to land-lines and ownerships. These maps show:

FIRST, the actual divisions of property; not where the lines are supposed to be, but where they have been found to be marked on the trees after careful survey.

SECOND, the lakes, rivers, and mountains are then depicted in their proper places. The elevations are not simply marked by occasional figures on the map, but, by means of continuous fine dotted lines traced over the surface of the map, the line of exact height of five hundred, or one thousand, or one thousand five hundred, or any other height in feet above tide is shown, and even the slope of the ground, whether gradual, steep, or precipitous. From such maps—actual miniature representations of the country covered with lines and measurements, showing ownerships, latitude and longitudes, and all the irregularities of ground—a better idea can be obtained of the uses to which any portion of the country can be put, than can be gained from an inspection of the region itself; for such a map is a collection of ideas, as well as a representation of the ground.

THIRD, the question of assessment and laying of taxes, of the con-

*Adirondack Survey — Trail Up Black Mountain*

struction of roads and railroads, or of the bringing of water for canals or public purposes can be settled by a single glance at the map and a reference to the figures.

## Land-Lines and Measurements

Of equal importance is the restoration and preservation of the great corners of the vast land patents upon which depend the titles to all real estate throughout northern New York. In the place of the old lines of marked trees by which the whites (following the fashion of the Indians) in Colonial times separated the lands of the Crown from those of private owners, great monuments of stone are now set. In the centers of these great monuments of granite (sometimes weighing half a ton or more), are set copper bolts, brightly nickel-plated, showing on their surfaces inscriptions describing the corner thus preserved. By means of the trigonometrical observations these monuments are referred to as astronomical stations, and so connected by measurement with other copper bolts set in the summits of mountain peaks that, were these monuments destroyed, new ones could be reset with accuracy in the same locations.

### Results of the Survey

The present cost of the Survey is but $10,000 annually. Out of this sum, all the field and office expenses have to be met, including the compensation of the several large corps of engineers and surveyors and their assistants, aids, guides, chainmen, axemen, and laborers. The work is done by special and local engineers, under the instruction and orders of the Superintendent. The expenses of the work are settled and audited by the Comptroller of the State, who has the final financial settlement of the accounts. No payments are made until examined and allowed by him.

In the preservation, by substantial monuments, of the land-lines and the great corners alone, the Survey already pays for itself many times over.

Among its important special geographical results may be mentioned the discovery by Superintendent Colvin, in 1873, of the highest lakelet source of the Hudson river at Lake Tear of the Clouds, just southward of Mount Marcy, and the tracing of the sources of the Raquette river, the Au Sable river, with the Cedar, Oswegatchie, Beaver, Schroon, Moose, Sacandaga, and other rivers of the wilderness. The ascent and first measurement of scores of great mountains—which until the inauguration of the Survey were not shown upon any map— are among other results, of which Mount Seward, Mount Haystack, Mount Algonquin, Mount Iroquois, the Gothic mountains, Mount Colvin, the Boreas mountains, Mount Macomb, etc., are prominent.

Accounts of these explorations, with a narrative of the experiences of the explorers, will be found in the published volumes of reports on the progress of the Survey, issued by order of the Legislature from time to time. Of these, seven reports have now been published, and about ten thousand of each have been distributed to public libraries, foreign governments, savans, etc.

These reports are to be finally followed by the maps and volumes of field-notes, and measurements and records that will be permanent works of reference in regard to this great district; which—by reason of its mines of iron, its magnificent richness of forest, its enormous water powers and pure lakes, natural reservoirs of health, and its mountain peaks, raising their granite crests far into the region of the clouds—forms the wonder and pride of New York, and, ultimately, will be its greatest source of wealth.

## Officers of the Survey

The officers of the Survey are as follows:

Verplanck Colvin, Superintendent—appointed by the Legislature— office in the New Capitol, at Albany.

The Staff, during 1881, appointed by the Superintendent, were as follows—the triangulation and map work being under the immediate supervision of the superintendent:

M. Blake, assistant in charge, Division of Levels; N. L. Rush, Aid.

NORTH WESTERN DIVISION—S. J. Farnsworth, C. E., in charge. Includes St. Lawrence county and a portion of Franklin county.

NORTH EASTERN DIVISION—H. K. Averill, C. E., in charge. Includes Clinton county.

MIDDLE EASTERN DIVISION—William H. Case, C. E., in charge. Includes eastern portion of Essex county and great iron-mining district.

SOUTH EASTERN DIVISION—D. M. Arnold, C. E., in charge. Includes Warren county and lines bordering on Washington county.

SOUTH WESTERN DIVISION—S. H. Snell, C. E., in charge. Includes Lewis and portions of Herkimer, Hamilton, and adjoining counties.

# The Adirondacks

SPEECH DELIVERED BY THE HON. VERPLANCK COLVIN,
AT THE ANNUAL BANQUET OF THE NEW YORK BOARD OF TRADE
AND TRANSPORTATION HOTEL BRUNSWICK, NEW YORK,
WASHINGTON'S BIRTHDAY, 1885

*Extract from the proceedings of the Annual Banquet of the New York Board of Trade and Transportation, Hotel Brunswick, New York, Washington's Birthday, 1885 (celebrated Feb. 23d).*

The President read the next toast on the programme, and called upon the Hon. Verplanck Colvin to respond to same, viz.: "The Adirondacks—the land of magnificent mountains and lovely lakes; the source of the Hudson River, the feeders of our canals."

Mr. Colvin spoke as follows:

*Mr. President and Gentlemen of the Board of Trade and Transportation:*

I thank you heartily for the kind and graceful courtesy shown me, which I attribute to your interest in my field of labor among the grand, granitic crests of New York.

The Adirondack—the land of magnificent mountains and lovely lakes, famous in song and story, the land which is now the summer home of thousands, who there drink in renewed health and vitality with each breath of fresh, forest air, has become the pride and glory of New York; and I ask you to drink this health in the clear, cold water of the mountain springs. The ice that tinkles in your goblets, and the pure water which upholds the ice, are both fresh from the head-waters of the Hudson. Two days since, the great block of snow-encrusted ice, which decorates this table, formed part of the wintry bridge across the Upper Hudson, in the gorge among the mountains at the very spot whence it is proposed to conduct the water into the great aqueduct to supply all the cities of the valley of the Hudson, from the

29

very sources of our noble river. It is 13 years since I suggested this source of water supply for the metropolis, and now the construction of the aqueduct is under consideration, and to-night we drink the first glasses of the pure Adirondack water ever tasted in the banquet halls of New York.

It is fit that the memory of Washington should be connected with the wilderness region of the Appalachian chain, for their rocky battlements and foot-hills guarded the flanks and rear of his suffering and heroic army; and, pure as are the waters of the crystaline trout brooks and well springs of the Adirondacks, they are not more pure than was the high patriotism of our General, whose character, virtue, and devotion secured the salvation of our country, and the reformation of the English-speaking people.

The eloquent speakers who have preceded me have already recalled the glorious incidents of his noble life; and, while our soldiers justly claim that Washington was "first in War," and our statesmen demonstrate, as they follow in the paths that he laid out, that he was "first in Peace," the records of his early life prove that he was among the first and most eminent of the Surveyors who systematized the equitable sub-division of the wild territory of our young nation.

The work of the Surveyor is the work of the practical mathematician, and it cannot but be believed that the application of the exact sciences to practical business purposes leads to systematic methods and accuracy of thought; and it may be confidently assumed that these studies contributed largely to the formation of the character of Washington.

Not to be *exact* is really to be false; and the truthfulness of Washington was a proof of the precision of his habits of thought. He lived at a time when the best of the stern rules of Sparta and republican Rome were believed, by the wise and thoughtful, to be worthy of study, as containing the rudiments of a better form of government. The stern simplicity of his habits may be traced to his studies and his camp life among the mountains; for, coming from among the most wealthy, he had mingled also with the humblest and knew the good and the essential from the gaudy and the meretricious.

It is proper that the Board of Trade and Transportation especially should honor his memory, for no American has ever lived who was more appreciative of the importance of commerce to the welfare of the nation.

Had not New Hampshire chosen his name for the highest peak of the White Mountains, Mount Washington might have been located as the most commanding summit of the Adirondacks; looking down upon Mount Iroquois and Mount Algonquin, and the lofty summit of Mount Clinton, which perpetuates the memory of the founder of our canals.

Here, under the shadow of Mount Tahawus, is the highest lakelet source of the Hudson—4,321 feet above the sea. From this lakelet the waters descend over many a cataract to the place where commerce has diverted its surplus volume to lift the boats from the Hudson to Lake Champlain—the natural route for the great ship canal to the lakes, where the passage of ships will be less hindered by cross roads and bridges, by cities and villages than on the Erie, and with the whole volume of the Hudson and St. Lawrence available for navigation barely a hundred and fifty feet above tide.

We must hope to see, at no distant date, the great ships sail up the Hudson, into the great canal, and by one short step reach Lake Champlain; then traversing that inland sea and entering the new "Northwest Passage," a ship canal skirting the northern limits of the Adirondacks to the great river St. Lawrence, and so, grandly and easily to Ontario and the West.

There is abundant water in the Upper Hudson for the purposes of this great canal, as well as for the great aqueduct which shall bring the pure water of the mountains to every city along the valley of our noble river; but the navigation of the shallow portions of the Hudson, from Castleton to Troy, can be best secured by great river locks near the head of deep water above Athens. Gigantic locks, with machinery controlled by the hydraulic power of the river itself could be constructed, which would carry through at one lift an entire fleet of boats, and render the river channel uniformly navigable.

Five years since, in my annual report to the Legislature for 1880, I called especial attention to the remarkable facts which the rain-fall observations of the Adirondack Survey had revealed. The increase of the rain-fall, with the increase of altitude, was shown to be very remarkable.

Along the borders of Lake Champlain at 100 feet above the sea a rain-fall of 23 inches was found. At an elevation of 1,000 feet, a few miles back in the Adirondacks, the average rain-fall of a number of years has been found to be about 30 inches, and at an elevation of

2,000 feet, at Edmund's Ponds in Essex County, one year's observations give a rain-fall of 46 inches.

These results indicate that the conditions which govern the rain-fall in our mountains are similar to those controlling the rain-fall of Europe; and with the data obtained by the Adirondack Survey and the known laws of rain-fall, we may arrive at just conclusions as to the exact commercial value of the actually available hydraulic power of the Adirondack region.

I have been urged to quote from my report to the Legislature of 1880, upon this subject, as an evidence that these views were maintained by me five years since. On pages 19 and 20 of that report I said:

> The laws of rain-fall of this region are very similar to those of other mountain regions, having an approximately similar environment. We can therefore assume—by analogy—in advance of the perfected knowledge afforded by a long series of rain-fall observations, that the whole upland area of mountain streams and lakes actually possess a rain-fall vastly in excess of what the same area of low lands in our State would afford, and that the reservoirs for water supply to fill future aqueducts conveying the cold, pure water of the wilderness to our cities, can depend upon a constant supply from these trout streams and mountain brooks.
>
> As a source of pure water for our cities, or for the moderate needs of our canals and mills, the Adirondack streams and lakes may be safely relied upon; but the practicability of furnishing a continuous flow to keep up the volume of our larger rivers in summer is questionable; while, from an engineering point of view, it seems more practical to look for a remedy for the low waters of summer in such streams as the Hudson, in the more simple mechanical resources of a channel restricted by wing-dams, or even to temporary river-locks with permanent piers, to which the gates could be attached when required in summer.

We must guard our water supply, secure the reservoirs to store the surplus water, and maintain the forests which protect the springs at the river sources from evaporation; yet we must remember that it is chiefly the Mohawk branch and its affluents which supply the eastern division of the Erie canal with water, and that the Upper Hudson is to be the feeder of the short and perfectly feasible ship canal route to Lake Champlain and the St. Lawrence.

The influence of forests as conservators of moisture, modifying it or to a certain extent, it may be said, regulating the rain-fall, has led many to regard State ownership of all the forest lands at the sources of the Hudson as essential to the maintenance of that water supply upon which the commerce of our canals depends. This subject is too broad for present discussion, but I must call your attention to a startling phase of the question which affects the interests of every landholder in the State.

The recent decision of Judge Tappan, regarding the title of the State to certain "tax lands" in the Adirondack region, shows that grave defects exist in the tax laws, and the decision virtually throws a cloud over the ownership of vast sections of territory both of private and State lands.

This state of affairs proves the need of immediate legislation to secure equitable taxation, with simple and less technical proceedings, and the passage of laws confirmatory of titles in cases of sales where every possible requirement of the statutes has been complied with.

Unless this important matter be at once attended to, the foundation of the ownership of property on tax sales will be undermined, and fraudulent evasions of the equal burdens, apportioned among us for the maintenance of the commonwealth, will ensue in many cases.

Let the spirit of Washington imbue us with the desire to secure only just and equitable laws, favoring no single locality, but conferring equal advantages, equal benefits upon all—and we shall prove by the evidence afforded by good works that he is indeed "first in the hearts of his countrymen."

The surveyors of America can never forget the memory of him whose birthday we celebrate to-night. Those whose duties have called them among the forests of the Appalachian Mountains; who in the search for the ancient boundary lines of the Colonial land patents, have found the old boundary trees still bearing the scars left upon them by the axes of the Colonial surveyors over a century ago; who have carefully cut into the wood, counting each woody ring of growth, back to the years 1748, 1760, 1768, and 1772, will remember that the hearts of hundreds of trees of old Virginia carry the veritable axe marks of Washington the surveyor. The child who marked the tree with his hatchet in his father's garden was probably already in

his day dreams a surveyor in the wilderness, and I had hoped this
evening to be able to lay before you a block cut from a tree, showing
the original survey marks of Washington, found by one of my assistants now engaged in surveys in Western Virginia.

Thus we trace an interesting fact connected with one of the legends
of the youth of Washington, in his association with the early surveys of
the wilderness region of the Appalachian mountain chain, and find
everywhere the evidences of careful and conscientious labor, and of
that truth and fidelity which have formed the foundation of our system
of government as firm as the mountain masses of the Adirondack.

## PART TWO

# Early Explorations

Call not a mountain range the backbone of the earth; to man the world is not a being, but a dwelling; rather liken these great ridges to the dome, the strange, weird, fantastically ornamented pinnacle and ridge-roof of his vast treasure-house. This was indeed the divide—the great water-shed of the continent, whose gutters are mighty rivers, whose cisterns are the seas!

But oh! how wonderful this mountain architecture—the unmarred handiwork of our God! Gazing down upon these frosty peaks, they seemed a sea of monstrous icebergs, a frozen ocean—a spectacle whose only equivalent would be such a scene as an ocean's bed laid bare, its waters driven back and stilled, and its deepest and most secret chasms all revealed.

— VERPLANCK COLVIN
"The Dome of the Continent," 1873

# The Helderbergs

Verplanck Colvin enjoyed an idyllic boyhood. His family had means — not on the grand scale, but comfortably so. His education was varied; he studied at home, with private tutors, and at the Albany Academy for Boys and the Nassau Academy. He read for the law at his father's behest, but found time to develop and pursue other interests. Perhaps it was his family's move to rural Rensselaer County when he was fourteen that prompted this independent streak.

Verplanck's neighbor was Mills Blake, an orphan boy one year younger than he, who lived with a guardian across the street. They had similar interests in the out-of-doors and tramped the fields and forests over the rolling hills of the near and far countryside. When the Colvins returned to Albany a few years later, Blake was hired as a clerk in the Colvin law office. The two of them sometimes accompanied Verplanck's father and his partner, Anson Bingham, to the Helderbergs, where they were deeply involved in representing settlers and farmers caught up in the Anti-Rent Wars.

Blake and Colvin became adept at interpreting deed descriptions and locating boundary lines and corners of the farms that were in dispute. It was in the Helderbergs where Colvin found his life's calling.

About the same time he developed a deep interest in the Adirondacks. He began annual visits to these northern mountains in 1865, intrigued by the old survey lines that sought to divide them into patents and tracts and lots. However, he didn't lose interest in the Helderbergs and, with Blake's help, conducted an extensive geographical and geological survey of the mysterious escarpment. The result was an illustrated article, written and drawn by Colvin, that appeared in the October, 1869 issue of Harper's New Monthly Magazine.

Colvin's own opinion was that it "excited much attention" and raised him to "a high position in American literature." It is difficult to disagree.

— NJVV

In the State of New York are three principal mountain chains. The Adirondacks cover the northern, granite region of the State, of rock which had been violently heated, if not melted, by the earth's internal fires. They are igneous, plutonic mountains, with peaks perhaps 6,000 feet above tide-level. The Catskills are an isolated group of peaks on the Hudson, more than a hundred miles south of their granite elder brother of the Adirondack. They are principally of the old red sandstones and shales which underlie the coal formation. These are sedimentary rocks, the silt of ancient ocean currents; their peaks exceed three thousand feet in height.

Between these, north of the Catskills, not twenty miles distant, is a line of small mountains known as the Helderbergs, the third though not the least of the mountain systems of New York. They are a long angular range of solid blue limestone cliffs, running nearly east and west. Their geographical name exists only in Albany county; but, geologically, they are over three hundred miles in length, their unbroken strata reaching from the Hudson to Niagara and on into Canada. Their greatest altitude is one thousand two hundred feet.

These calcareous cliffs, filled with fossil, petrified sea-shells, answer to the European Silurian and Devonian ages. By its peculiar fossil shells the Helderberg, like other rock, is known when met with in distant regions. In subterranean darkness it stretches, a hidden, undulating sheet of strata, an inner mantle to the continent, cropping out here and there, and leaving its wooded "Silurian ruins" to render picturesque the scenery of many a State.

In the far West a geologist picks up a fossil shell, examines it, and says, "Helderberg"—surmises that good limestone may thereabouts be found; and gypsum for the plasterer's art, and iron pyrites—fool's gold—useful for sulphur and sulphuric acid manufacture. Caves also may be expected, and sulphur springs, strontian, or barytes, if not more valuable deposits, may be near.

A Tennessee geologist also picks up a petrifaction, and makes note of it as "Helderberg." In Britain Sir Roderick Murchison, mentioning the existence of his favorite Siluria in America, will not fail to speak of the Helderberg formation. Yet it is possible that of these three not one had ever seen the Helderberg.

Reprinted from *Harper's New Monthly Magazine*, vol. 39, October 1869.

"Helderberg" is a Dutch corruption of the old German *Helle-berg,*
meaning "Clear Mountain." This name was given by the first settlers
of Schoharie county, who had the bold and distinct *berg* constantly in
view during their first day's journey westward into the then wilderness. Though plainly visible, and but ten or fifteen miles from the
ancient city of Albany, few of its citizens appear even to know of their
existence, let alone their traditions and their beauties. Helderberg
to many Albanians means "anti-rent," "sheriff's posse," military,
blue uniforms, bright muskets and bayonets, and shackled prisoners,
against whom no crime being proved they are always released.

Most of the farms on these hills were what was once called "manor
land." It had its feudal lord and manor-house after the fashion in
England prior to our Revolution. The farmers were peasantry, of
whom feudal rents in the shape of wheat, chickens, and "days' service" were exacted, though the land was indentured, or deeded, to
them, their heirs, and assigns forever. Ignorant emigrants were led to
purchase, invest their all, clear and improve the land, and give it
value, not dreaming that they would have to pay the interest on their
own improvements. Alas! they found that they had exchanged the
hard lot of a Holland "boor" for one even harder. Shrewd Yankees,
living on free soil, jeered at them as slaves.

The Revolution came, the battles of liberty were fought, and down
went Tory and Royalist. After that, feudal exactions seemed hard and
oppressive, as well as unrepublican and monarchical. Some now re-
fused to pay the "quarter sale"—one quarter of the price received by
the farmer each time a place was sold. If the farm was sold four times
the "Lord" received the cash value of the farm, and still pretended to
own it! Threats not sufficing, they were called "Anti-Renters," and
war was levied upon them. But since then the conflict has raged, nor
is it ended yet; but quarter sales are abolished.

The Susquehanna Railroad trains, as they leave Albany crowded
with tourists bound for Sharon Springs, the beauteous Susquehanna
river valley, or distant Pennsylvania, are forced to follow the wall-like
precipices facing the Helderberg almost along their whole extent, far
to the north and west, before they are able to climb it. It is its romantic wooded rock scenery, dark caverns, and sprayey waterfalls, its
varied landscape and accessible mountain grandeur, that render the
Helderberg interesting to artist, author, poet, tourist, or rusticator.

*Mountain Spurs*

The traditions herein written are at least as true as traditions ever are, and I tell them substantially as they were told to me. The sketches may give some idea of the scenery.

To those who desire to escape for a day from the oven-like city in summer; who wish to enjoy a scramble among romantic cliffs, in shady woods, beside cool mountain brooks and waterfalls; to view spots sacred to legends of wild Revolutionary days, of Tory and Indian depredation, naming place, precipice, and mountain; to gather the fossil corals and shells (univalves, bivalves, and brachipods) which, forming the very soil the farmer tills, cropping from out the sod, are reared as farm walls or burned to lime; to visit and explore known caves, and search for new ones, possibly existing unknown and unexplored, among the cliff ledges, the "Indian Ladder" region of the Helderbergs offers superior inducements.

Taking an early train on the Susquehanna Railroad and stopping at Guilderland Station brings one within a mile of the Indian Ladder Gap. Even from that distance the mountain spurs are visible. Wondrous are the deep, black shadows that they cast early in the day. A scarcely discernible zigzag ascending line, not unresembling a military siege-approach, shows the Indian Ladder Road crawling up the mountain and along and beneath the precipices.

It is but an easy two hours' drive, however, from Albany, and many may prefer to visit it in the saddle or with a pleasant party. If the weather be dry and not very sultry the jaunt will well repay you. If your horses are brave and steady you may drive up the mountain road—it is a mile to the summit—or you may lead your horses up, the party walking leisurely after. Still some descending team may be met, and it is ill passing on that narrow cliff road. Notwithstanding many accidents, this road is the highway, winter and summer, of the country folk.

If, however, you have a desire to "foot it," and wish to see the wildest, most romantic scenery the place affords, abandon the road and follow the stream, called by some Black Creek, up the valley to the foot of the gorge—a savage stairway up the mountain slope, of broken rock-fragments and great water-worn boulders. Then, if your heart fails you not—for any place more difficult to climb is impassable—you will ascend for a breathless, dangerous, exciting three or four hours to the foot of the cliff and the falls—an escalade which will bear comparison with any thing climbable.

But you should not return without mementoes of your visit. Carry then a satchel, unless you have capacious pockets; for curiosities will meet you on every side. Besides the fossil medals of creation—petrifactions and minerals—the collector will find a thousand objects of interest. If he have keen eyes he may note some curious grafts, great hemlocks on huge pine-trees, perhaps of Indian handicraft. Large slow-worms, unknown lizards, insects, perhaps black-snakes, toads, and eels, mingled in strange confusion, swarm amidst the rocks. The place was once renowned for the multitude, size, and venom of its rattlesnakes.

The damp, thick woods of oaks, hickory, red (slippery) elm, basswood (linden), butternut, ash, beech, and birch, with white pine, hemlock, and some spruce, give color to the scenery heightened by the green, graceful frondage of the scarlet-fruited sumac, the trailing cordage of the wild grape-vines, and the numberless other rarer wild plants—annuals, biennials, perennials, every where luxuriant.

Your satchel may contain some luncheon; a geological hammer and a chisel would not be inappropriate; your sketch-book by all means. Gun or fishing-tackle here are useless, hunting there is none save foxes, "coons," some ruffled grouse (partridge), and at times wild pigeons. The fishing is also poor, except for pickerel, perch, sunfish, and the like, in lakes and brooks amidst the hills back from the summit.

What is this Indian Ladder so often mentioned? In 1710 this Helderberg region was a wilderness; nay, all westward of the Hudson river settlements was unknown. Albany was a frontier town, a trading post, a place where annuities were paid, and blankets exchanged with Indians for beaver pelts. From Albany over the sand plains—Schen-ec-ta-da (pine barrens) of the Indians—led an Indian trail westward. Straight as the wild bee or the crow the wild Indian made his course from the white man's settlement to his own home in the beauteous Schoharie valley. The stern cliffs of these hills opposed his progress; his hatchet fells a tree against them, the stumps of the branches which he trimmed away formed the rounds of the Indian Ladder.

That Indian trail, then, led up this valley, up yonder mountain slope, to a cave now known as the "Tory House." The cave gained the name during the Revolution: of that more anon. The trail ended in a corner of the cliffs where the precipice did not exceed 20 feet in height. There stood the tree—the old Ladder. In 1820 this ancient ladder was yet in daily use. There are one or two yet living who have climbed it. Greater convenience became necessary, and the road was constructed during the next summer. It followed the old trail up the mountain. The ladder was torn away, and a passage through the cliffs blasted for the roadway. The rock-walled pass at the head of the road is where the Indian Ladder stood. The Indians had once a similar ladder near Niagara Falls. There were probably many such among the cliffs. It was possibly the resemblance of this wild mountain scenery to that of father-land far away that induced its early settlement by the Swiss, and gave the name of Berne to the neighboring town.

You have followed the rapid brook up the valley through the shadowy woods, and have reached a little prairie—an opening surrounded almost on every side by the great mountain slopes which rise grandly to the impregnable cliffs walling the summits. It seems a window whereby the crag-climber may observe the whole extent of his labors. This spot was known as the "Tory Hook" or Plat, and in days gone by was their rendezvous, a lone, sequestered glade of the savage forest. Above you, in front and to right and left, is a colossal natural amphitheatre, the long, wooded slopes rising tier on tier to the base of the circling precipices. Two rocky gorges, which ascend like the diverging aisles of an amphitheatre, part the wilderness of green. The steep slopes have four-fifths of the mountain height.

Towering above the uppermost tree-tops are the gray, battlement-like cliffs. Many a dark opening, gloomy recess, and inaccessible ledge can be seen which human foot has never trod; once, probably, the pathway and home of that blood-thirsty savage, the nimble and stealthy-footed cougar. Two lofty waterfalls stream down, milk-white, from the cliff-top at the head of each dry, rock-filled gorge. Your way lies to the right, up the gorge to the smaller of the two falls.

Following the stream and entering the opposite woods you commence the ascent of the gorge. It is no light undertaking. The bed of the stream is your best road; keep to the right. Difficulties begin; you are frequently compelled to cross the rapid stream on stepping-stones. At length you reach what may be termed the foot of the gorge. The stream rushes down in a number of little cascades— above it is lost amidst the huge rocks. Look upward, your labor lies before you.

Up, then! Up! Ah—it is fatiguing? Look below! It seems easier to climb up than down. Retreat appears impossible, if not recreant. Up-ward, then! no longer over fallen rocks merely, but over prostrate cliffs rather. Huge blocks as large as little cottages or backwoods log cabins are heaped in wild confusion; up them and over them! More toilsome, nay, dangerous, becomes the ascent; but now the novelty and danger give new zest, and "Forward!" shouts one. Where at you all, with vigorous competition hurrying, climb and scramble upward; sometimes on foot, oftener upon hands and knees, and frequently prone, with aid of fingers and toe of boot making slow progress up the face of some fallen mountain.

To climb, some aid themselves with sticks snatched up from where they were cast by the last great freshet that foamed down the wild gorge. The barkless pole, dry and withered, often fails the user, who scarce has time to drop the worthless fragments, snatch a firm grip upon immovable rock, and thank his stars that he has not followed the fragments of his staff that rattle down half a hundred feet before they reach a cranny large enough to hold them. Do not take each wriggling thing among the rocks to be a snake. Once thinking to cap-ture what I took to be a serpent sunning himself on the rocks, I found I had a sleek, fat eel! An eel there on those dry rocks? Assuredly. For, hark! do you hear that steady rushing sound, as of a subterranean waterfall? Hours of toilsome climbing have passed. Look upward, the falls are before you at last.

From the brink of the dark cliff drops a spray-white stream, about 80 feet, unbroken. Lost for a moment to sight it issues from a rocky basin, and ripples down in two streams brightly over a series of little stone steps, the angular and parallel edges of abraded schist strata, seldom over an inch in thickness. Suddenly the smooth descent ceases; the rock drops perpendicularly 15 or 18 feet. Down the face of this wall or "fault" dash two little cascades; they fall upon another series of the miniature rock steps, and, glittering and shining like a magic stream of crystal, hurry down to lose their waters among the huge rocks of the gorge; lost for a thousand feet of that dread mountain slope ere coming forth to light again as the stream in the valley below. At last beneath the precipice you stand in the cool shadow of the dark dripping rocks, at the foot of the falls, the top of the gorge—that goal for which you have so arduously labored.

This is the Small Fall, sometimes called the "Dry Falls." The latter name you will hardly appreciate should you visit it when swollen by recent rains. Here you may enjoy an unequaled shower-bath; but the stream carries pebbles, and the dashing water itself stings like a shower of shot.

Below (and on the cliffs above) this fall is one of the best localities for Helderberg fossils or petrifactions. Among these fossil shells of ancient seas are many peculiar to the Helderbergs. The names and features of these shells once mastered, two of the most important of geological ages are known to you. On the Pacific slope, amidst the Sierras, throughout the north American continent, even in foreign lands, knowing these fossils you will be able to recognize the Silurian and Devonian rocks. The Helderbergs are principally Silurian; above this, on the summit of the hills and on their southern slopes, Devonian rocks are found.

When, years ago, Lyell in his geological travels visited these hills, he was struck with amazement. It seemed a new, a forgotten world. There is a stratum of the cliff rock, sometimes fifty feet in thickness, entirely composed of one variety of fossil shell—the *Pentamerus galeatus*—the shells massed together in a way astounding. This, once the shell-covered bed of an ocean, is now a portion of a mountain cliff. It is this that gives such interest to Helderberg precipices, more than to basalt Palisades, or even dread Wall-Face of the Adirondacks.

If you are fortunate you may find the outcrop of that stratum and bring away a "chunk" of shells. Besides the *Pentamerus* a dozen or more varieties of fossils may here be found. *Spirifer* and *Athyris*, whose delicate internal spirals art has brought to light. The well-named *Platyceras dumosum*, a flat horn covered with spikes, as its name implies. The beautiful minute *Tentaculites* that resemble little petrified minnows or fishes just hatched—they fairly swarm on the thin, clinking fragments of the water-lime stone. *Encrinoids* (stone lilies), ancient *Trilobites (dalmania)*, with their numberless eyes, perhaps a rare, odd-looking thing called a *Cystad*, a beautiful little *Euomphalus*, a butterfly-like *Strophomena*, an *Atrypa* or *Rynchonella*, cornucopia-like *Zaphrentis*—Corals (favorites), *Bryozoans*, *Fucoids*, and others valuable to the geologist, surprising and interesting to any one.

These rocks (or rather the rocks of this age) were till within a year called *Palaeozoic*, as containing "the most ancient life." Fossils have since been found in the older, granite *Azoic* (without life) rock. Those names, having lost their meaning, are now obsolete.

Along beneath the cliffs runs a narrow path. The debris of the mountain drops on one side (a steep wooded slope); on the other the overhanging precipice forms a wall. Westward this path leads to the Indian Ladder road; and, going that way, you pass a curious spring. At the base of the cliff is a dark opening, about three feet high by six or eight in width, narrowing inward. From the dark interior of the cliff a clear, sparkling stream issues, constant summer and winter. This place I once explored in a boat built for the purpose, narrow and coffin-like, carried thither from the road along the ledges. I found a black, narrow passage—no deep water, lakes, or large rooms—nothing to reward me for my pains.

Eastward the path leads to the "Big," "Mine Lot," or "Indian Ladder Falls." Have a care when following this path; the overhanging rocks are often loose and trembling. Sometimes your mere approaching tramp will be sufficient to cause their rattling fall. Suddenly you turn a corner of the cliff and pause in admiration of the scene before you.

From the edge of the overhanging precipice, more than a hundred feet above your head, streams down a silvery rope of spray, with a whispering rush, sweeping before it damp, chilly eddies of fugitive air that sway the watery cable to and fro. Back, beneath the rocky shelf from off which the fall precipitates its unceasing stream, is a black, cavernous semi-circle of rock, its gloomy darkness in deep contrast with the snow-white fall. Below, to the left, the woods are swept away to the base of the mountains, and in their place a wild and desolate descent of broken rocks falls sharply—rendered more savage of the eye by the shattered trunks of dead trees mingled.

Back of the fall at the base of the precipice is a low, horizontal cavity in the rock, from four to six feet in height, 50 or 60 feet in length, by 15 in depth. Stooping and clambering in over a low heap of rubbish—probably the old waste of the mine—you enter. Mine, strictly, there is none; but the marks of mining implements and the excavation show that operations of some kind have been carried on. There is a massive vein of iron pyrites (bisulphide of iron), fine-grained and solid, and well suited for sulphuric acid manufacture. The bed or vein of pyrites has evidently been much thicker, but it has decomposed, a yellow oxyd of iron and sulphate of lime (gypsum) resulting.

The particular appearance of the bed is interesting. At the bottom of the excavation can be seen the glittering masses of pyrites, above them calcareous incrustations, over which appears the yellow oxyd of iron, resulting from the decomposition of former pyrites, seamed and segregated with veins of gypsum—mis-named "plaster of Paris." There is no sulphate of iron (proper) or green copperas resulting, but a white, acid, crumbling substance answering to *Coquimbite* (white copperas) may be found; and a yellow incrustation, in one place at least, resembling sulphur flowers. The oxydized sulphur of the pyrites, as sulphuric acid, has united with the limestones to form the gypsum, of which there are sufficient indications to warrant a search. As the limestones are frequently magnesian, another result has been the formation of sulphate of magnesia, and beautiful acicular crystals of the Epsom, or "hair," salt have here been found. Almost all the "plaster" used in the State comes from the western Helderberg limestones. California is said to have imported from New York in 1868 nearly 25,000 barrels of gypsum.

Long years ago wild stories were told about this mine and its workers; of two strange, taciturn, foreign men who frequented the spot, who kept their mouths shut, and minded their own business in a way astonishing and irritating to the country people around. Nay, more incomprehensible, they lived there beneath these silent rocks, and often in dark nights strange lights were seen flashing and moving among the dangerous precipices—wild, heathenish shouts and noises heard among the cavernous recesses of the cliffs. At times in the misty haze of early morning they had been met upon the road with heavy packs upon their sturdy shoulders, wending their way toward some mart, and all who saw them muttered "a good riddance." But suddenly some night lights would again be seen flashing far above the farm-houses among the gloomy, night-hidden rocks. At length they vanished, never to return. The object of their labors is unknown; the ruinous remains of a stone structure resembling a vat, said to be of their construction, yet exists; it is called "The Leach." The mine is known as the "Red-Paint Mine," and it is asserted that the miners were engaged in the manufacture of a red paint from the yellow, ochery oxyd of iron there existing. How they managed it seems now among the lost arts.

Were the Helderberg rock but slightly metamorphosed, with here and there a dyke of trap or basalt, what minerals might it not contain? The Almaden mercury mines of Spain (red cinnabar, vermilion, "paint") are in metamorphic Silurian limestones. The White Pine and Treasure Hill silver mines of Nevada are in a metamorphosed, crinoidal limestone of the Silurian age, the quartz veins containing the familiar fossils silicified. Old Dutch Colonial Governor Kieft protested that there was gold in this region. Nay, it is said that he found it; and doughty Van Der Donck, the historiographer of the New Netherlands, swears to it.

You may reach the cliff top from here by going further east, where the precipices decrease in height. Search till you find the ascent to a narrow ledge that leads to a square embrasure-like break in the cliff; it seems as though a huge block twenty feet square had been carried out. In one corner you will discover the crumbling fragments of a tree-ladder; it can not exceed twenty-five feet to the summit. Ascend, and you will have an idea of the Indian Ladder.

Westward now along the cliff tops, back toward the falls again, and the Indian Ladder Road. You reach the stream which forms the Big or Mine Lot Fall, and, stepping through the bushes which obscure your view, stand upon the verge of the precipice. To your left, from the lowest ledge below, the fall leaps the cliff brink, and pours in a steady stream.

Recline here and rest. Six inches beyond your feet is the mossy, weather-worn, blackened cliff edge. A wild flower growing in some cliff below, never once trodden by now living man or beast, raises its unpretending head just above the precipice brink. Out beyond is empty air; below, the dark afternoon shadows of the perpendicular mountains are already casting the valley in shade. The wild, rock-filled gorges seem but tiny gutters; the forests shrubbery; all below miniature.

Leaning head and shoulders over as you recline, you see that the rock on which you rest is a projecting shelf but a foot or so in thickness. Should the table-rock yield beneath your weight, rushing with it through mid-air you might light upon the cruel jagged tops of those dead hemlocks, thrust upward from below, whose withered points, lightning-scarred, and broken moss-wreathed limbs, seem waiting, bristling, to receive your fall.

It is grand, thus reclining on the cliff brink, to view the wide-spread landscape to the north of the mountains—the joint basin of the Hudson and the Mohawk—a deep valley more than 60 miles in width. From here you see a wide-spread level country, a true basin, bounded by distant mountain chains; not the bewildering sea of lesser peaks and hills visible from Tahawus. You see, nearest, the deep savage valley, with shades predominating, mountain-walled; the checkered fields and woods beyond, in vast perspective; the distant white farm-house and the red barns, and half forest-hidden steeple of the village church—all vanishing in hazy distance; last, the blue, ragged outline of the northern granite mountains, a bright sky flecked with feathery cirro-cumuli, ever changing, lit with a rich, warm, mellow North American sunlight, brighter than which can not shine either in Italy or on South Sea palm groves.

The cliff, measured by cord and plummet, is here about 126 feet in height; that of the waterfall may be estimated at 116 feet. Here you may lunch beside the brook, and gaze out past the Hanging Rock, across the valley, to the opposite mountain spur, where a faint ascending line shows the Indian Ladder road again; by it you will soon descend the mountain. Amidst the bushes back from the falls is a deep, narrow crevice. A stone dropped in rattles and clatters and hops till lost to hearing. To what gloomy cavern is this the sky-light? Some careless person may yet tumble in and learn; yet no one else would ever be the wiser. Such crevices account for the numerous springs at the cliff base. The rock must be ramified with caverns.

Leaving the fall, westward again along the cliff tops, bring you to

*The Dome*

the Small Fall and a road; following this you come out upon another
road. Look to your right: that deep angular cut through the rock is the
Pass, the head of the Indian Ladder road.

Descend the defile; you are below the cliffs again in gloomy
shadow. Here stood the Indian Ladder. Observe the semi-Alpine character of the road; off this built-up, wharf-like way more than one team
has dashed. The trees on the long, steep slope beneath have their
history: "The horse struck that one; the man was found just here."

As you descend the road the cliffs increase in height, and the
Dome, a mantle-piece-like projection, fairly overhangs and threatens
it. Climb the debris beneath the Dome and you will find a path. Fol-

low it. It leads to a cave, the resort of Tories and Indians during the Revolution.

"The Tory House" is a large circular or semicircular cavity in the cliff, just above the road, a good view of which it commands. It is a single room, perhaps 25 or 30 feet in diameter, open on one side; looking out over a block of fallen stone—an imperfect rampart—down the wooded slope to the road, and beyond, into the deep valley between the mountain spurs.

Here Jacob Salisbury, a notorious royalist spy, is said to have been captured, about the time that Burgoyne was marching his army toward the now historic plains of Saratoga, visible from the mountaintop. The capture of this spy was deemed of considerable importance. It was with difficulty that his lurking-place was discovered and his projects frustrated.

No road then climbed these cliffs. In these wild, unsafe days the wolves were left in undisturbed possession, and the cave was almost unknown. Imagine the darkness of night enveloping the scene. Within the cave, the dusky figure of a man who kneels before a feeble and smoking fire, which ever and anon gives forth a lurid flash—lights for a moment the dungeon-like cave—shines from the brass-bound butts of the huge pistols decorating his belt; then disappears in more mysterious shadow. The thick smoke irritates, he sneezes, how melancholy and hollow is the echo! how quick suppressed the sound! Hark! a twig snaps without; the rattling fall of a stone is heard! The flame leaps up once more as he turns his savage, bearded face; mark the knit brows, the glaring eyes—a desperate *spy*. His right hand reaches toward his musket, yet he hesitates. A heavy tread outside; the rattling of many stones; a brushing through the bushes. He starts defiantly to his feet; though trembling, cocks his musket—at bay! There is an muttering of human voices in the impenetrable darkness without; an ominous clicking as of many rifle-locks; and suddenly some one cries out, "Jacob Salisbury, lay down your arms! You are surrounded and can not escape. A dozen rifles are leveled at your breast." He hesitates. "Down with your musket!" shouts one without. "Do you love treason better than life?" As he dashes his musket, with a curse, to the ground, the flame leaps brightly up and shows the shadowy forms of his foemen; their leveled rifles, steady aim; their leader, sword in hand, in front. Disarmed and bound, the spy is hurried down the mountain, and the lonely cavern abandoned to wild beasts again.

In the roof of the Tory House is a dark, tubular or spire-like cavity, which has, apparently, no connection with any other chamber or cavern. You may, returning, descend the mountain by the road, having seen the more prominent places of interest of the Indian Ladder region.

I will now locate and slightly describe a few of the numberless Helderberg caves. Indeed, without such guidance, the visitor might never find any of them; for to discover caves appears to require a cave-hunting instinct, a learned eye. The under-world has its peculiarities. It differs from the upper-world. Its rivers run at right angles beneath the surface torrents, and are generally little influenced by surface storms and changes. Some run a clear, cold, unaltering, constant stream; others ebb and flow with the seasons; are impassable, muddy, furious in spring flood-time; and the waters vanish, dry up, and are lost in seasons of drought.

The limestone rock of the Helderberg is the cave rock of the world. Other names it may have beyond the oceans; but the rock is of the same age, and contains fossils similar to these found here. Only in Silurian limestones is there space for a region of extensive caves— "Silurian," on this continent, carries Helderberg with it. The Mammoth Cave of Kentucky appears to be in the corniferous, upper Helderberg limestone, which is, however, Devonian. In England, on the Continent, in Palestine, are caverns in limestone, and some in other rock, but rock which has been changed, having by heat been metamorphosed into marbles and the like.

Within thirty miles of the Indian Ladder one may count twenty caverns large and small. Among them, in Schoharie county, Ball's or Gebhard's Cave—brightest of alabaster caverns—whose gloomy portal drops perpendicularly over a hundred feet to a region of large lakes and wondrous waterfalls; and Howe's or the Otsgaragee Cavern, which strives to rival Kentucky's Mammoth Cave.

The caves of the Helderberg are not glittering crystal grottoes. Though often extensive, they are dark and dungeon-like, damp and muddy; on every side they show the means which made them. The hollow, constant rushing of the water also tells the story of their formation.

Among the cliffs, however, are some caves comparatively or quite dry. Many a dark hole and crevice may be seen on the face of the impregnable precipices; and the water-worn appearance of the rock just below these openings proves them the entrance of unknown caves. None have explored, none save the fool-hardy will explore, their passages.

Sutphen's Cave, near the Indian Ladder, is reached by descending a narrow crevice through the rock to a ledge a few inches wide. Along this you crawl, the cliff above and below you, a dangerous path in winter, ice and snow covered. Reaching a chill recess beneath overhanging cliffs, you are at the cave entrance. The cave is said to be of some extent, and perhaps it is—under water. A short distance in, after wading at one place knee-deep, icy cold, the cave becomes spacious, and you reach a deep, clear body of water. It is said that in a heavy rain-storm this cave fills up suddenly, and pours a perfect torrent from its mouth. One of those savage, rock filled gorges descends from this cave's mouth down the water-worn mountain slope.

Westward, among the cliffs, above the village of Knowersville, is Livingston's Cave, a small, dry, and romantic cavern. Should you happen to be near, it is worth a wait. West and east there are many more caves which you may find by seeking. Near the Hudson, toward Coeyman's there are several.

At Clarksville, 12 miles from Albany, and eight or 10 miles southeast from the Indian Ladder, are more caves. Two of these are well known; the entrance of one is in the back-yard of one of the village houses. The subterranean river is the house well; a pair of steps lead down into a crevice in the rock. They have no other water. For drinking it is unsurpassed; but it issues from lime rock, and is therefore hard and unfit for washing. This same river bursts forth near by in the bed of the Oniskethan, and aids that stream to run a saw and paper mill. Chaff thrown upon the river in the cave is soon found floating on the mill-pond. The stream empties into the Hudson at Coeyman's. I once heard it remarked that an amphibious animal might make its way through the caverns from Hudson river to Niagara Falls without once coming forth to daylight!

These two caves are said to be respectively one-eighth and one-half a mile in length. They should not be called two caves, however, for the "river" seems to flow from one to the other, and forms a connection which a person who likes ice-water baths might explore. Taken as one cave they may exceed a mile in length. The smaller cave is dry and airy, and has some spacious corridors. Squeezing your way down through the narrow entrance you reach a sort of room—the vestibule—faintly lit with the few white rays of daylight which glimmer down through the entrance. You have suddenly passed into a dim region of silence, only broken by the faint tingling and murmuring of the subterranean stream below. You light your lanterns, and the red flames guide your footsteps. A short way through a narrow passage and you ascend into a lofty chamber—the "Room of the Gallery." Should you visit it in winter, as I once did, you may start horrified back. Two or three ghostly, white columns rise here and there from the floor! There are no such stalagmites in this cave. What, then, are these white columns gathered in a spectral circle? You approach; they move not. Nearer, nearer still, and the white columns resolve themselves into fantastic stalagmites of ice—beautiful yet fragile. The water dropping from the roof, the frost which reaches in thus far, account for them.

That dark hole plunging downward to the right is the continuation of the cave; descend, and turn in at and climb the first side passage to your left, and you will reach the "Gallery."

It is related that a villager, venturing in to pass a hot summer night, having but a solitary tallow-candle, his light became extinguished, and he thought himself all but lost. Feeling along in the dark to find some means of exit, he was suddenly precipitated into a dark pit. A while after, as he sought to ascend, he fell again, deeper, receiving severe injuries. Dreadfully alarmed, he rushed hither and thither, only to fall a third time, and still deeper. He swooned from terror; and when he awoke he observed a faint light opposite. Scrambling toward it, he entered a room; it was the cave entrance! Some assert that he mistook the passage in returning, and merely climbed to and fell from the gallery several times.

There are other large rooms and corridors in this cave, but there are few stalactites or stalagmites, if any. In one place are some beautiful incrustations of spar; and in another spot a vein of the massive calc-spar, with large crystals, is found. The latter sometimes contains the Silurian anthracite, supposed to have had its origin in the organic animal life of that age. The rock inclosing the calc-spar is a granular or sub-crystalline limestone—the Upper Helderberg.

A singular feature of the cave are the waterworn pot-holes in the rock ceiling. Every one knows that rational, common-sense brooks or rivers of the surface world make them according to law of gravitation in their water-worn beds. Here natural laws seem laughed to scorn; and these pot-holes, as though from very perverseness, are set inverted in the roof. They were formed undoubtedly when the cave was filled with water, whirling and rushing against the roof.

A narrow passage leads to the extremity of the cave. Where it enlarges is a steep and rather slippery descent to water. This is called by some a lake; the rock roof comes so close to the surface that its lateral extent can not be seen. Naptha poured upon the water and ignited, though it makes a singular sight, burning with a blue, lambent flame, shows nothing, and the darkness is deeper when it dies away. The water is very clear and still, and increases in depth, gradually, off the shore. There are here no "eyeless fishes."

The "Half-mile Cave"—the larger cave, or the longer end of the cave, if they are but one—is about a quarter of a mile from the hotel in Clarksville. This cave is often visited, and has a large, wooden, cellar-like door, and wet, slippery steps, which lead in winter down into warm, steaming darkness.

Mind your steps; I speak literally. Now go down the dark hole on your right; it is a steep descent. You are in darkness again, and your lights but feebly illuminate the place. There is a sickening damp warmth; it is not unlike charnel-house, a catacomb. This mouldy earth beneath your feet, lixiviated, would probably yield much nitre; the earth of caves generally contains it. Notice those black strata veins of flinty hornstones; they may have served their time in the days of flint-lock rifles. Here is flint, there saltpetre; pyrites through heat will yield sulphur; the alders and willows from beside mountain brooks give choice charcoal. Here is gunpowder in the raw, for those adept in its manufacture.

It was these veins of brittle, translucent flint, called hornstone, which gave the name of "corniferous limestone" to this rock, from the Latin *cornu*—horn. It was not the fossil shell, the cow-horn shaped *zaphrentis*, which originated the name; though that is the most prominent of the many brown, weathered shells incrusting the roof and walls of the cave. These same shells—*zaphrentis*—project similarly from the walls of the great Kentucky cavern. This corniferous (upper Helderberg) limestone is peculiar as being the oldest rock in which the fossil remains of fishes have been found.

You may have a mile or more of clambering in and out from this cave, and that is as good, though not quite so bad, as 25 miles. There are long passages where you might drive a team of horses and a wagon; narrow, muddy passages in profusion; bats, overhead and fluttering past you, every where.

The bats hang from the ceilings separately, and from one another in curious festoons. They are now hibernating. Aroused by your approach, some take wing and occasionally strike against your lantern, shattering the glass. On all sides you hear them squeaking and chattering and grinding with their teeth; it is horrid. How they live there is a mystery; no suitable food is visible, and the door of the cavern is kept closed. Some of the bats seem withered and half dead; others are more lively. The gray or frosty bat is sometimes found here. The *cheiroptera* of this cave have been described in Goodman's "Natural History;" for this is the one therein mentioned as "an extensive cavern about twelve miles south of Albany, New York." They have quite changed their habits since sketches were made of them by that reliable naturalist. In his time, it is evident from the engravings, all bats hung themselves cozily head up; now the contrary vampires all hang head down, in a way that could not fail to be alarming to apoplectics—a vile rebellion against the naturalist. Bats, sleeping, hang then with their heads downward, holding fast by the little paws they have behind, and not by the hooks attached to their membranous wings. In their flight near the roof they stop and flutter for a moment, then hang correctly. It is thought that they catch by their hooks, and, if the place suit them, assume the upside-down posture. If they fall to the ground they are for the while helpless; however, with the aid of their front hooks, they climb to some little eminence from which, by turning a sort of somersault, they fall down, and, as they fall, take wing and search for better quarters. Nature has given them instinct so to repose that, when disturbed, they may be able to take to flight and escape.

If you determine to see the end of the cave and the lake, and are not afraid of mud and low, flat passages, you will go further, perhaps fare worse. Again the cavern enlarges, a black emptiness is before you. Approach. You stand upon the shores of "Styx." A vaulted roof of dripping rock, a silent, echoing cavity, scarcely illuminated by dim lantern-light. Unruffled are the still, deep waters, green, though clear. The silence only broken by the sudden, occasional tinkling of a drop

*The Styx*

of water falling somewhere in one of the dark side passages only to be explored in a boat. The boat is wrecked.

In returning you have to repeat the crawling and scrambling through the low, narrow, or wet and muddy passages: it seems endless. You halt to await the approach of a loitering companion. His lantern is seen, in distant perspective, far down the dark corridor. You shout for him to hurry. Hark to the distant, echoing answer, "Coming!" Turn your lantern this way, and look down the long, shadowy passage of the cavern; in the dim vista he seems an imp, dancing along with a fire-brand. Suddenly, while you think him yet at a distance, he seems to enlarge, and is close to you.

I once fired a pistol-shot in this cave to hear the echoes; instead of the sharp crack which should have followed the flash came a volley of deep, echoing, hollow thunders, a rolling and swelling roar, a musical, harmonious earthquake, deafening. One of our party who was on ahead took it for heavy, celestial thundering.

Cave explorations are interesting to those who love to see the wonders of nature—things before unseen, new and surprising. Who knows, some one thus exploring may discover a great, subterranean, transcontinental river; an underground, round-the-world canal, cheapening freightage between New York and San Francisco. Whether you should find this wondrous stream or not, a visit to the under-world will not be forgotten; the hornstone and the fossils collected, nay, the grimy, shattered lantern that you carried, will ever remain objects of interest.

Winter is the best time to visit caves; it is certainly the most healthy season, for it is dangerous to enter a cold, damp cave in hot weather. Nevertheless, ice closes the entrance of some caves in winter, and, if among the cliffs, the climbing is dangerous.

In winter the Indian Ladder or Mine Lot Fall is one huge icicle from the cliff brink to its base; the water pours down—an unceasing stream—through the huge frost-proof conduit it has formed for itself. A pyramid of pure green-white ice, glittering, resplendent with icicles, which in fringed sheets, strange and fantastic shapes, adorn the translucent column, one hundred and sixteen feet in height. Have a care how you climb up among the rocks in winter; it is almost impossible to descend again, and dread indeed is the ascent. Upward may prove your only path to safety over slippery ice and snow-capped rocks; below you the cliff, the tree tops, the dread craggy mountain slope! Hands icy and stiffened, useless and bleeding, my only reward for the climb depicted was a bit of rare moss (the *Hamelia gracilis*) which I found on the rock above.

Frequently upon the brow of the mountain, you will see a ruined tower perched; surprised, you draw near. The door is low and narrow, and seems to be almost closed by the debris; it has a very ancient look, and resembles some old feudal watch-tower you may have seen in Europe. The slope below is white with rubbish and covered with fallen stone—the tower itself blackened with fire. It is a Helderberg lime-kiln. The lime made here is the best known; many of the poorer farmers burn lime in the winter. It replaces the charcoal burning of other regions, and though quite as laborious and scorching, is more remunerative. The fuel used is wood, and the great heaps of ashes thus obtained are greedily sought by agriculturists and potash makers. The kilns are of refractory rock; blocks of clay-slate are preferred; and they are generally built near the quarry where the limestone is blasted out. These lime-burners will tell you curious stories of the "animals" they have seen in the rocks; some of them have singular collections of the fossils.

The limestone, when blasted, breaks into large, regular blocks, well suited for building purposes. This is generally owing to the cleavage, but frequently huge blocks are quarried which are perfectly loose and need no blasting. These owe their origin to "shrinkage clefts," which, as another singular feature of Helderberg scenery, is worth explanation.

Often the roads on the summit of Helderberg are of solid, level rock; the mountain top is a plateau as smooth as a table. Cantering along on horseback the constant ringing clatter of iron against stone is painful. In places the rock is jointed and in small blocks and resembles a Belgian pavement; again it changes, and a singular sight meets your eyes.

The rock plateau is split by numberless parallel crevices, stretching only either side in perspective; if you view them with half-closed eyes the dark clefts resemble railroad tracks. The sutures between the long blocks or trunks of stone are often 20 feet or more in depth, though sometimes choked with rubbish, and generally six, eight, or 10 inches wide. In storms the water rushes down into the caves below. On the mountain (above the village of New Salem) these clefts extend perfectly parallel for miles. At times rectangular or diagonal sutures cross the main ones; then the rock is cut in blocks a yard square on the surface; downward—twenty feet, more or less—it is a pillar; you may teeter it where it is; a thousand like you could not lift it out. These barren, arid rocks refuse to grow aught save stunted cedars, ground-hemlocks, and white birches, though now and then a larger kind of tree supports itself in a rock cleft. The foxes also find excellent hiding-places in these clefts. Near Clarksville, on the slope of Copeland Hill, the clefts are two, three, or four feet wide; sometimes black, bottomless looking pits, unexplored. Below are often other subterraneous rivers, flowing no one knows where from or whither. A robber once had a boat there, and in a cavern deposited stolen goods; his secret was discovered, and himself and plunder captured. The sudden and mysterious disappearance of obnoxious men is mentioned in connection with these dark pits. There is a stream which dashes, full-bodied, into a great pit or sink-hole in the rock, travels an unknown course, and issues at once from a cliff three quarters of a mile distant.

The slippery or red elm (*Ulmus fulva*) is or used to be, very abundant, and tons of the bark have from hence been brought to market. Maple-sugar making is another industry common here. In frosty spring, smoke rising here and there over the woods tells of the fires crackling and flaming under the great iron kettles in the open forest, or—as at old Peter Ball's, near Berne, on the slopes of Mount Uhi—in a well-built sap-house. In early frosty morning the "Sugar Bush" is a bright scene; the sunlight streams down over the mountain, and the old trees cast long shadows. The sugar-maker hurries hither and thither, collecting the buckets of clear, colorless sap, throwing out the ice which has frozen on the surface overnight (for experience has taught him that in freezing it has lost its sugar), placing empty buckets under the taps—ever busy.

But there is not space to mention every thing of interest in this forgotten range of hills—the numerous waterfalls and caverns and mountain-split gulfs.

If but a few learn from these scant notes that there is something new to be seen at home as well as abroad I am satisfied.

# The Dome of the Continent

*Those familiar with the life and career of Verplanck Colvin assume his world extended only from Albany to the Adirondacks and back with a side trip now and then to the Helderbergs. He did travel as far as New York City on occasion to lobby for continued support of the survey and for an Adirondack Park. Notable among these efforts was his speech before The New York Farmers in December of 1890. Some "farmers" these — numbered among the membership were two Vanderbilts, a Stuyvesant, a Colgate, John Jay, Pierre Lorillard, W. Seward Webb, and J. Pierpont Morgan.*

*Colvin, however, did make two extensive journeys that took him far away from his beloved Adirondacks. His half-brother, James, had served with distinction in a series of battles during the Civil War, rising to the rank of Colonel as an aide-de-camp to General William Tecumseh Sherman at war's end. As a teenager, Verplanck had followed his brother's exploits with great interest and plotted his marches and countermarches on a collection of campaign maps.*

*In the summer of 1870, Colvin traveled south, visiting Richmond, Wilmington, Charleston, and other sites where James had fought. He continued to Florida, New Orleans, and up the Mississippi before returning home. All this is set down in itinerary/diary form in one of his field books and entitled, "The Southern Journey."*

*In 1871, Colvin toured west and visited "the crest of the Snowy Range of the Rocky Mountains." His article describing these explorations was published in the December to May 1872, issue of* Harper's New Monthly Magazine *and added to his fame "as an artist and literary man" and "obtained for him election to honorary membership of the Rocky Mountain Club of Denver, Colorado."*

*An interesting historic aside to this expedition is that Colvin passed through Chicago on his way west the day before Mrs. O'Leary's cow kicked over the lantern and started the Great Chicago Fire.*

*— NJVV*

In these days, when every one may travel, and the great plains, the Sierra Nevadas, and even the beauteous Yosemite valley are becoming trite and common, it will please the tourist to learn of new routes of travel, fresh sights and places to be seen. Some who have rushed across the continent to see the wonders on its western shore will yet gaze with amazement upon equal or greater wonders which they have hurried past without even imagining their existence; for men may journey and see nothing, may travel and have little for their pains. Thousands boast their overland passage from the Atlantic to the Pacific Ocean, and return, who never saw the Rocky Mountains! Not that they traversed them in the night, nor that some of the mountain ridges were not seen; but that the sea of towering snow-clad summits which mark the eminent majesty of this great range were to them distant or invisible, hidden by the foot-hills through which they passed.

Of the whole Rocky chain Colorado Territory possesses the chief mountains—certainly the most famous; for here, amidst a multitude of others, each one a monarch in itself, rise Pike's and Long's Peaks—names linked with the earliest history of the West—the landmarks of prairie voyageurs in days gone by. Further west, Gray's Peaks, Mount Lincoln, and a host besides tower, with summits crested with eternal snow, and, circling, surround those beautiful and wondrous valleys, which Rasselas might envy—the North, Middle, and South Parks. Here is the snowy range, the icy mountain wall which parts Orient from Occident—the "divide," as it is popularly called, where melting snows discharge their waters east and west to the world's greatest and most widely separated oceans.

The days of danger are past in Colorado. Upon most of the stage routes the traveler is as comfortably kept and cared for as at many Eastern summer resorts, and already Saratoga trunks are seen where but a dozen years since the bear and deer only were met. Many tourists come to see the gold mines, perhaps longing to pan out some "dust" for themselves; mineralogists and geologists here find the earth's wealth thickly spread before them; the botanist meets a new and splendid flora, and cactus growing thriftily beside the snow; the eyes of the ornithologist are dazzled with the dark blue-green iridescent plumage of the bold and fearless Rocky Mountain blue jay, and

Reprinted from *Harper's New Monthly Magazine*, vol. 46, December 1872 to May 1873.

*The Snowy Range*

he starts at the sudden cry of the large, garrulous, black and white jackdaw. The sportsman looks to his rifle as he sees the monstrous tracks of the cinnamon grizzly, and by the camp-fire listens with surprise to stories of adventures with "mountain lions," of hand-to-hand encounters with huge elk, or of thrilling climbs amidst the cliffs in pursuit of the big-horn or mountain sheep; regrets the absence of his fly-rod as he hears of cold crystal brooks swarming with speckled trout of the same old habits and as vigorous in their play as those that haunt the Adirondack lakelets or the streams of Maine. The Alpine tourist feels anew the longing for adventure as he hears of untrodden summits vying in altitude with the loftiest of the Swiss Jura; and the artist longs to stand in the presence of those scenes which have inspired the pencil of Bierstadt.

It is a great pleasure-ground, and soon to be the resort of those that leave the stale and hackneyed routes of European travel to see and appreciate the fresh glories of their native land; the summer home of those who, loving mountains, prefer to find *their* Alps this side the stomach-troubling ocean.

The visitor to Denver has at least a distant view of the mighty mountain chain, some of the peaks and ridges of the snowy range showing slightly above the darker foot-hills. Numerous interesting routes into the mountains diverge here; but passing most of them, we will go westward on the unfinished Colorado Central Railroad 17 miles, over the last piece of prairie land, and entering the foot-hills, rest at Golden City.

Golden City is not as auriferous as its name implies. Its mineral wealth is principally coal, and its mills and well-utilized water-power make it the manufacturing town of Colorado. It is just within the foot-hills, which, edged with vertical sandstone precipices—from which one prominent summit gains the name of Table Mountain—almost surround the valley where it lies. From here a stage can be taken for Central City or Georgetown; and while Georgetown should be the objective point, those desirous of visiting the gold mines will proceed by way of Black Hawk and Central City, regaining the other stage at Idaho, the celebrated soda springs. This is the route for the Middle Park *via* the lofty, snow-bound Berthoud Pass. On this line also lies Guy Hill, famous with all stage-travelers in the region for the steep, almost dangerous piece of road descending it westward—a zigzag way carved in the face of the mountain—down which the six-horse coach is driven at full speed.

The scenery of a mining region is proverbially barren and desolate; yet here, though the axe has swept the timber from the mountains and left them a wilderness of stumps, the grand surroundings, the wonderful views of crests and chasms, compensate for the vandalism. Dinner is taken at a way-side inn, a small white frame building; then, after a few hours of up and down hill journeying, the gold mines are reached.

Suddenly debouching from a valley, we turn into a road running at right angles with our previous course. The mountains rise steeply up on either side, and along the road a stream, the north branch of Clear

Creek—here any thing but *clear*—runs pent in a wooden trough, leaving dry and bare a rugged bed of cobble-stones, once its home. Among this drift men are shoveling and delving, wheeling barrow-loads of gravel to the trough or sluice-way—for this is "sluicing," a variety of placer gold digging or gulch mining. In one spot two men, apparently engaged in undermining the road, step back and look up, as though to stand from under, as we drive above; near by another stands beside the sluice with a sort of steel-pronged stable-fork in hand, and working the ringing tines through the swift-running muddy water, throws out the larger stones and gravel. All the peculiar features of a gold-mining region were here: little water-courses in board troughs ran upon stilts in various directions; skeleton under-shot and overshot water-wheels abounded; and in the hills on either side were dark, cavernous openings, the mouths of tunnels or deserted claims. Now the bottom of the narrow ravine or canyon is choked with mills, furnaces, and buildings, which often stand among the rocks and perch in almost impossible places. Through all this the road and the creek with difficulty find a passage, and while the one is frequently blockaded by teams, the other is forced through many a mill and compelled to do a deal of dirty work in the "washing way." Beyond are stores and shops and a Chinese laundry; and this is Black Hawk, the first of the string of village "cities," which are indeed but one, crammed into this red, gilded gulch, in three miles ascending 1,500 feet, one town beginning where the other ends—Black Hawk, Mountain, Central, and Nevada Cities, each one greater in altitude than the other—having together a population of 4,000 or 5,000 souls.

Central City is well named: on all sides of it are mines, which are often as profitable as their names are singular. The Groundhog lode, on Bobtail Hill, is a veritable and wealthy mine, and, together with a host of others, is well worth visiting.

The Illinois may be taken as a type of what is here called a "quartz mine"—it being first understood that very little quartz mining is done in Colorado, the "pay rock," or ore, being principally iron and some copper pyrites, together with what is here commonly called brittle copper, with black-jack, or zinc-blende, and galena, all forming ores of the class called *sulphurets*. It is not often that all of these minerals are found together. Though quartz always accompanies them in some form, the gold is here chiefly associated with the pyrites, and such is the unreliable nature of popular names that a lump of the glittering yellow "fool's-gold" is often called quartz by unlearned miners, while the same name is commonly applied to the pay rock, heavy with the cubic pyrites, by those who should know better. Native gold does occur in pure quartz rock, but it is seldom that very fine specimens are seen.

Gold mining here becomes systematized, and the history of a mine may thus be traced: The formation, or "country rock," is a common gneiss, apparently of Laurentian age; a vein or lode is found in it exhibiting "blossom rock," a yellow, spongy mass, charged with iron rust formed by the oxidation of the pyrites. The discoverer stakes out his claim, and if the "dirt pans well" the rest of the lode is soon taken up. At length the "top quartz," or "blossom rock," is worked out, and even iron mortar and pestle fail to pulverize sufficient of the now hard and refractory ore to pay the prospector for his trouble; water, too, invades the mine and drives him out. Now comes another phase: either the claim owners effect a consolidation—a mining company being formed—or the capitalist steps in and purchases the whole. Lumber and machinery are then brought over the mountains, and presently buildings appear, and steam hoisting and mill machinery, and true mining has commenced. Shafts are sunk, levels and tunnels made, the mine is drained, the ore brought out, and, if available, put through the stamp mill. The product of the mill would not readily amalgamate with pure mercury. It issues from beneath the heavy stamps a grayish, sparkling, thin mud, and flowing over gently inclined sheets of amalgamated copper, bright with quicksilver, passes off under the name of "tailings," leaving the gold-dust amalgamated, fixed to the surface of the wide copper trough plates. From the surface of these plates the amalgam, thick with gold, is wiped at regular intervals, and when sufficient is collected it is placed in a cloth, the ends of which are gathered together and twisted. Upon squeezing the bag thus formed much of the mercury passes out through the pores of the cloth, while a heavy, pasty mass of gold, still silvered by the mercury, remains within. This last, with the cloth holding it, is now placed in a cast-iron crucible-like cup, to which a flat iron top is fastened, a bent pipe of the size of small gas tubing passing out at the center, forming the neck of the retort. Upon the application of heat the mercury is expelled, and collected under water at the end of the tube for future use; the cloth is consumed, and the gold in its pores thus saved, while, if the heat be not raised to a height sufficient to melt the gold, its exterior still shows the shape and impression of the folds, seams, and texture of the rag or cloth which held it. In this condition is most of the raw gold in the possession of the banks of these mountain cities, though the tin pail or box in which they obligingly exhibit it will often contain at the bottom a gleaming yellow metallic sand and gravel, which have an intrinsic beauty, and are the "dust" from many a placer miner's pan.

The gold of Colorado is thus obtained; but wealth and fortune are gathered by many gold miners and companies who never see the metal that they dig. Capital has introduced a division of labor, and much of the poorer ores, in which the metal is altogether invisible—locked up and hidden in the sulphurets—never enters the amalgamator, but, after having its value ascertained by assay, is sold at fifty dollars and upward per ton at the smelting furnace. Black Hawk has the fame of possessing both the first stamp-mill and the first reduction-furnace of Colorado. The smelting-works, erected in 1867, and in charge of Professor Hill, their projector, are famous throughout this region, and are to the miner the equivalent of the grist-mill and the factory of the agriculturist. In each case the master of machinery and of skilled labor buys the crude material from the producer. At the smelting-works the poorer ores, and especially those of auriferous copper or argentiferous galena, with the tailings of the stamp-mills, are purchased. The process is the reduction of the unmanageable sulphurets by fire to a condition suitable for the rapid extraction of their precious contents. This disintegration and destruction of the pyrites is but a shortening of that natural process which has made the outcrop of every vein of the sulphurets a porous mass of blossom rock. Even at the smelting-works the pyrites are compelled to aid in their own destruction, and in the open yard of the works, broken in small lumps, they are heaped in dome-shaped piles, perhaps eight or 10 feet high, in form not unlike charcoal kilns. A layer of wood underneath the pile serves as kindling, and before it is entirely consumed the pyrites themselves take fire and, burning slowly, give off dense, stifling vapors of sulphurous acid gas, sufficient, one would think, to bleach even the dirty hats of the bull-whackers passing on the road. As this slow combustion proceeds, especially in cold weather, the tops of the heaps become incrusted with a bright yellow coating of brimstone; but at length the action ceases, about half the sulphur having disappeared. The once hard, brilliant, and sparkling pyrites—bisulphide of iron—have become black, clinker-like masses—protosulphide of iron, like that used in the laboratory for evolving sulphurated hydrogen. This particular protosulphide is too valuable for laboratory purposes; and after calcination in a long range of brick ovens, where, under intense flame-heat, it is kept stirred with iron rods, an additional portion of sulphur is expelled. It now assumes the form of a black or brown powder, and is finally thrust into the smelting furnace, which is of the reverberatory kind, strongly built of fire-brick, supported and held by a system of broad iron bars passing around and over it, and bolted and clamped together. The work of this furnace is constant, the temperature maintained terrible to contemplate, and gazing in at the small door by which the process may be observed, nothing is seen, when the heat is greatest, but a white glare as dazzling as the sun. Into this furnace the roasted ore is put, an average similarity in its composition being secured by the mixture of auriferous, argentiferous, and cupriferous ores, as may be necessary, the design being to form a compound which, when melted, will react and separate into an upper and lower liquid, the one rich and heavy, the other light and containing almost all the dross.

The charge having been introduced, the intense heat, *which acts upon its surface,* soon reduces it to a molten condition; but the process does not stop here, for the heat continues and grows *more* intense, till it seems to threaten the destruction of the furnace and of the great tower-like chimney, up which the white-hot blast rushes furiously. After some hours the watch-door is opened, and when a peculiar brightening of the surface of the lake of molten metal is observed the fire is withdrawn, and presently an opening on one side of the furnace, till now stopped with fire-clay, is tapped, and the lighter surface metal allowed to pour out into rough moulds of dry sand. This is worthless slag, being a mixture of silicate and protosulphide of iron, and it is moulded merely that it may be more easily handled when cool, and carted away to form roads or fill gullies. It is remarkable for its hardness and brittleness; for, while glass may be scratched with it, a mass of a hundred pounds' weight or more will fall to pieces under the boot. After the slag has been drawn off an opening is made at the other side of the furnace, and the lower liquid, the brilliant fluid metal, is led into open sand moulds similar to those that held the slag. This product is called *matt*, and though of the same dark iron-color of the slag, is a mass of gold, silver, copper, and iron, with a small amount of sulphur, which seems to remain in combination with the iron. The Colorado treatment is over, and the precious black *matt* is forthwith started upon a journey across the world by rail and sea to England—or rather to Swansea, Wales—where the gold and silver are extracted, and the copper remaining is sufficient to pay not only the expense of transportation, but the cost of the various processes through which it has passed.

But let us turn from the consideration of gold extraction to gold mines. One bright October afternoon, accompanied by Mr. Bela S. Buel, of Central City, I examined a mine of which my companion was principal owner. The mine was situated on Quartz Hill, south of and above Nevada. In the superintendent's office we exchanged coats and hats for less worldly habiliments, and, provided with overalls of a color uncertain from the dry mud upon them, prepared to descend. The costume was nearly as picturesque as that of the oiled-skin-en-veloped neophytes who haunt the rocks beneath Niagara. Having lighted our candles, a small trapdoor in the platform covering the mouth of the shaft was opened, and disclosed a dark pit, perhaps eight or ten feet square at the mouth, dropping apparently fathomless into the depths of the earth. A steep ladder fastened to one of the walls showed the means of descent, and we went down into the pit; the trapdoor closing left us in inky darkness, which the light of the feeble tapers we carried but partially dispelled. The steep, muddy ladders led on down till to the imagination the depth below was awful. Not a ray of light could penetrate it, not a sound or echo came up from it to indicate the existence of life below; the water dropping from the oozy walls, the scrap of rock detached, were lost and gave no sound. O gold! beloved of men, bright, glittering gold, gloomy and desolate are the pathways to thy home!

At last some slippery boards received our feet, and we paused to rest; then down again by shorter and more inclined ladders, with platforms at intervals of 25 or 30 feet. Occasionally dark, horizontal tunnels led off into the rock, which now formed the only walls of the deep shaft. These *levels* were passages to upper *headings,* and were not provided with rails or cars, the ore being cast below to another level, where conveniences for carrying and hoisting existed. Passing along one of these levels, we came to what was known as the skip shaft; for here, boxed off in one half of a shaft the huge *Cornish skip* carried the ore to the surface. This vessel, which has a carrying capacity of twenty cubic feet, here replaced the less spacious and heavier kibble buckets of old-time mines, and was of boiler iron, strongly bolted or riveted together, forming an oblong box, open at one of the smaller ends, which was also uppermost. A prolongation of the metal at one of the upper edges gave it a lip like that of a rectangular coal-scuttle, and served a similar purpose, preventing the spilling of the ore when the top of the shaft is reached, and the skip, by an automatic arrangement, discharges its contents. One engineer above, by levers ready to his hand, controlled both engine and skip, and, at a signal from below—the ringing of a gong-bell at the shaft mouth, by means of a cord or bell-rope passing down the shaft—would bring the skip with a rush to the surface, see it discharged, and send it swiftly down again.

Descending further, we reached another tunnel, and then a short ladder brought us to the lower level and the bottom of the shaft, a well hole, called the *sumph,* all the drainage of the mine being led this way, and the water here raised by the skip to the surface. Entering the level, which was partially floored, and had a narrow wooden railway, we went toward the heading, encountering a subterranean breeze which threatened the extinction of our lights. It was a singular avenue we traversed. Much of the ore above had been removed or worked out, and as only the ore had been taken, the bent, overhanging, and recurved walls rose above us till lost to sight in the gloom, making plain to the eye the form of a true fissure vein. The hanging wall, propped everywhere with short but heavy timbers, threatened us as we passed beneath, and ever and anon trembled responsive to the distant thunder of blasting. Now we passed an upward-leading shaft, arranged for ventilation, and called a *winze;* then a board boxing was seen at one side, descending from some upper level, and crammed with ore, held back by a sort of slide-gate at the lower end. This was a *mill,* but more resembled a strange sort of hopper; it held the ore cast down by miners from above, and kept it from the rail track till a car was ready to receive it; when by simply raising the gate the ore poured forth into the car.

The heading was an interesting sight: numbers of miners were engaged, some "pushing the level," and some on slight platforms of poles picking the gold rock from overhead; while the numerous lights, reflected with a thousand minute scintillations from the glittering walls, bright with mirror-like crystals of golden-colored pyrites, made the place appear a very cave of Monte Christo, and the walls rather of royal metal than of gleaming ore. Gold was every where; the very rock seemed to have taken a bright color, to make it a fit dwelling for the metal king. Gold under foot, gold on the walls, gold in the roof, *but really very little visible,* the brilliancy of the tawdry, tinsel associates hiding its less brazen beauty. Seldom is it here seen until the stamp-mill and the furnace have done their work. The appearance of a sulphuret vein is worth description: the *vein-stone* does not entirely fill the fissure, and on either wall are lateral cavities containing drusy quartz, the slender crystals thickly bristling on the rock. Far more beautiful, however, are the large cubes of iron pyrites, which for perfection of shape and polish are unrivaled, while their size is a surprise to the Eastern mineralogist. No glass or metal mirror can equal the polish of their faces; but often I noticed them superficially inclosed or boxed in sheets of quartz as thin as writing-paper, which at a touch from the finger slipped aside and showed the gleaming facets of a virgin crystal, on which light never shone before.

It was late evening almost before we knew it. The miners had all left, and we hastened upward. Slowly climbing, laden with specimens, we found the ascent more toilsome than the descent; and pausing now and then to rest, noticed where the white sperm of the miners' candles had dripped upon the wet rocks of the shaft, and, changed in color by the copper salt in solution to a verdigris-green as vivid as the spring foliage of the forest, showed the mineral richness of even the water of this region.

Above-ground once more, we bade the superintendent good-night and went quickly out into the frosty darkness on our return to Central City, and a comfortable though late supper at the Connor House.

Much may be seen at Central City even in a day or two. If the inquisitive traveler escape falling into some one of the numerous disused pits which make the mountainsides a dangerous region after dark—if he has seen the famous silver mines at Caraboo, some 20 miles away, and the wild and beautiful Boulder Creek Canyon—he may take the stage that every afternoon goes rumbling off to Idaho, and, leaving mines, proceed in search of mountains.

Up, slowly up, we go, leaving behind Central and Nevada, till, gaining a lofty ridge, we see before us the whole bright, sun-lit southward picture, where, prominent and picturesque among other scarcely less romantic summits, rise softly and dreamily the Indian Chieftain, with Squaw and Papoose mountains at his side. Who would think that in that neighborhood lies the scenery of Bierstadt's "Storm in the Rocky Mountains," the Chicago Lakes and Chicago Mountain? Who would dream that that cloudless sky could ever be convulsed in such dark magnificence? Away to the westward are loftier, haughtier summits, dazzling in their spotless robes of white. But we have crossed the ridge, and to the crack of the whip go hurrying and jolting down to Idaho and the hot soda springs.

Idaho, named from the "purple flower" of the Utes—a rich, wild columbine here growing in profusion—is a quiet little village, and though 7,800 feet above the sea, is at the bottom of the valley of Clear Creek, whose shallow, sparkling waters sever it, and give occasion for a rude, picturesque wooden bridge, over which the main road up from Golden and Denver has its way.

The springs, three in number, are on the south side of the creek, and the steaming alkaline water, issuing from the rock at a temperature of about 109° Fahrenheit, trickles down and forms a little brook of soda-water, better suited for washing than for drinking. This is genuine *soda*-water—cooking soda with nearly an equal amount of sulphate of soda (Glauber's-salt), and a considerable percentage of Epsom salt and salts of iron and lime, besides common chloride of sodium, forming together a mixture *probably* of great medicinal value, but certainly not agreeable when taken internally.

Idaho, being a quiet and cozy place, has become quite a resort, and few of the tired and dusty tourists from the East pass it without enjoying a hot bath. The waters have also the reputation of being curative in rheumatic and paralytic diseases, and for cutaneous affections no one can doubt their efficacy, for it is a most cleansing solution.

But now away for Georgetown and the end of civilization on the Atlantic slope, the place where silver bricks are used as paperweights upon the public desk of the bank counter: fearlessly used, not because the spirit of absolute honesty has settled dove-like on the heads of teamsters and miners, but because the bricks of precious metal are much too large to pocket, and rather heavy for any one man to carry off.

Away, then, fast as six horses can whirl the lumbering coach, up a deep canyon valley sunk between almost precipitous mountains, along beside the flashing, hurrying creek. Spanish Bar, and Fall River with its wonderful Profile Rock, the semblance of a fierce human

*Humility with Wealth*

head, sharply projecting from the opposite mountain crest, were passed, and, as the sun's shadows lengthened, a canyon opened to the right, showing a long vista through the dark mountains up to where two white slopes bent grandly down to form the Berthoud Pass over the snowy range, its lowest point more than 11,000 feet above the sea.

It was evening when the deep valley widened, and the mountains, parting to right and left, made space for a small plateau or upland prairie—a *bar,* in mountain parlance—then, circling and closing in darkly and gloomily, seemed to forbid further progress. Picturesquely spread and scattered on the plain which forms the pit of this great natural amphitheater was Georgetown. Beautiful little city, nestled in this last romantic nook of the mountains, with its broad streets and neat white houses, and Clear Creek winding through it like a ribbon of flowing metal from the mountain's silver veins! Beautiful valley, land-locked with granite ridges, up which the scanty evergreen forest creeps to meet the frosts of a perennial winter, and draw back, dwarfed and withered, down the steeps! It hardly seems to be a mining town, so little crowded and so quiet. How the thin air startles one! Strange spot to build a city! Europe has no place like it, for it is more than 5,000 feet higher than the glacier-walled vale of Chamounix, and it is even higher than the far-famed snow-girt hospice of the St. Bernard. Yet it is *not* altogether a mining town, for already it has become a centre of resort for tourists, and in the Barton House it possesses one of the best hotels between the Rocky Mountains and the Missouri river.

Just above the town is the famous Devil's Gate, a deep chasm, cliff-walled, through which this branch of Clear Creek—Vasquies Fork—foams and leaps.

Twelve or fifteen miles from Georgetown are Gray's Peaks, perhaps the loftiest of the true Rocky Mountains, rising, it is said, to an elevation of 15,000 feet above the sea. Securing the services of Mr. Bailey, of Georgetown, and two of his gallant black steeds, early morning found us on our way to make the ascent, cantering along the well-kept and firm though narrow road which followed the valley or canyon of the stream westward and upward. It must not be supposed that the road is maintained for the accommodation of tourists visiting the snowy summits. It leads to many a rich silver mine, and teams toil along it daily, dragging wagons heavily laden with gray, glistening ore.

A zigzag path ascending the mountainside from the road attracts attention. It is a trail from some silver mine among the cliffs, where wagon teams can not be brought. A dangerous path even for human foot: but see, here come *its* travelers, a sober-looking set of silver-gray donkeys! In single file, without bit or bridle, they come leisurely on, bearing upon their backs bags of silver ore slung across the pack-saddles. The sure-footed beasts neither slip nor stumble, and day after day toil on, receiving many kicks and no caresses; on Sundays only, gathering in squads, standing idly side by side with crossed necks, fondling one another; on week-days at their work, laden with precious ore, the very pictures of humility with wealth.

And here we notice a "tunnel claim," a slight excavation made into the rock, with a few timbers put up before it—two sides and a top piece—representing the commencement of the timbering of a tunnel, or adit level, to the lower portion of some vein opened on the surface further up the mountain. Such a tunnel claim, under slight rules, entitles its owner to a plot of land one or two hundred feet square around its mouth, and to property in any lodes, or metallic veins, he may discover.

The valley now opened beyond, and suddenly gave us a near view of the snowy range, which we had imperceptibly approached. How strange and solitary the aspect of the white slopes and ridges of that mountain desert! Yonder a peak of bold, sharp outline stands high above the rest; long, narrow ridges, ice-edged, leading upward to the summit, and dread crevasses and chasms forming defenses on its flanks. Is that our goal? "No; it is only the Little Professor," a much less summit than the one we have to climb. Now we turn sharply to the left, up into the mountains, following a narrow, steep, winding road, through the evergreen forest. Strange, though at Georgetown there was no snow, here the road is deep and heavy with it, and the whole scene is one of midwinter in the Eastern Middle States. The road, winding and turning, constantly ascends; and the dull trampling of the horses in the snow is the only sound heard in the silent and shadowy forest. This is October; at home the brilliant joyous season of ripe fruits and gleaming, gaudy foliage; *here* already chill and joyless winter. We had left far below the groves of aspen—trees of the fluttering leaf—and had now around us only the tall, majestic pines, the slender and graceful *Menzies* and *Douglass* spruces, and the gleaming silver-firs, that answer to the balsams of Canadian forests. Beneath the trees the snow was marked with rabbit tracks, and now and then the animal itself was seen—the great Northern hare, in fact—here already changed in color, and at times so white as to be hardly distinguishable upon the snow, while some but partially changed, mottled white and brown, were the more readily seen. To one acquainted with the habits of the animal this apparently premature change of color is remarkable. At this season of the year and in this latitude only here amidst the lofty mountains does the change occur thus early, those inhabiting less elevated regions much further north still retaining their brown summer pelage; and in the lowlands it is only when we reach the arctic circle, and the lowland zone of perpetual snow or ice, that we find the "varying hare" assuming at this season his white winter coat.

I was surprised to learn that wolves were not found in the mountains, and, from description, became satisfied that the mountain lion—which is here sometimes met with—is the panther or cougar of the Eastern States. Here, however, was the home of the monarch brute, the cinnamon bear, or cinnamon grizzly, as it is more properly termed.

It is a little remarkable that even the great savage of our continent grows less and dwindles in our estimation as we near his home. We learn not only that he does not always seek the encounter, but nowadays often has the discretion to scamper off upon the sight of man. We are not so much surprised to learn that he is not absolutely carnivorous, and that he is even capable of sustaining life upon a diet altogether vegetable; but what have we to say when we learn that this mighty beast, at certain seasons of the year, devotes the whole of his majestic mind and body to the capturing and eating of grasshoppers? It is but another example of the great law of nature, the preying of the strong upon the weak; but the strangest thing is the way he gets the gryllidae. In the summer season these pests of plain and valley swarm up among the mountains, as though inspired with the desire which every living, progressive being has to press westward. At length in some of their airy flights they are caught by the winds, and wafted swiftly upward to the snowy range, their own strong wings assisting. Here, alas! fortune and strength fail them, and, chilled in that unaccustomed atmosphere, they fall upon the snow lifeless. The winds that previously aided and beguiled them here now gather and drift them into funereal piles in hollows and crevices amidst the snow. Thus wonderful masses of them accumulate, and at this season Master Grizzly wanders over the snow fields, peering into crannies and crevices, and finding a hoard, deftly conveys pawfuls to his capacious mouth.

We saw nothing of these monsters, however; and now the strange and wondrous scenery withdrew my mind from them. We had reached a wide upland valley walled by naked precipitous mountains of dark gneissoid rock. The forest had grown thinner, the trees were smaller, and looking back over their tops, the depths from which we had ascended were seen, while other valleys, opening in various directions, diversified the solemn landscape. Before us the broad chasm valley came sloping down in a great curve, its terminus hidden by an intervening mountain at the right. At the left, sheer and rugged, rose McClellan Mountain, one long curved ridge of precipices; while on the slopes below—the *talus* of the cliffs—were scattered the last stunted, twisted, and gnarled trees whose nature enabled them to stand the climate—the pitch-pine *(Pinus contorta)*, of shriveled and dwarfed growth.

A little further, and we crossed an ice-bound brook by a crumbling bridge of logs, which told us that even here man had come in search of gain and profit. We were nearing our object, and the day was bright, clear, and so far favorable; yet the labor was still to come. Breaking a hole in the ice, beneath which the little stream went gurgling and murmuring, we gave our horses drink. A faint cry, almost lost even in that stillness, came softly quivering down as if from the sky or from the cliff-tops of McClellan Mountain. Glancing upward, a keen scrutiny at length discovered a small building (shed or shanty) clinging apparently upon the face of the precipice, more than five hundred feet above our heads! What could it be? What were those long ropes that sloped down at an angle of seventy degrees to a building which we now noticed in the valley?

It was the famous Stevens silver mine, located 12,000 feet above the level of the sea—nearly twice the height of Mount Washington, which, with the Baker mine upon the less precipitous mountain at the right, is probably the highest point in Colorado—perhaps in the United States—where mining is carried on. Those cables which seem but threads are endless wire ropes, moved over drums and pulleys by machinery in the lower building. The one descending carries buckets of ore; the empty buckets are returned by the ascending portion. Against the rocks hang other ropes, and there is some sort of pathway up which men, clinging and scrambling, may climb. Few care, even if permitted, to slowly pass up through the air in nothing but a kibble bucket, hung from a quivering, trembling wire cable. It was a giddy spot to look at, and I learned that it was considered the hardest place of labor in the Territory. The thin air saps the muscles and energy of the miner, and a single stroke of the pick tires his whole body. After three or four days' labor in the mine the haggard and nerveless workman is pulled up, and sent off down the mountains to Georgetown, to get breath and strength for another struggle; while if he have a trace of consumption, one effort is sufficient to send him back a corpse.

It was past, and out of sight; and we almost seemed to have reached the boundaries of the world, and the drear, barren, rocky wastes that lie between it and the blue ether of the heavens. We had reached the timber-line. I turned my horse, and looked, and wondered. The dark green forest had crept up into this high valley, and here ceased suddenly; in places it reached forward in short strips like courageous, undaunted squads of infantry pressing onward before their comrades upon the foe. How wonderful a war between natural forces—how obstinate the contrast where they meet! The few daring trees that stood forth solitary before their fellows had been seized by some strong invisible power and twisted and contorted into shriveled, writhing agonies of dead, bleached limbs. Their tops resembled dry and weather-beaten roots, and all their life was near the ground, where some branches crept out horizontally, groveling to obtain the growth and breadth that were denied to them above. Dread clime, where even the hardy evergreen is forced to yield!

We were above the timber-line, here rising to 11,000 to 12,000 feet from the sea, above the limits of tree life, in the open valley where only the dwarfed forms of arctic or Alpine vegetation found existence. There was no road now, hardly a trail. At times our horses trod in snow, then their hoofs turned up the deep brown peaty soil of the Alpine bog, with its surface of microscopic plant growth, and now their iron shoes rang against fragments of stone. Suddenly we entered a forest—but what a forest! It hardly rose to our horses' knees, yet the trees were full grown. They were deciduous, their leaves all fallen, but their unmistakable growth and cottony catkins showed them to be willows. It was, in fact, a growth of the mountain willow (*Salix phylicifolia?*) which, like the varying hare, is only abundant on the lowlands of the frozen North and the equivalent frosty regions of high mountains.

Hark! what are those strange ventriloquistic, chirping sounds, now near, now far, now like the cries of prairie-dogs, now like the piping of the partridge grouse?

"It's the conies—see!"

A little gray, mouse-colored animal, not larger than a guinea-pig, thrust his head up out of the snow, and, motionless, as though he thought himself quite unobserved, glared at us with his wild-looking little eyes.

"Watch him; he's coming out."

With a slight awkward scramble, the tiny beast emerged, and took his place upon a fragment of stone projecting above the snow. Oddest of creatures, he had absolutely no tail!

It is peculiar to these lofty mountain deserts, and their little communities make them to the eye the equivalent of the prairie-dog of the plains. They are said to be a true cony, however, and no marmot, and consequently can not hibernate like the common woodchuck, but must remain amidst or under the deep winter snow, cutting galleries and tunnels through it to the herbs and stems on which they feed. Such channels or subniveous passages I found among the thick growth of mountain willows, but did not establish their object. The Rocky Mountain cony should not be confounded with the Scriptural animal, for, as already stated, it is a true cony, and is classed by naturalists with the rabbit kind (Lepus), whereas that called Shapan by the Hebrews owes its present name merely to a mistake of the English translators of the Bible.

"What was that?"

Something resembling a hand-breadth of snow fluttered up from among the willows, and flying a short distance, lit and was lost again upon the earth's white covering. Another and another followed, till presently the surface of the snow seemed animated.

"White partridges!" cried the guide. "How tame they are! See them, walking within stone's-throw!"

Truly it was an interesting sight. It was a flock of the rare willow-grouse, or ptarmigan (Tetrao [lagopus] saliceti), another habitant of subarctic regions, here finding a congenial home. Like the Northern hare, it had already lost shade and color, and its spotless winter plumage made it all but invisible against the snow. We had roused them from their feeding ground, for they were living upon the buds of the dwarf willow. After a vain attempt to shoot some with a revolver, for specimen for the taxidermist, we proceeded, satisfied that with a fowling-piece most of them could have been secured, for they are but little acquainted with man, and so tame that it is said that they have been taken by hand.

Here the valley was finally closed in and ended by the mountains, prominent among which were two lofty summits, towering and im-

*Gray's Peaks*

posing still, and yet we stood more than 12,000 feet above their deep foundations!

We saw the summits of Gray's Peaks. Grand, awe-inspiring spectacle! crests of a continent! The nearer, stern, dark, and precipitous; the other, still afar off, soft in outline, and sloping easily down to a great bed of snow and ice—the hidden, crouching, shadow-loving remnant of a glacier.

But how are we to reach that crest of snow? Midway, just beyond the great moraine, are steep precipices, dropping at the left to the very bottom of the valley, while their edges, glary with ice, slope at the right to the fathomless snow-drift which covers all that remains— if there be any remnant—of the old glacier.

"There's no difficulty," says my companion, calmly; "the trail winds along the edge of the cliff, from which the wind has blown most of the snow, and, except where the ground is slippery, it's perfectly safe."

Another half hour of constant ascent and I was upon the brink of that precipice; involuntarily drawing rein, awaiting the coming of my guide. The silence here was awful. The deep drifts at the right, on the margins of which our horses floundered fearfully, had forced us from the trail to the very edge of the cliffs. The soft, new snow, of unknown depth, looked treacherously calm and beautiful, and where it met the opposite mountain wall had a névé glacier appearance, upholding fallen boulders, and here and there scored with a long drift of rock and gravel, cast down from the overhanging cliffs by frost, and which it was now its duty to slowly carry down, to form, perhaps, one last moraine. Beneath the other hand was the dark, dizzy chasm, the cliff descending sheerly six hundred feet and more.

We were above the region of plant or animal life, upon the margin of things inorganic; surely, it seemed to me, this might be termed "Life-limit."

But still far above arose the snowy crest which we designed to climb. The precipices passed, a long, steep slope of snow-clad rocks rose before us, and a narrow trail, winding in short precarious zig-zags on its face, led upward toward the summit. The horses were now exceedingly distressed, and panted painfully after each exertion; their bodies were swollen from lack of atmospheric pressure. The narrow trail was hidden beneath drifts, and could hardly be followed; its turns were so abrupt, and the mountain's face so steep, that, when our horses plunged into deep snow, or stumbled over hidden rocks, it seemed as though horse and horseman must dash down headlong after the hurrying, scudding masses of snow, helplessly over the steep, glary, ledgeless crust, to be ingulfed in the deep snowy tomb below.

At length the fresh snow became so deep, and further progress in the saddle so precarious, that, reaching a spot where there was standing ground, we left the horses loose, knee-deep in the downy drift, the guide sure of their remaining where we had placed them.

Making directly for the summit, in a few moments, chilled, breathless, and panting, we were compelled to rest. There was something startling about the thinness or rarefaction of the air. The lungs gasped, and yet, shuddering, almost repelled the cold, dry, strange atmosphere which offered itself to aid vitality. Too violent an exertion produced dizziness, and we were compelled to proceed with caution.

Suddenly, as we climbed, the western sky grew larger and more vast, increasing and growing as we clambered, till at once the whole westward view burst on us, and we were standing upon the very crest.

Before us, walled in by a vast mountain chain, whose average height exceeded 13,000 feet, whose passes (the Georgia, Snake River, and Berthoud) were from 8,000 to 11,000 feet from the sea-level, far below, stretched like a vast topographical map, was the Middle Park, with all its subordinate mountain ranges, and numerous streams and rivers—the springs and sources of the Rio Colorado. Thousands of feet below, trees and vegetation gave color to the scenery, and marked the limits of plant growth. At the right, half-way down, in a huge basin hollowed in the gneissoid rock, was Lake Colfax, a dark green, glistening mirror. The park itself, with its valleys, plains, and prairies, stretched away into the hazy distance westward, to where snow-crowned ridges, southward from the Rabbit-ear Mountains, were parted to give passage to the deep-flowing Colorado. Such was the view down the Pacific slope; eastward, fifty miles away across the mountain billow, like a calm ocean, lay the boundless prairies.

Spurned by our feet, heavy masses of snow sped eastward and westward down the mountain slopes, parting to the world's great seas. The one to thaw and glide through the dark canyons of the Colorado to the Gulf of California and the Pacific Ocean; the other to be hurried with the yellow spring floods of the Platte, Missouri, and Mississippi to the Gulf of Mexico and the Atlantic.

Call not a mountain range the backbone of the earth; to man the world is not a being, but a dwelling; rather liken these great ridges to the dome, the strange, weird, fantastically ornamented pinnacle and ridge-roof of his vast treasure-house. This was *indeed* the divide—the great water-shed of the continent, whose gutters are mighty rivers, whose cisterns are the seas!

But oh! how wonderful this mountain architecture—the unmarred handiwork of our God! Gazing down upon these frosty peaks, they seemed a sea of monstrous icebergs, a frozen ocean—a spectacle whose only equivalent would be such a scene as an ocean's bed laid bare, its waters driven back and stilled, and its deepest and most secret chasms all revealed.

The day was beautifully clear, a few light cirrous clouds only floating above. Away at the southwest were Mount Lincoln, the Sopris, and other peaks without number—a white sea of shrouded mountains; and far in the north rose Long's Peak, another chieftain, lacking only a few hundred feet of the height of Gray's Peaks. Below, in the glacial valley through which we had made the ascent, the limit of the forest was seen, at that distance appearing merely to be a dense carpeting of green; while it was remarkable that on the northern exposures of the mountains, and in the deeper ravines, the trees seemed to be more thrifty, and the timber-line to be higher, than on the more open, sun-lit plateaux, or the southern fronts.

After lunching on the summit to windward of some stones—supposed to represent a wall—we started downward, and found our horses shivering under their blankets. Then, leading them, we slowly but safely descended to the valley. Conies and ptarmigans were seen again, and the Alpine bogs passed; but there was no time to tarry: the sun, so bright upon the mountain-top, had here already left every thing to shadow. However, once below the snow and ice of this October winter, and upon good roads, we sped along at a swift canter, and shortly after dark dismounted before the Barton House, in Georgetown, receiving congratulations on our successful ascent at so late and unpropitious a season, while Mr. Bailey emphatically declared it the last trip which he would make that year.

Withal it was a delightful ride, entertaining and instructive; and a ride of about thirty miles, the ascent and descent of a monarch mountain—chief of its range, and fourteen or fifteen thousand feet in altitude—is not made every day between sunrise and sunset. The Rocky Mountains are not seen until these peaks have been climbed; but in the summer season access to them is less difficult, even ladies making the ascent.

Geologically, there is hardly a more interesting ground than the region around Gray's Peaks. I have referred to the evidences of glacial action in their immediate neighborhood: the proofs of such action are conclusive. There are moraines and moraine dams and frozen lakelets, and I was informed by miners of the Stevens mine that frost is found two hundred feet deep in the gravel, and that it seems to be rather increasing in depth than decreasing. If this be so, it is a sufficient refutation of the theory recently advanced—that there is no line of perpetual congelation among the Colorado mountains; and it would prove that the present lack of ice-fields and great glaciers is owing to the deficient rain and snow fall, and the dryness of the atmosphere consequent upon the great distance of the oceans. The accompanying map of this mountain neighborhood will be sufficient proof to any geologist of the previous existence of glaciers there, and exhibits, also, the timber-line, or height to which the forest rises.

The glacial evidences have, however, been obscured by subsequent dynamic action—frost force—the exposure to frost and heat having broken the cliff edges and shivered the rocks till moraines are covered and valleys filled with sharp angular fragments of stone. Nothing but glacial power could have grooved and cut the deep valleys through the mountains; nothing but frost could have made the crags as rugged as they now appear.

Again, Green Lake, three miles from Georgetown and some 10,000 feet above the sea, is said to have neither inlet nor outlet, and seems to be a veritable glacial pool. Singular to relate, it is called a "good place for trouting," though how the trout got there no one seems to know or care; and it is a favorite resort of the pleasure-seekers at Georgetown, who in sail or row boat pass merry hours on its crystal surface.

## PART THREE

# Adirondack Surveys

It is impossible for those who have not visited this region to realize the abundance, luxuriance, and depth which these peaty mosses— the true sources of our rivers—attain under the shade of those dark, northern, evergreen forests. The term "hanging-lake" will not be deemed inappropriate, in consideration of the fact that in the wet season a large mass of this moss, when compressed by the hands, becomes but a small handful, the rest of its bulk being altogether water; often many inches deep, it covers the rocks and boulders on the mountain sides, and every foot-print made has soon a shallow pool of ice water in it.

With the destruction of the forests, these mosses dry, wither, and disappear; with them vanishes the cold, condensing atmosphere which forms the clouds. Now the winter snows that accumulate on the mountains, unprotected from the sun, melt suddenly and rush down laden with disaster. For lumber, once so plentiful, we must at no distant day become tributary to other States or the Canadas. The land, deprived of all that gave it value, reverts to the State for un-paid taxes.

— VERPLANCK COLVIN
Ascent of Mt. Seward and
Its Barometrical Measurement, 1870

# Ascent of Mount Seward and Its Barometrical Measurement

*The first four of Colvin's trips north (from 1865 through 1868) took him to the southern Adirondacks, where he spent much of his time attempting to unravel the intricacies of the lines of Totten and Crossfield's Purchase and adjoining patents. In 1869, he headed northeast and explored the High Peaks, climbing Whiteface and tramping to Indian Pass, Avalanche Pass, and Lake Colden.*

*In 1870, he started at Blue Mountain; went down the Marion River to Raquette Lake, where he hired on the guide Alvah Dunning; continued through Forked Lake and Long Lake; and up the Cold River to the lower slopes of the Mt. Seward massif. On October 15, Colvin and Dunning reached the main summit, after spending an uncomfortable night just below the final peak.*

*"The view hence was magnificent," wrote Colvin in a report to the state's Board of Regents that was published in April of 1871 in the* Twenty-fourth Annual Report on the New York State Museum of Natural History. *It consisted of three parts; the first being a diary narrative of the trip to the mountain, its ascent, and descent. The second part records Colvin's barometric measurements taken during the climb and at the summit together with a determination of the height of the mountain (4,462 feet) made by the Dudley Observatory.*

*It is, however, the final six paragraphs that are historic. Here Colvin began his campaign for "the creation of an ADIRONDACK PARK or timber preserve." Others would join in as years came and went, but it was the publication of this plea in an official state report that is the point of beginning. The long road ahead eventually led to the establishment of the Adirondack and Catskill forest preserves in 1885 and the "creation" of the Adirondack Park in 1892. All that is, of course, significant, but the wonder is that Colvin was only twenty-three when he climbed Mt. Seward and commenced his life's crusade.*

— N J V V

SAMUEL B. WOOLWORTH, LL.D.,
*Secretary of the Board of Regents of the State of New York:*

DEAR SIR.—I herewith respectfully submit to you the report of my recent explorations in the Adirondack Wilderness of Northern New York.

The main object of the expedition was the barometric measurement of Mount Seward, a lofty peak, of the ascent of which there is no record, and the height of which remained in doubt. Professor Emmons, while engaged in the survey of the second geological district of the State, estimated the elevation at 5,100 feet above tide; but as he neither ascended the mountain, nor attempted its measurement by triangulation, there seems to have been no basis for such a conjecture.

Mount Seward—called by the Mohawk Indians *Ou-kor-lah,* or the "big-eye"—is nearly upon the most southern boundary of the county of Franklin, in Great tract No. 1, township twenty-seven of Macomb's purchase; north latitude about 44° 10', and longitude, west from Greenwich, 74° 0'. It is, with the numerous lesser peaks connected with it, the most westwardly of the Adirondack, hyperite group. East from it is Wallface mountain of the Indian Pass, and more distant, Mount Tahawus or Marcy, the summit of the range and of the State, raising its gray peak 5,467 feet above the sea. South of Mt. Seward are the Preston ponds and their outlet, Cold river, which empties into the Raquette just below Long lake. The Raquette river might, perhaps, be called its western boundary; its northern limit, but for Moose mountain and Ampersand pond, would be the well-known Saranac lakes.*

In this expedition my route was from Albany, via Saratoga up the

Reprinted from *Twenty-fourth Annual Report of the New York State Museum of Natural History,* Albany: The Argus Company, Printers. 1870.

*In the accompanying plate the numerous lofty peaks forming the back-ground of the picture, taken together constitute what is locally known as Mount Seward. Some of the highest points are here shown, but the summit, looking back, nearly eastward of them, is probably not visible from any point on Long lake. The ascent was made from the right, up and along the range of minor peaks shown. *Inca-pah-cho* is the old Indian name for Long lake, and has heretofore been little used. It implies lake-of-basswoods, or linden-water.

Hudson, and to Indian lake in Hamilton county; thence crossing the woods to the beautiful and deservedly famous Blue Mountain lakes. Here guide and canoe awaited me, and, after tarrying to make the ascent of Blue mountain (Mount Emmons), I passed over the lakes, and, by way of Marion river, reached Lake Raquette. It may be here re-marked that the whole distance, from Blue Mountain to the foot of Mt. Seward, might almost be made without leaving the canoe or boat; lakes and rivers, for some fifty or sixty miles, forming the tortuous highway.

At Lake Raquette I found the guide whom I had selected to accom-pany me in the ascent of the mountain,—an elderly man, muscular, energetic, born and bred a hunter and skilled in wood-craft. A short day's journey, by Forked lake and Raquette river, brought myself and guide to the settlement on Long lake. Here I consulted Mitchell Sab-battis, the famous Indian, and others acquainted with the region near Mount Seward, and was confirmed in a plan which I had formed of attempting the ascent at the southside, from the direction of the Preston ponds. Sabbattis affirmed that Mount Seward had never been as-cended, and certainly never measured, or he would have known of it. One of the lower peaks had been ascended and called Mount Seward.*

The morning of October 13th, 1870, was bright and pleasant, and found us struggling to push our boat up the rapids of Cold river; a beautiful crystalline stream—haunt of the trout—which fed by the springs on the mountain slopes, rushes sparkling down to pour its icy flood into Raquette river, a short distance below Long lake. From the foot of that lake we had seen the outlying ridges of Mount Seward; now the forest which walled in the river concealed it from view. At length our progress became so slow, and the rapids so frequent, that drawing the boat ashore, we hid it, with my rifle and other luggage, in a thick copse.

Having lunched, we started to follow the north bank of the river, toward the Preston ponds, taking a sled-road leading to certain de-

---

*Since writing the above I have been informed that Professor A. Guyot had previously made the ascent of Mount Seward, and, in answer to an inquiry, he has kindly given me some notes of his expedition. The starting point was Adirondack village, and the time occupied two days. Mr. Ernest Sandoz, his nephew, undertook the ascent and measurement, but had the misfortune to cut his foot, which made the ascent the more difficult, after which he suffered an additional disheartening misfortune, in breaking his barometer before reaching the top of the mountain. My observations, therefore, seem to be the first ever taken upon the summit of Mount Seward.

serted lumber shanties, distant seven or eight miles, where we expected to camp that night.

We were armed each with a hunting knife and revolver,—the
guide carrying in a pack three days' provisions, rubber and woolen
blankets, and in his hand a hatchet. I was encumbered only with my
barometer and satchel containing sketch-book and maps.

Our course along the river bank was a slow but constant ascent, as
was proved by the numberless rapids and several falls which at short
distances made the hurrying water whiten with foam. Step by step
the stream descended its channel, and now our approach to the true
Adirondacks became obvious. In the bed of the river were numerous
huge boulders of labradorite rock or feldspar—sometimes called hypersthene granite—of the familiar bluish, ashen hue, which gives the
beds of these mountain streams so peculiar an appearance. Before
nightfall we had reached the terminus of the sled-road, not far westward from the Preston ponds, but returned to make our camp in one
of the old, long deserted lumber shanties. During the night sparks
from the camp-fire caught in the roof; fortunately the flames were
extinguished before they were beyond control, or the instruments on
which the success of the expedition depended, might have been
destroyed.

| Hour. | Barometer. | Attd. Ther. | Detd. Ther. |
|---|---|---|---|
| 8.30 A.M. | 28.150 inch. | 52 5 Fah. | 53 0 Fah. |
| 8.42  " | 28.175  " | 53 0  " | 54 5  " |
| 8.45  " | 28.200  " | 53 0  " | 54 5  " |
| 8.50  " | 28.225  " | 54 5  " | 54 0  " |

October 14th—The camp was about thirty feet above Cold river,
the banks of the stream being very steep. When we awoke clouds and
fog enveloped everything, and a drizzling rain was falling. Before 9
A.M. the fog lifted, the rain ceased, and finally, the clouds broke a
little, though the mountains were still obscured. There was no wind.
This was the first station where observations were made, four readings being taken.

I had previously determined the compass direction of the mountain, and notwithstanding the dubious state of the weather, set out
immediately to commence the ascent. At the south, or south-east,

Mounts Henderson and Santanoni were, alone of all the peaks, visible; and even their summits were hidden in the clouds. Taking a north-easterly course, we struck directly into the forest toward a small mountain, whence we might be able better to select the way. Our progress was slow for, as there was no trail, my guide took the precaution to blaze the path, by chopping upon the trees every fifty or a hundred feet, and continued so to do, with great labor, throughout the day.

At length, reaching the height we had in view, we were disappointed to find it overlooked by another crest, more lofty than the one which we had climbed, and separated from us by a slight depression. Believing that from its top we would be able to discover Mount Seward, we addressed ourselves to the task and laboriously climbed it, only to discover two loftier peaks towering opposite, beyond and above which the clouds, as they drifted, at times opened to view a misty summit higher than all. It was evident that we were already upon the slopes of the mountain. A narrow valley was between us and the opposite peaks; descending into it, we found the forest carpeted with deep, wet, sphagnous moss. Again ascending, the slope became all but precipitous; yet, by means of small trees, mainly silver-birches, we drew ourselves up.

Here the guide called my attention to a tree with its bark and wood torn by the claws of some large beast. In another place a bear had bitten a fallen tree to the core, and elsewhere left marks of his teeth on the wood. The tracks of deer and other wild animals were also observed, some of which were very recent; the deep moss was like snow and retained the impressions.

With much labor we at length climbed a ridge and saw no more peaks above us; the valley we had left was far down, and the surrounding country, wherever the eye could reach, spangled with lakes. Now the forest began to show that we had attained an altitude where vegetable life recoiled; the trees, principally Canadian balsam, spruce, and white birch, were dwarfed and stunted, being barely fifteen or twenty feet high. The abundant, deep moss was a sponge of icy water, so cold as to make our feet ache as we stood. In clambering upon our hands and knees as we were often compelled to do, we were wetted to the skin, waist high. Our breath was visible in the cold air, which chilled us through our wet clothing; yet the day, though windy, was now bright and clear.

After a hasty repast, we hurried along the ridge to gain the highest point upon it, being anxious to accomplish our work and descend part-way the same afternoon; not wishing to camp in that wet, cold region, where sleep, if possible, would be extremely hazardous.

About 3 P.M. we seemed to have gained the highest point on the ridge, though the thick, miniature forest, obscured the view, telling by its presence—before I had glanced at the instruments—that we were still far beneath the height ascribed to the mountain. Barometrical observations were here taken; cloud fragments drifting through the forest, the while.

| Hour. | Barometer. | Attd. Ther. | Detd. Ther. |
|---|---|---|---|
| 3.26 P.M. | 25.900 inch. | 44 0 Fah. | 40 0 Fah. |
| 3.30  " | 25.940    " | 42 0   " | 38 0   " |
| 3.35  " | 25.950    " | 40 0   " | 37 0   " |
| 3.40  " | 25.950    " | 39 5   " | 37 0   " |

Hardly had the above been noted before my guide, who had wandered off, returned to announce a still higher point in view. The barometer was returned to its case, and we hurried on. The balsam trees continued to dwindle in height, until we stood upon an open crest. The world seemed all below us; but northward, half mile way, a lofty summit reared itself, grizzly with dead and withered balsams, struggling to keep their hold upon the rock that here and there looked out gloomily; it was Mount Seward. Between us and it was an abyss through which clouds floated.

It was a grand, though disheartening spectacle; so near, yet seemingly inaccessible. The afternoon was nearly spent; it was evident that we would now be compelled to camp amid the clouds. However, evening and twilight continue upon the mountains long after the valleys are dark with shadows, and we determined to improve the time by attempting the passage of the gorge. At length, as the clouds parted, we noticed a narrow ridge, or "horse-back," far below, which crossed the deep valley, and on which it seemed that one might pass over.

Starting to descend, we discovered snow in small quantity, the remains of a last winter's drift, lying exposed to the air, discolored and icy. Its preservation thus must be exceptional. Descending amidst precipitous rocks, we reached the "horse-back," and, by hastening, were able at nightfall to cross the deep valley. With the last rays of the sun upon us, we formed a camp just below the true summit of the mountain, on the edge of the impenetrable thicket of dwarf balsams.

There was no spring, but water was easily procured by pulling up moss; the space thus made being soon filled with excellent cold water which, when settled, was sufficiently clear for use. The night came down dark and chill, and a strong westerly wind made the camp-fire burn fiercely. The rubber blanket, spread upon a thick bed of balsam boughs, kept me from the wet moss and some of the small trees, piled bodily to windward, tempered the blast; the rear of the camp being a large rock.

At about eight o'clock in the evening the sky was lightened by that brilliant aurora borealis which excited such attention throughout the northern hemisphere by its wonderful iridescence, and brought the inhabitants of beleaguered Paris upon their ramparts, to gaze with awe at a manifestation by many deemed of dire import. It shot up from the north-west and, passing over to the east, formed a broad crimson belt overhead; while the whole dome of the heavens was lit with silvery glory, which flashed and swayed in seeming concord with the eddies of a gale then whirling round the mountain. With every wave and brightening of the aurora a sighing, whispering sound was heard, like the rustling of great folds of silk, which my guide assured me was the "noise of the northern light." At the north-western horizon pencils of blue darted up toward the zenith, but I was in doubt whether the color was not that of the sky, seen through intervals in the auroral cloud. The rays seemed to center a few degrees south to the zenith. The display lasted long into the night. The guide, who was without coat or blanket, kept himself warm by chopping fire-wood, and we hailed the day with pleasure.

October 15th.—We had not far to ascend from our camp, before we reached a dense growth of dwarf balsam trees, which form a barrier to the summit. They were at first about seven or eight feet high; with much labor we pushed or chopped our way through them, their branches being stiff and numberless and intricately locked. At 8 A.M. we walked upon the trees, which had dwindled to great shrubs, flattened to the ground, with long, spreading, lateral branches, and stood at last upon the summit.

The view hence was magnificent, yet differing from other of the loftier Adirondacks, in that no clearings were discernible; wilderness everywhere; lake on lake, river on river, mountain on mountain, numberless. Northward was Whiteface Mountain; then shone the lower Saranac lake, half hidden by Moose Mountain, while below glittered Ampersand* pond. Looking eastward the mass of the Adirondack was seen, a sea of peaks; nearer, the serrate crest of Mount McIntyre reared itself; but nearer still was Wallface Mountain, viewed not from the east, but from the west; the reverse slopes descending steeply into a dark but broad valley, which seemed even deeper than the Adirondack or Indian Pass upon the other side of the mountain, yet, though gloomy with precipices, lacking the tremendous cliffs which give so much interest to the more famous gorge. A similar locality, somewhere in this neighborhood, was called by the Indians *Ouluska.* As Indian terminology is now generally preferred to modern names, I suggest this for the pass discovered.

The day was clear but cold, and a strongly westerly wind blowing. The hypsometric observations were as follows:

| Hour. | Barometer. | Attd. Ther. | Detd. Ther. |
|---|---|---|---|
| 9.10 A.M. | 25.600 inch. | 47  0  Fah. | 45  0  Fah. |
| 9.12  " | 25.600  " | 46  0  " | 44  5  " |
| 9.15  " | 25.625  " | 44  0  " | 43  0  " |
| 9.17  " | 25.625  " | 43  5  " | 42  0  " |
| 9.20  " | 25.640  " | 43  0  " | 42  0  " |
| 9.30  " | 25.600  " | 42  0  " | 42  0  " |

The height of the mountain had indeed been over-estimated. Of the 5,100 feet attributed to it, it lacked 638 feet; the elevation as measured being 4,462 feet above tide-level, or the sea.

The substance of the mountain was found to be labradorite rock; fragments broken from the summit exhibited crystals of opalescent feldspar, with beautiful play of colors; magnetic iron also occurred in small fragments scattered through the rock. It was late in the season for botanical observations, but the flora appeared similar to that of the neighboring summits which I have visited.

---

*"Ampersand." I believe this to be incorrect etymology, and do not think that it is derived from the *and-per-se-and* termination of old alphabets; but attribute the name to the bright, yellow sandy shores and islands, which make it truly *Amber-sand lake.*

Of the provisions carried with us, there now remained only sufficient for one light meal. Since leaving the boat, it had taken us two
days and a portion of a third to make the ascent, and we were now in
the depths of the wilderness.

About 10 A.M. we commenced the descent, taking a new course
west of south, and, under powerful incentives, by dint of rapid and
hazardous traveling, at nightfall reached the boat, where our extra
provisions and luggage were found undisturbed.

During the descent, near the foot of the mountain, we observed
some scattering giant white-pines, some of which seemed to be between 100 and 200 feet in height, with diameter in proportion. The
rest of the forest was dwarfed by their presence. On my return to
Albany, I passed out of the wilderness by the Fulton chain of lakes,
into Lewis county, and thence via Utica.

The barometer used was a mercurial cistern instrument, deer-skin
bottom and brass scale. Before starting upon the expedition it was
compared with the standard at the Dudley Observatory, and fortunately, for in returning it was broken. The deductions from the observations hereinbefore given have been calculated by Professor
Hough of the Dudley Observatory, which was the station for corrections. I include a note giving the results:

"DUDLEY OBSERVATORY,
Dec. 15th, 1870.

"DEAR SIR.—In accordance with your request, I have computed the
height of your stations on Mount Seward, from the barometrical observations you furnished me.

"The observations were reduced to 32° Fahrenheit, and compared directly with the records given by our automatic registering
instruments.

"The following is the data used:

| Date | | | | Mt. Seward | | Dudley Observatory | |
| --- | --- | --- | --- | --- | --- | --- | --- |
| October, 1870 | Stations | No. of readings | | Barometer 32 | Temp. of air | Barometer 32 | Temp. of air |
| 14th, 8.45 A.M. | No. 1 | 4 | | 28.144 | 54 | 29.769 | 55 |
| 14th, 3.30 P.M. | No. 2 | 4 | | 25.905 | 38 | 29.779 | 56 |
| 15th, 9.15 A.M. | No. 3 | 6 | | 25.580 | 43 | 29.980 | 50 |

"As your barometer had previously been compared with our standard, and found to give essentially the same readings, no correction for scale has been necessary.

"At the time of the observations at the three stations, the variation of pressure was as follows:

Station No. 1, barometer rising  0.004 inches hourly.
      "     2,     "     rising  0.010   "     "
      "     3,     "     falling 0.002   "     "

"As the longitude of Mount Seward does not differ more than one minute of time from that of the Dudley Observatory, the observations may be directly compared with our own, without any sensible error.

"The following results have been deduced:

| Station | Height above the Dudley Ovservat'y | Height above the tide-water |
|---|---|---|
| Number 1 | 1544 feet. | 1714 feet. |
| " 2 | 3773 " | 3943 " |
| " 3 | 4292 " | 4462 " |

"The height of the barometer at the Dudley Observatory is assumed to be 170 feet above tide in the Hudson river.

Very truly yours,

G. W. HOUGH,

*Director.*"

"VERPLANCK COLVIN, Esq."

Before closing this report, I desire to call your attention to a subject of much importance. The Adirondack Wilderness contains the springs which are the sources of our principal rivers, and the feeders of the canals. Each summer the water supply for these rivers and canals is lessened, and commerce has suffered. The United States Government has been called upon, and has expended vast sums in the improvement of the navigation of the Hudson; yet the secret origin of the difficulty seems not to have been reached.

The immediate cause has been the chopping and burning off of vast tracts of forest in the wilderness, which have hitherto sheltered from the sun's heat and evaporation the deep and lingering snows, the brooks and rivulets, and the thick, soaking, sphagnous moss which, at times knee-deep, half water and half plant, forms handing lakes upon the mountain sides; throwing out constantly a chilly atmosphere, which condenses to clouds the warm vapor of the winds, and still reacting, resolves them into rain.

It is impossible for those who have not visited this region to realize the abundance, luxuriance, and depth which these peaty mosses—the true sources of our rivers—attain under the shade of those dark, northern, evergreen forests. The term "hanging-lake" will not be deemed inappropriate, in consideration of the fact that in the wet season a large mass of this moss, when compressed by the hands, becomes but a small handful, the rest of its bulk being altogether water; often many inches deep, it covers the rocks and boulders on the mountain sides, and every foot-print made has soon a shallow pool of ice water in it.

With the destruction of the forests, these mosses dry, wither, and disappear; with them vanishes the cold, condensing atmosphere which forms the clouds. Now the winter snows that accumulate on the mountains, unprotected from the sun, melt suddenly and rush down laden with disaster. For lumber, once so plentiful, we must at no distant day become tributary to other States or the Canadas. The land, deprived of all that gave it value, reverts to the State for unpaid taxes.

The remedy for this is the creation of an ADIRONDACK PARK or *timber preserve*, under charge of a forest warden and deputies. The "burning off" of mountains should be visited with suitable penalties; the cutting of pines under ten inches or one foot in diameter should be prohibited. The officers of the law might be supported by a per capita tax, upon sportsmen, artists, and tourists visiting the region; a tax which they would willingly pay if the game should be protected from unlawful slaughter, and the grand primeval forest be saved from ruthless desolation.

The interests of commerce and navigation demand that these forests should be preserved; and for posterity should be set aside, this Adirondack region, as a park for New York, as is the Yosemite for California and the Pacific States.

VERPLANCK COLVIN.

Albany, *Dec. 16th,* 1870.

# First Annual Report of the Commissioners of State Parks of the State of New York

Travelers on the long road to the Forest Preserve reached a few steps closer to their goal in 1872. The law that then created a Commission of State Parks directed it "to inquire into the expediency of providing for vesting in the State the title to the timbered regions within [seven named Adirondack counties] and converting the same into a public park."

Seven commissioners were appointed — among them a former governor of New York, Horatio Seymour; a former state engineer, William B. Taylor; a future vice-president of the United States (under Rutherford B. Hayes), William A. Wheeler; Franklin B. Hough, who would be appointed forestry agent in the federal Department of Agriculture in 1876, which single position evolved into today's Forest Service; and Verplanck Colvin, who was selected to serve as secretary.

The commission's report — submitted in May of 1873 — was clearly written by Colvin. The prose is distinctly his, the facts are thoroughly presented, the reasoning is persuasive, and the verbiage throughout, while in the style of the day, could have come only from his pen.

The order of the report is contrary to most dry, rambling, governmental documents — the main recommendation is offered first instead of last, quickly bringing the reader to the conclusion before losing his interest in page after page of facts and figures. In the second paragraph, Colvin says the commission is "of opinion that the protection of a great portion of that forest from wanton destruction is absolutely and immediately required." Surely, this wasn't written by committee.

The commission (or Colvin) was plainly optimistic in titling the report as being the First Annual. . . . Alas, it was not to be; it was the only report. It was filed, as are most such commission reports then and now, and still languishes on some shelf in a dusty state archive known only to historians.

*Colvin, himself, may have quickly forgotten it. Another 1872 law sent him off to the Adirondacks, where he spent most of the next twenty-nine years.*

— N J V V

State of New York No. 102: In Senate, May 15, 1873.

SIR—I herewith transmit the annual report of the Commissioners of State Parks of the State of New York, for the year 1872.

VERPLANCK COLVIN, *Secretary*

**Report**

*To the Honorable the Legislature of the State of New York:*

The Commissioners of State Parks of the State of New York, having been directed "to inquire into the expediency of providing for vesting in the State the title to the timbered regions lying within the counties of Lewis, Essex, Clinton, Franklin, St. Lawrence, Herkimer and Hamilton, and converting the same into a public park," respectfully present the following REPORT.

After careful consideration of the projected forest park, with its practical bearing upon the interests of the people of the whole State, we are of the opinion that the protection of a great portion of that forest from wanton destruction is absolutely and immediately required.

We do not favor the creation of an expensive and exclusive park for mere purposes of recreation, but condemning such suggestions, recommend the simple preservation of the timber as a measure of political economy.

The conclusion that the permanent preservation of a large portion of this forest is necessary, is based upon numerous considerations intimately connected with the great business interests of the State. Before proceeding to the discussion of the reasons which have brought us to this conclusion, a statement of the facts in regard to the region is desirable.

The ancient *Cough-sa-gra-ge*—the beaver hunting country of the Indian Six Nations—now known as the Adirondack Wilderness, is essentially a great and almost primeval forest, covering the mountainous and semi-mountainous elevated region of Northern New York. The northern portion of the county of Hamilton is the approximate center of the wilderness, while the western portion of Essex county contains the most elevated lands and the highest mountains of the State. From Lake Champlain on the east, the Mohawk river on the south, the Black river on the west, and the St. Lawrence on the north, the land slopes upward toward the wilderness, whose marked peculiarity is the multitude of its lakes, of greater or less degree, and the vein-like ramification of its crystal brooks and rivers. The surfaces of the principal lakes throughout this upland are generally elevated from fifteen to sixteen hundred feet above the sea, whence some writers have been erroneously led to term the whole region a plateau or table land; viewed from some lofty peak it is seen as a silent expanse of mountains, shrouded in unbroken woods, vast and quiet, and stretching to the apparent limits of the sky.

Throughout this forest, game is still abundant: the deer, bear, and panther, with smaller animals, find shelter and support, and their presence gives to the magnificent scenery a strange, wild, and romantic element, which has contributed to make its more accessible portions a choice summer pleasure ground for those of our people who travel, and who admire the natural splendors of their native land.

A few settlements only have as yet been formed in this wild territory, although during the two hundred years past, numerous attempts have been made to recover and cultivate it, all of which have signally failed and recoiled with disaster upon the projectors. The cause of the failure of these enterprises is to be attributed to the deplorable ignorance that has existed in regard to the climate, soil, and general capabilities of the region, which rendered unwarrantable the expenditures made. Amid the mountains, granite rocks, sparsely covered with vegetable mould, soon become bare and almost arid when deprived of the dense growth of trees and the network of roots and fibres which hold the soil together. Ages will have passed before the slow growth and death of minor plants upon the naked rocks will again afford sufficient soil to enable the second growth of timber to attain the size and value of that destroyed.

It must not, however, be supposed that all this region is a mass of rock. There are extensive tracts of gravelly and sandy soil, intervales, and near some of the lakes and rivers, alluvial lands, which are sometimes covered with a dense growth of wild grasses, often cut and cured by the lumbermen for the use of their oxen and horses in winter. Nevertheless, owing to the elevation and the coldness of the climate, there is no profitable farming carried on anywhere upon this upland; for, seldom is there a year in which the temperature does not fall so low as to prevent the ripening of corn, while frost is not unfrequent even in summer. The potato, that hardy vegetable which may be grown even far toward the Arctic zone, in Labrador and British America, is here produced of fine quality, in some locations. Oats, also, grow thriftily, especially upon new lands or soils that contain even a small percentage of lime, which mineral—so important to the agriculturalist—is, unfortunately, not abundant. In fact, the agricultural products are absolutely nothing when compared with the products of the forest; which are indeed the only surface wealth of the region; and but for the need which the lumbermen and the summer tourist have for even the scanty amount of hay, oats, and potatoes produced, and provisions brought in and kept for sale at these slender settlements, those settlements would soon cease to exist. As it is, many of the inhabitants are forced to eke out their subsistence by hunting and trapping; and latterly since the value of the region as a summer resort has got to be understood by our citizens and the citizens of other States, the class of guides—hardy and intelligent men—has increased, and thousands of dollars, which have hitherto been expended in travel in foreign lands, remain in or are brought to our State.

The mineral wealth of the region is not inferior to that of its forests. It is practically limited to iron; which exists in remarkable purity and enormous quantities; but careful geological exploration has proved that the available deposits of ore are confined to the northern portion of this region, and that the ore-beds generally exist in the settled, cleared, or accessible portions of the country. Great activity in iron manufacture is now exhibited near Lake Champlain, at Port Henry, Mineville, Elizabethtown, Black Brook, and Dannemora. The beds which here supply the furnaces are of magnetic or octohedral ore. Passing westward, along the northern boundary of the region, the character of the rock changes, and the specular, *hematite* ores of iron are encountered, and the ore-beds, as at the Iron Mountain in the town of Oakham, St. Lawrence county, are often unworked, and far in the depths of the woods.

In addition to these masses of iron, there are beds of serpentine (so-called verde antique marble) steatite, or soapstone, and deposits of graphite. There are also superior grades of granite, or more properly gneiss, valuable for building purposes. Besides these products there are no mines or minerals of great commercial importance.

In the early days of iron manufacture in this region, all the iron was made with the aid of wood charcoal. When a pure ore was used, free from the sulphurets and phosphides, the "charcoal iron" produced was unsurpassed in quality, and commanded a high price. The result was that large sections in Essex county were entirely stripped of forest in order to supply the requisite charcoal. The mountains thus debosqued are to-day almost treeless, showing desolate flanks of naked rock; and some of the streams which once were trout brooks are now torrent beds, through which the water of each storm on the smooth sides of the mountains rushes swiftly off to leave them almost dry, instead of slowly percolating through a sponge of moss and tree roots, as a slow-running, cold, and constant spring.

To the introduction of coal from Pennsylvania by railroad may be partially attributed the present activity in the mining of iron near Port Henry, as in that immediate neighborhood the supply of wood was long since exhausted. It is not alone to coal, however, that this activity is owing; it is more directly attributable to the improved means of transportation. Instead of dragging the fuel far from the coal fields up steep grades to the mines, and then dragging the iron produced out again to market, a great portion of the ore is now transported directly to the cities, to the furnaces, to points where labor is cheap, and where repairs to machinery can be readily made. Instead of being overloaded with coal, the empty cars go easily up hill to the mines, to roll speedily down again laden with the heavy ore.

From this it becomes evident that, for the development of the iron mines of the region, railroads only are needed. Without railroads, neither the ores nor the products of the ore-beds of the interior can be brought to market. With railroads, and the easy access they afford to the coal fields, wood, which must be cut and drawn by team over a rugged country, and would at length give out, becomes a fuel far too expensive to compete with coal.

The advancement of iron manufacture, therefore, is simply a matter of railroads; and the development of the mineral wealth of the region does not in any way conflict with the projected preservation of the forest.

Vast portions of the wilderness are owned and controlled by the lumber interests, which, with that of the tanneries, is likely to be most immediately and radically affected by the creation of a State forest park or timber preserve. These lands are generally purchased, held, and valued solely for the timber growing on them. As soon as the pine, spruce, and hemlock trees have been taken off, the lands are often abandoned and revert to the State for unpaid taxes. The common and wasteful method among lumbermen, therefore, is to cut all the available timber from a given section at once. This enables them to escape further taxes on that piece by abandoning and throwing the same back upon the State. The small trees, even under ten inches in diameter, are cut, and thus the natural process of replacement by a second growth of the valuable varieties of timber, becomes very slow, if not impossible.

The mass of brushwood, the boughs and tops lopped from the trees in such quantities, dry and wither, and become in summer beds of tinder. The first spark from a hunter's fire kindles them, and now—spreading rapidly through the forest—commences one of those terrible conflagrations which have covered whole townships with a sea of flame, and, invading the settlements, have destroyed mills, dwellings, and human lives. These fires reveal the slenderness of the soil, which—though sometimes several feet in depth—is often totally consumed, even down amid the crevices of the great boulders, which after the fire stand out red and burnt, like the uncovered bones of the world. The soil, apparently so rich and strong, is here without base, substance, or solidity; being only the rich peat-like earth, derived from the semi-decay of the fallen timber and sphagnous (peat) mosses. In agriculture such a soil is fairly eaten up by the plants cultivated in it, and the boulders gradually appear above the surface, as when the soil is burnt. Great tracts in Franklin county have been swept by these fires, and the people of that section best know what a terrible infliction they are. It is interesting to notice that some of the people assert that they have detected a remarkable diminution in the usual flow of water in the streams of the burnt regions, and that sudden floods are more frequent now than heretofore.

The tanneries, which are scattered along the margin of the wilderness, require great supplies of bark, and, therefore, aid in the rapid destruction of the forest; though the hemlock is almost the only tree which is cut. So thorough in some sections has the work been made, that it is frightful to see the numberless crossed trunks of trees, lying one upon another, stripped of their bark and white as skeletons, left there to decay.

From an early day there have been numerous projects for building railroads through this region, most of which have been abandoned, and none of which have been completed.

At different times charters have been granted for such railroads, and, to some, special immunities have been given. Among these that now passing under the name of the "Adirondack Companies Railroad" is prominent. This company appears to have succeeded to the rights, privileges, and real estate of the old Saratoga and Sackett's Harbor railroad, organized April 10, 1848 (afterward known as the Lake Ontario and Hudson railroad, organized April 6, 1857) which became insolvent and passed into the hands of a receiver. Finally the present railroad, by certain amendatory articles of association, under the general railroad act, and by other means, has come to assume the character of a great landed corporation. A large portion of the land which they possess was originally obtained from the State at the price of five cents an acre; more than 250,000 acres being obtained by the Saratoga and Sackett's Harbor railroad in this way. The manner of their acquisition will, perhaps, be better understood by an examination of the following transcript from the report of the State Engineer and Surveyor (Assembly Document No. 60, Jan. 15th, 1857, page 202):

> Since the spirit of land speculation has subsided, to dispose of our public lands by wholesale was not to be expected, until by act chapter 207, Laws of 1848, and subsequent acts chapter 72 of 1851, and chapter 122, Laws of 1855, the Commissioners of the Land Office are authorized and required to sell and convey to the Sackett's Harbor and Saratoga Railroad Company 250,000 acres, belonging to the State in the counties of Hamilton and Herkimer, at the rate of five cents an acre, on the company complying with the conditions named in said acts. This claim has been satisfied in full, by lands granted in August, September and October, 1855, viz.:

| | Number of acres. | Per acre. | Amount |
|---|---|---|---|
| Hamilton and Essex counties | 205,202 | 5 cents | $10,260.11 |
| And on July 23, 1856: | | | |
| Hamilton county | 20,000 | 5 cents | 1,000.00 |
| Hamilton and Warren counties | 6,984 | 30 cents | 2,095.20 |
| Warren County | 15,974 | 30 cents | 4,792.20 |
| Warren and Essex counties | 7,042 | 30 cents | 2,112.60 |
| Total | 255,202 | | $20,260.11 |

As will appear from the following extracts from the minutes of the Land Office, on the 9th July, 1856, the Sackett's Harbor and Saratoga Railroad Company by their president, Mr. Waddell, made the following proposition:

"*To the Commissioners of the Land Office:*

"GENTLEMEN—I propose, for the Sackett's Harbor and Saratoga railroad, to take lands now owned by the State in Hamilton and Herkimer counties, in accordance with our chartered rights, 20,000 acres; the road having already received 205,000 acres, and claiming 25,000 acres adversely claimed by Dart, Kirby, Loomis and others; also propose to purchase 30,000 acres of lands belonging to the State, lying in other counties, and to pay for the same thirty cents per acre, under a stipulation from the road, to be filed, that in case our suit for the disputed lands is decided against the road the number of acres now purchased shall go toward the amount due from the State, in which case the excess over five cents per acre to be refunded."

Therefore,

*Resolved,* That the proposition herewith submitted by the Sackett's Harbor and Saratoga Railroad Company be accepted and the patents be issued, upon the payment of five cents per acre into the State treasury, for 20,000 acres of land lying in Hamilton and Herkimer counties, and not claimed adversely by other parties; and that the proposition to purchase from the State 30,000 acres lying in Warren and Essex counties, additional, to pay therefor the sum of thirty cents per acre, be accepted, and that patents therefor issue upon the payment of thirty cents per acre, and the filing of a stipulation, on the part of said company, that in case the suit for lands on the part of the company, and defended by the State, shall be decided against said company, the amount of their said purchase at thirty cents per acre shall go toward the amount due from the State, acre for acre, in which case the excess over five cents per acre shall be refunded said company.

The suit of the railroad company was decided against them, and they obtained these last—thirty-cent—lands in *Warren* and *Essex* counties also at five cents an acre.

These transactions show that the wild lands of this region are, intrinsically, of very little value; for a single acre of farming land, valued at the moderate price of $100, is equal to 2,000 acres at five cents an acre. The working of the iron ores would in no way interfere with the preservation of the forest, for the mining companies would only require those lands in which the iron lies, and the right of way for their railroads.

The area of the wilderness may be estimated approximately at one million seven hundred and thirty thousand (1,730,000) acres, or, about two thousand seven hundred and three (2,703) square miles.

These wild lands are distributed among the several counties in about the following proportion:

| County. | Acres. |
|---|---|
| Hamilton . . . | 750,000 |
| Herkimer . . . | 350,000 |
| Lewis . . . . | 60,000 |
| St. Lawrence | 40,000 |
| Franklin . . . | 300,000 |
| Essex . . . . | 200,000 |
| Warren . . . . | 30,000 |
| Total . . . . . | 1,730,000 |

The county of Clinton, though containing much wild land, lies in a measure separated from the main portion of this great forest, and has not, therefore, been included in these estimates.

About eight hundred and thirty-four thousand four hundred and eighty (834,480) acres, or one thousand three hundred and three (1,303) square miles, are upon the Hudson river side of the mountain divide which separates the head-waters of that river from the streams flowing to the St. Lawrence. This would be the approximate area of the region which would be required for the purposes of the forest park, in case it should be determined that the preservation of the forests covering and protecting the sources of the Hudson is all that is necessary for that purpose.

The following is a statement of all the lands now owned by the State and remaining unsold:

| County. | General Fund. Acres. | School Fund. Acres. |
|---|---|---|
| Clinton . . . . . . | 8,315 | 3,027 |
| Essex . . . . . . . | 2,824 | 9,954 |
| Franklin . . . . . . | 1 | 180 |
| Hamilton . . . . . | 7,397 | 3,558 |
| Herkimer . . . . . | 780 | 26 |

| County. | General Fund. Acres. | School Fund. Acres. |
|---|---|---|
| St. Lawrence . . . . | 66 | |
| Warren . . . . . . | 645 | 3,081 |
| Total . . . . . . . | 19,962 | 19,892 |

In all, 39,854, or nearly 40,000 acres.

Having now given an outline of the more important facts and statistics in regard to this region, we will proceed to a review of the considerations which have brought us to the conclusion that these great forests should be permanently preserved.

Foremost among these considerations is the question of water supply—of the maintenance of that quantity of water in the navigable rivers, in the streams that supply the canals and afford power to mills and manufactories, which from time immemorial has flowed in undiminished volume in their channels, and which only in these later days begins to slowly fail and disappear. This is, of course, a question of rain-fall, for it is to the precipitated moisture of the air that all streams or rivers owe their origin. There is nothing of greater importance to the agriculturist than rain at the proper season and in proper quantity; and science has demonstrated that the forests of a country are potent in the regulation of storms, the formation of clouds, and the descent of rain. Any thing which vitally affects the interests of the farmer and producer affects the whole State, and demands the earliest attention of the people's representatives.

The State of New York is, perhaps, the most remarkable water-shed of the eastern half of North America. Northwardly its waters descending the St. Lawrence wash the coast of Labrador, while, far at the south, waters, which reached the earth from the self-same shower amid the Adirondack highlands, pour through the Hudson valley to the sea; and, in the western portion of the State, the sources of the Allegheny river rush, foaming, from their mountain springs to the Ohio, flowing thence through the Mississippi to the Gulf of Mexico. It is noteworthy that nearly every stream in this State, if traced to its source, will be found to originate in some lake or pond—of greater or less degree—from which, if in a forest region, it pours in an unfailing stream. South of New York there is no lake region till the brackish, dead-water bayous of Florida are reached; and it is to this system of lakes, of natural reservoirs, bosomed in the cool primeval forests, that our State is indebted for that water supply which has *created* our canals, and that steady water power which is the wealth of so many manufactories.

Without a *steady, constant* supply of water from these streams of the wilderness, our canals would be dry, and a great portion of the grain and other produce of the western part of the State would be unable to find cheap transportation to the markets of the Hudson river valley. In Erie, and the neighboring western counties, grain would decrease in value, and the farmers would be in the power of the great railroad monopolies. The merchants at Albany would also suffer, their summer trade would be ruined, and the hundred propellers which now make the Hudson foam before the fleets they tow, might be idly tied to the wharves and left there to decay.

We believe that the great Adirondack forest has a powerful influence upon the general climatology of the State; upon the rain-fall, winds, and temperature, moderating storms and equalizing throughout the year the amount of moisture carried by the atmosphere; controlling, and in a measure subduing, the powerful northerly winds, modifying their coldness and equalizing the temperature of the whole State.

It is now generally conceded that forests do not increase the amount of *annual* rain-fall. Their influence is to cause a distribution of the rain in frequent showers at short intervals throughout the year, while their absence induces droughts, followed by sudden and tremendous storms which are the origin of disastrous floods.

The record of the rain-gauge, year by year, shows only the amount of annual rain-fall. Let the total rain-fall of any year be supposed to be forty inches. If about every ninth day during the year there occur a shower—or forty annually—depositing only one inch of rain, aggregate rain-fall of the year will be forty inches.

If, on the other hand, but eight storms occur, each precipitating rain to the amount of *five inches,* the amount of annual rain-fall is as before, viz., forty inches.

It thus becomes evident that the amount of annual rain-fall is not the question to be discussed, but "how, and in what manner does it fall?"

In the first instance, the rain coming in gentle showers refreshes and revives the earth, forwards agriculture, and is a blessing.

In the second instance, there are long periods during which rain does not fall; the land is parched by the sun's fervent heat; evaporation proceeds rapidly; the air, though clear, is saturated with invisible moisture, heavily charged with electricity, which finds the moist upper air a better conductor than the heated, dry, repellant surface of the earth. The drought continues; nature is silently becoming exasperated, for there are now (in this case) no broad, cool forests, nor cold, wooded mountain sides to condense the vapor into cloud. The only chance for the relief of the atmosphere from its burden of moisture is the advent of some cold north wind. It comes at length, and the region of the air is convulsed. Black, gloomy clouds rapidly gather, and the suspended vaporous ocean overhead drops suddenly in one grand deluge, while the released electricity flies back to earth, cleaving the air with dreadful detonations. Down hill sides, the furious turbid waters rush to the streams and rivers, cutting and carving ravines through grain fields or gardens, and then, with a united swollen volume, sweeping before them and destroying bridges, dwellings, cattle, and human beings.

We have only to turn to France to see realized, as the actual result of forest slaughter, the very disasters which we have here described. There, though the government has been called upon to contribute large sums, and great contributions have been collected to aid the peasant farmers, suddenly made destitute by such floods, the means seem to have been inadequate to relieve the suffering originated by the reckless wasting of the woods.

All floods, however, are not to be attributed to the destruction of the forests; for in this, as in other things, there are exceptions to the rule. Nevertheless, upon the Hudson river, the destruction of the Adirondack forest would have a calamitous effect. The deep winter's snows, accumulating upon the disafforested uplands, would remain unmelted till the thousand and three hundred square miles of the present wilderness might have a compact covering of snow equal to twelve inches of water. Spring, with its sunshine and showers, would suddenly release this latent ocean; thirty-six billions, two hundred and forty-one millions, nine hundred and twenty thousand (36,241,920,000) heavy, cubic feet of water might rush at once down through the valleys to the sea. More than a quarter cubic mile of water hurled furiously into the narrow valley of the Hudson, it would sweep before it fields of ice, to crush and sink the strongest vessels, and ruin

the warehouses on the wharves. While the Adirondack forests remain, these deep snows will be protected from the direct rays of the
sun in spring, and will slowly and gradually melt away. The general
temperature of the region will, consequently, be low: the air will not
be overcharged with moisture, and sudden heavy rains will be im-
probable. Such vapor as exists will form light drifting clouds, which,
influenced by the forest, will act the part of one vast shielding canopy
above the snow-bound earth.

While, in our opinion, the chief and very important influence
which forests exercise upon the rain-fall is their power to moderate
storms and distribute the annual quantity of rain more equally
throughout the year, there are not wanting, among the greatest of
scientific men, those who strenuously advocate the theory that the
presence of great forest increases, and their absence diminishes, the
amount of annual rain-fall. Among those who have given the weight
of their names and influence to this theory may be mentioned Humboldt, Bonpland, De Sausure, Bousingault and others, who, in support of their opinions, have recorded facts so remarkable that they
cannot be passed without notice.

De Sausure early came to the conclusion that the great diminution
of water in some of the lakes of Switzerland was directly owing to the
destruction of the forests covering the slopes of the Alps.

The Spanish historiographer Oviedo, in his account of Venezuela,
states that the city of Neuva Valencia was founded A.D. 1555, about one
and a half miles from the lake of Tacarigua. The lake is peculiar as
having no outlet, though numerous streams empty into it. The climate
of the surrounding country is favorable, and the soil productive. In A.D.
1800, Humboldt visited it, and learned that for thirty years its waters
had been gradually decreasing, being then distant three and one-third
miles, the difference being proved by absolute measurement. The great
philosopher recorded his conviction that the disappearance of the water was owing to the destruction of the vast forests in the neighborhood
of the lake. After the period of Humboldt's visit, wars and dissensions
paralyzed the industries of the country, and the tropical forests quickly
grew again. In 1822, Tacaraigua was visited by Bousingault, who found
that the waters were rising, the people showing places which had been
farms, but which were now covered by the lake.

The astronomer Herschel, while in Africa, at the Cape of Good

Hope, made careful meteorological experiments, and is said to have remarked with surprise that rain fell plenteously upon the forest, while the neighboring plains received no showers.

More recently an unpretentious botanical publication of New York has made public new and important information: the famous West Indian island of Santa Cruz is at the present moment, it seems, suffering from the former vandalism of its inhabitants; its eastern portion, which twenty-seven years since was rich, populous, and of tropical luxuriance, now deprived of its forest, has become dry, arid and worthless. It is now found to be too late to retrieve the previous error, for of a thousand trees, recently planted upon an estate on this island, not one survived. The statements in regard to the Island of Curacoa are still more interesting:

> In the year 1845, it was found to be an almost perfect desert, where, according to the testimony of the inhabitants, had once been a garden of fertility, abandoned plantations, the recent ruins of beautiful villas and terraced gardens, and broad arid wastes without a blade of grass, showed how sudden and complete a destruction had fallen upon this unfortunate little island. The cause was the cutting down of the trees for export of their valuable timber; the effect followed even more rapidly than at Santa Cruz, as the island lies five leagues further to the south, and the heat is more intense. The rains have almost entirely ceased, and fresh water is among the luxuries. Almost within sight of Curacoa is the coast of Spanish main, covered with the rankest vegetation, over which the burdened clouds shower down abundant blessings.

In a recent paper of the British Association for the Advancement of Science, an author states his belief that forests have little or no effect upon the rain-fall; but, at the same time, he records the fact that wherever forests have been cleared from the slopes of the Alps, destructive torrents have arisen, which disappeared when the trees were replanted. The author further relates the result of an experiment touching the influence of forests upon evaporation. Two open-mouthed jars of water were sunk so as to be nearly level with the surface of the soil, the one in an open field, the other amidst bushes. An equal quantity of water was placed in each jar, and after five days it was found that the jar in the field had lost by evaporation twice as much as that partially sheltered by the bushes.

But it is not necessary to enter more fully upon this subject. One thing seems to be beyond the possibility of doubt, viz.: That the destruction of a forest covering the sources of a stream or river, by exposing the moist earth, the springs, rills, and brooks to evaporation, diminishes the supply of water in those streams. It is a principle of natural law and equity that no man has a right to take from others, without compensation, any property or privilege. Again and again streams have been diverted from their natural beds by selfish, ignorant men, who, as often, have been compelled by the stern mandate of law to restore and turn back the stolen water. The Indian savage, dependent for food upon the forest game, knew nothing of such questions; they were intangible and far beyond his comprehension. We, in the semi-barbarism of the present, are putting aside or passing by as incomprehensible the self-same question in another form. The mass of mankind do not see or fully comprehend that the rivers flowing down hill past them are forever, in the clouds, flowing up hill overhead. Like a long, endless wire rope moving over pulleys in some deep mine, the water descends the stream only to return. Destroy a pulley, and the slack rope stops, catches, and, perhaps, is broken; destroy the forests, and the rain first stops, then falls suddenly in flood torrents, which are succeeded by hot, blasting droughts. It is a continuous process, this evaporation, cloud, rain and river, yet it is only one of the many perpetual motions which the Creator retains as his prerogative, and which man can merely apply and modify.

It has been shown that the forests preserve and protect the springs and streams among them. No man has, therefore, more right to cut away those forests absolutely, and thus divert, by evaporation, the water they protect, than he has to conduct it away, for his own selfish purposes, by canal or tube. Those below him upon the stream, the mill owner and operator, and the farmer and his cattle, are as much entitled to the water as the lumberman is to the timber. When we find individuals managing their property in a reckless and selfish manner, without regard to the vested rights of others, it becomes the duty of the State to interfere and provide a remedy. Here, by ruthless destruction of the forest, thoughtless men are depriving the country of a water supply which has belonged to it from time immemorial, and the public interest demands legislative protection. The canal interests of the State are very great, and are already suffering from this wrong. The water supply of the Champlain canal is entirely obtained from the streams of this wilderness, and the Erie canal, from Rome to Albany, is almost entirely supplied from the same watershed. In the Hudson, near Albany and Troy, navigation, at midsummer, has become very difficult. The mill owners at Glen's Falls and at other points find that their water fails them; and the farming hands throughout the State suffer from the storms and droughts already noticed. It is of no consequence that, through ignorance of the natural laws governing rain and rivers, men have hitherto permitted, without protest, the injustice which they have felt, but the cause of which they did not understand. The State must apply the remedy, and, to protect their interests, preserve the forest.

The supply of timber which a State possesses within its own limits is one of the measures of its wealth. The lumber trade of New York was among the earliest sources of income, and our people will have cause ever to regret the hour when that trade shall cease to exist. At first sight it may appear that the absorption of all this vast forest (practically the only lumber region now remaining in the State) into a State park would amount to the immediate annihilation of that trade. The idea of such an unproductive and useless park we utterly and entirely repudiate. The park should be eminently a timber preserve and reserve. The carefully protected forests of Europe afford their States large annual incomes; the timber is cut under the direction of officers charged with the care of the forests, who mark the old and mature trees for cutting, and see that as little injury as possible is done to the growing timber. In England, and more especially in Ireland, forest *culture* has received much attention; for as early as the 17th century the cultivation of forest trees for industrial purposes was commenced. In Ireland, barren hillsides and hitherto desolate regions have, by arboriculture, become rich with forests, and the native trees are now in some sections less abundant than the foreign varieties, the very scenery being changed. In France and Germany there are natural forests which are preserved and properly cared for, affording supplies of valuable timber for house and ship building. Should an Adirondack park be created, careful consideration should be given to the utilization of the forest.

If the present wasteful use of lumber be continued, even the forests of Canada and the West will fail; and even now our supply from those quarters may be any year destroyed by another series of those forest conflagrations which have, in Wisconsin and Michigan, already been so extensive and disastrous. Unless we desire to be reduced to the use of inferior timber—of balsam-fir and other trees which we now regard as worthless—we must preserve our forests.

In addition to these weighty considerations of political economy, there are social and moral reasons which render the preservation of the forest advisable. Its effect upon the general healthfulness of the State is great. The philosopher, Boyle, long since remarked that in the Dutch East Indian island of Ternate, long celebrated for its beauty and healthfulness, the clove trees grew in such plenty as to render their product almost valueless. To raise the price of the commodity, most of the spice forest was destroyed. Immediately the island—previously cool, healthy and pleasant—became hot, dry, and sickly, and unfit for human residence. It is well known that the general clearing away of the forests in this country has had a tendency to raise the temperature, which in summer reaches such a height as to be barely endurable. In our cities, these great heats—acting upon garbage in those miserable quarters which are but cesspools and sinks—give rise to the probable source of cholera and other epidemics, the foul miasmatic effluvia which could not exist in the presence of living vegetation. Anxious to escape, our citizens hasten either to the country, the sea-shore, or the mountains, while those whose avocations will not permit their absence, find a purer air in the semi-rural suburbs, or in those elegant parks which modern culture and civilization have come to consider indispensable in any city.

The accessible portions of the Adirondack Wilderness have already become favorite resorts for those seeking health or pleasure. The field sports of the wilderness are remarkably exhilarating, and strengthen and revive the human frame. The boating, tramping, hunting, and fishing expeditions afford that physical training which modern Americans—of the Eastern States—stand sorely in need of, and which we must hope will, with the fashionable young men of the period, yet replace the vicious, enervating, debasing pleasures of the cities. It is to their eager pursuit of field sports that metropolitan Englishmen owe their superiority in physical power, with that skillful use of firearms, independence, fearlessness, cool presence of mind, and ability which they possess to bear the fatigues of war and exigencies of military service.

To foster and promote these natural and healthful exercises among the young men of the State, it is necessary in some measure to pre-serve the game, and the forest which affords it shelter.

In seasons of cholera the wilderness has been thronged with peo-ple, who have thus been preserved from that disease, and this is but one of the many additional considerations which might be urged as reasons for the preservation of the forest.

The area of the proposed park will not appear so immense when we compare it with that of the United States park at the head-waters of the Yellowstone river, in the Rocky Mountains. When we remem-ber, also, that the great reservation was made by the Government, not from any motives of political economy or public necessity, but simply in order to preserve it as a pleasure ground for the people, then the claims of the Adirondack Park to consideration become apparent.

The little settlements already existing in the region are not incom-patible with the project, but are, on the contrary, indispensable to the completeness of the park. They would keep provisions, as now, for tourists and lumbermen; and the people of these settlements, many of whom now earn a livelihood as guides, having a direct interest in the welfare of the park, would voluntarily protect the game and tim-ber from unlawful destruction.

A summer residence in this wilderness has been found so favor-able to health, and has become so popular, that people come even from St. Louis and Chicago, and more distant points south and west, and remain throughout the season. The mass of travel, however, comes from Philadelphia, Boston, and New York city. Should these wild lands become the property of the State, it is thought that leases of woodland points in lakes, and of islands near certain favorite lo-calities, to citizens desirous of erecting rustic summer villas or hunt-ing lodges, would form a very considerable source of income, and more than repay any expenditures which would be necessary.

There is no need, however, for any expenditures, save, possibly, in the improvement of a few of the principal roads leading to the settle-ments. The forest is in itself a natural park, and it would be improper to think of enclosing and fencing it, for it should be a common unto the people of the State.

The question before your commission is one of great importance to the State, and requires their further consideration. For the present we deem it advisable, and recommend, that the wild lands now owned and held by the State be retained until this question is decided.

ALBANY, *May* 14, 1873.

HORATIO SEYMOUR,

PATRICK H. AGAN,

WILLIAM B. TAYLOR,

GEORGE RAYNOR,

WILLIAM A. WHEELER,

VERPLANCK COLVIN,

FRANKLIN B. HOUGH,

*Commissioners.*

# Report on the Topographical Survey of the Wilderness of New York

Verplanck Colvin and his Adirondack Survey left two legacies. One is the "tracks" of the survey left variously as copper bolts set in the summit rock of the higher Adirondack peaks that once served as triangulation stations; large stones set on end with stones piled around to mark lot, tract, and patent corners; other bolts set in rocks along the lines of the original land divisions; and numerous field books and maps that document the work of the survey.

The second legacy is literary. The 1872 law that first funded Colvin and the survey required him to "render . . . a full report of his explorations and survey." And he did, in full measure. Today, these annual reports are much sought after by collectors, researchers, and others interested in Adirondackiana. A complete set is hard to come by.

The reports vary in length and quality. The one for 1896 consists of two volumes, the first running to 617 pages and including 54 photographs and 39 maps; the second volume consists of 15 maps in a hard-cover folder. The report for 1881 is only 5 pages long. A few years are missing; no report was printed for 1886, 1897, and 1899. The one for 1898 was not printed until 1989, after the manuscript was found in the archives of the New York State Department of Environmental Conservation.

The first report is the classic. It is fresh and hopeful. Colvin was obviously elated at having his dream funded by the state; he had not yet run into the difficulties of funding shortfalls that were to plague him in following years and cause his work to suffer. Some of the later reports had to be printed at his own expense. His prose is eloquent and picturesque as when describing his discovery of "the summit water of the State, and the loftiest known and true high source of the Hudson River. . . ."

Perhaps most important and long overlooked is the map inserted at the

117

*back of the report. On it is inscribed a thin blue line. In the text, Colvin says this "blue line . . . may be of value in the determination of the area of forest which it is necessary to preserve in order to protect . . . the source of the Hudson." There it is then, the first blue line — twenty years before some later draftsman drew it around an Adirondack Park.*

*What follows is that first report as it was submitted by Colvin to the state legislature on March 10, 1873. He was then only twenty-six.*

—NJVV

*To the Honorable the Legislature of the State of New York:*

Pursuant to a provision contained in chapter 733 of the Laws of 1872, to aid in completing a topographical survey of the Adirondack Wilderness of New York, I have the honor to submit, accompanied with maps, the following

## Report:

Since the completion of the primary geological survey of New York there has not been even an attempt at an exploration of the whole of the vast forest now known as the Adirondack Wilderness.

For almost all the exact knowledge that we possess of the topography and physical character of the region, we are indebted to Professor Emmons and those who so ably assisted him. Through them we first learned that Whiteface Mountain, beforetime placed at about two and a half thousand feet above the sea, and, consequently, supposed to be far inferior in altitude to the Catskills, really overtopped, by more than a thousand feet, those more famous and familiar mountains, while, southward, towering amidst the clouds, arose a sea of summits grander and still more magnificent.

There, guarded by the mountain peaks and ridges, arose Mount Marcy, which, by barometer, they found to be 5,467 feet above the sea; and there, hidden, lay Lakes Colden and Avalanche, long thought to be the highest bodies of water eastward of the Rocky Mountains.

This was almost the first scientific exploration of the mountains; for though the Indian and white hunters had long traversed the region, and had, even for the unvisited summits, names which many of them

Reprinted from *Report on a Topographical Survey of the Wilderness of New York*. Albany: The Argus Company, Printers, 1873.

still retain—despite subsequent re-naming—the only recorded measurements of mountains, on which is placed reliance, are those of Professors Redfield, Emmons, and Benedict, during the progress of the geological survey. These altitudes were all taken with mountain barometer, the last reported measurements being made in 1839, and recorded in the report, Assembly Document No. 50, for the year 1840.

The heights measured at that time were few; two mountain summits only—Mount Marcy and the Owl's Head—being recorded in the valuable report of Professor Benedict. A few other summits were measured by other observers with the inferior instruments of the day, and to many unvisited mountains, lying in the depths of the wilderness, an estimated altitude was given by guess, more as a means of comparison than as an exact statement of their altitude.

Beyond this hypsometrical work and the taking of a few magnetic bearings of important points, no addition was made to our knowledge of the topography; nor was such a result to be expected, the labors of geology requiring undivided attention.

Since that period, maps of the wilderness region have appeared, generally compiled from the notes of tourists and the statements of hunters or guides; in which the publisher has often so mistaken his informant as to place some mountains in the wrong towns or counties, or (as in one instance), to make space for three large and magnificent lakes, where, in reality, but two exist; while a thousand of the most prominent features of the wilderness, cloud-capped mountains, broad-stretching ponds, and rushing streams, are totally omitted.

Previously to the granting of the appropriation for which this report is rendered, by continued exploration of my own in the wilderness, a mass of typographical material had been gathered. The general positions, names, and shapes of most of the unmapped or wrongly mapped mountains, lakes, and rivers, had been ascertained, and the general character of even the hitherto unvisited portions of the country noted.

It was designed to found upon these observations a map of the wilderness more correct in its topography than any previously published, and, consequently, more useful; a contribution to the geography of a portion of the State which, as has been shown, is mathematically almost unknown.

In the endeavor to properly locate on paper, this mass of material, the gravest errors were detected, even in maps founded upon actual surveys; and the points which I had selected as topographical centers were found to be themselves undetermined. For instance, the position of Mount Marcy, the summit and center of the Adirondack range, and the highest mountain in the State, was found to have never been established; the place of that great mountain landmark upon the maps being miles distant from its real location. Compass bearings had been found generally worthless, owing to magnetic disturbance, peculiar to this region, and to the local attraction, probably attributable to the great masses of magnetic iron ore, so abundant among the mountains.

In this condition of affairs the only resource was a triangulation of these semi-alpine mountain summits, connected with some known base. The vastness of such an undertaking, necessitating the re-tracing of so great an extent of wilderness, the ascending of numerous mountains, several of which have a perpendicular height of 5,000 feet, the labors and fatigues, the dangers of exploration in the great ocean of woods, of accident and of hunger, can only be appreciated by the surveyor, who has passed through such an ordeal.

There remained, therefore, but one resource; a survey with theodolite or transit, entirely independent of the magnetic compass; the object in view being, as heretofore stated, the discovery, by trigonometrical measurement, of the relative angular position of the mountain summits, and other important landmarks, for use in the preparation of a map of the wilderness.

In addition, it was deemed advisable to organize a department of hypsometry, in order that, with the improved mountain barometers, the value of the old measurements could be ascertained, and the altitude of numerous unmeasured mountains discovered. The present survey, being necessarily rapid, would not admit of altitude determinations by trigonometry.

For the use of the very superior theodolite made by Troughton & Simms, of London, and employed in effecting the primary triangulation, I am under obligation to the trustees of the Albany Academy.

The sextant was an instrument of my own, and was useful in the measurement of horizontal angles. It was also occasionally used with artificial horizon in the approximate determination of latitude; but both the latitude and longitude of stations will be best determined by the results of the triangulation.

The mercurial mountain barometer, used at the upper stations on the mountain summits, in effecting their measurement during this season, was new, and of James Green's best construction; scale adjusted for capillarity, and vernier reading to one-thousandth of an inch.

The barometer employed at the near lower station for corrections was the same which I used in the first measurement of Mount Seward.

The detached thermometers, large and very sensitive instruments, were made by James Green. Each was carried in its case, carefully packed with cotton.

The large, compensated aneroid barometer was also my own. An azimuth or prismatic compass, telescopic spirit-level, with other numerous smaller instruments completed the mathematical equipments.

At some stations, where signals were required to indicate with precision the position of important points, red, white, and black flags were employed. At others, more distant, cones of bright tin were used, so placed as to be given a slight vibratory motion by the wind. These, when the sun shines brightly, may be distinguished at a distance of several miles, sparkling like minute stars. Some of the mountain summits, however, whose relative position it was desirable to locate, were distant from the designed point of observation some 50 or 60 miles, and were, consequently, difficult to distinguish. It was therefore determined to attempt their location by the night observation of lights simultaneously kindled upon their summits. The oxyhydrogen or calcium light, at first suggested, was rejected as entailing more expense than was warranted, and as impracticable. It was thought advisable to attempt the same result with beacon fires, and, in addition, ribbon or wire of the metal magnesium was procured, with the hope that the dazzling blaze which it affords while burning, would subserve the same purpose as the calcium light.

Copper bolts were provided for use upon five of the more important mountain stations, and sunk in holes drilled for their reception in the rock. Being of pure, soft copper, they will be almost indestructible by weather, and will serve to show the position of the theodolite to such other and further surveys as may be made. The words "Adirondack Survey," etc., in sunken letters are cut in the flattened heads of the bolts, together with the number of the station.

Bolt No. 1 is in the summit of Mount Marcy, the center of the mountain system, and of the great quadrilaterals of this triangulation.

Bolt No. 2 is in the summit of Whiteface Mountain.

*Station on Bald Peak*

Bolt No. 3 is in the summit of Owl's Head Mountain.

Bolt No. 4, intended for Crain's Mountain, Warren county, was not sunk; the station not being satisfactory.

Bolt No. 5 is in the summit of the Bald Peak, in the town of Moriah, Essex county, near Lake Champlain.

Three gentlemen, at different times, gave their services as assistants, their expenses being paid: R. Prescott, C. E., taking barometrical observations on one mountain; T. James making the barometrical observations on the summits of Bald Peak, and at Whiteface Mountain, and at Bennet's pond synchronous with those taken at Lake Placid; M. Blake making, during the survey at near lower stations for corrections, barometrical observations, showing the change or variation of atmospheric pressure. The barometrical observations at the more important mountain or lake stations, and the measurement of all the angles, by theodolite, sextant, or prismatic compass, were made by myself. The reconnaissance maps of topography are also my work.

More than twenty experienced woodsmen, or guides, were employed at different times during the season in carrying theodolite, baggage, and provisions. The lighter and more delicate instruments, sextant, barometers, etc., were carried by myself and assistants.

**Field Work.**

The field work was commenced in the neighborhood of Lake Pleasant, Hamilton county, in the latter part of July. It was intended that, starting here, in the south-western portion of those mountain ridges which form the Adirondack chain, the triangulation should be advanced north-easterly, station by station, to Lake Champlain, and a perfect connection thus preserved throughout the survey. It was estimated that the leveling by mountain barometer and the topographical mapping could be advanced with the primary triangulation, thus avoiding the expense of more than one survey party.

Topographical reconnaissance was carefully made of the neighborhood of Lake Pleasant, several map sketches secured, and three triangulation stations made. On the 31st of July, I ascended and barometrically measured Speculator Mountain, a prominent summit not to be found on any map, an assistant taking observations for corrections at the foot of the mountain. The altitude of this summit is computed at 3,004 feet above tide.

In the preparation of reconnaissance maps of topography, several summits near Lake Pleasant were ascended and measured with the large aneroid barometer. Burnt Mountain, according to these observations, has a height of 2,085 feet, Rift Hill 2,104 feet, and Holmes Hill 2,085 feet above tide.

On the first of August, with three guides or packmen, carrying theodolite, provisions, etc., we left Lake Pleasant for Lewey lake, an unsettled point, situated further in the forest.

There is some question of the proper orthography of the title "Lewey." It is derived from the name of a Canadian Indian hunter, at one time a resident upon the lake shore. His name has long been written *Lewey,* and as the name thus spelt has appeared upon the State maps, it is best to retain it, and avoid hypercritical correction.

Near this lake arises a lofty mountain, which I had long regarded with interest. The best maps hitherto published show either level ground or slight hills where it really arises to the clouds. Its measurement was desirable, for I suspected that it might be even higher than some of the famous Adirondack summits. In 1868 it first particularly attracted my attention from Lewey lake. In 1870 I ascended and made a barometrical measurement of Mount Emmons, or Blue Mountain, eight or nine miles distant from this peak, and found that it was really lower than his estimate, or about 3,595 feet above tide. From Mount Emmons, I was again surprised at the great height of the unmapped mountain thus towering where the maps show nothing but a plane, and, determined to visit it at the first opportunity.

It is known to the guides and hunters as Bald Face, or Snowy Mountain (the snow remaining on it late in the spring), and has also several other titles.

August 2d was stormy, but by noon on the third the weather improved, and gave promise of being fair enough for work. Leaving an assistant to take observations at a lower station on the shore of Lewey lake, accompanied by two guides carrying theodolite and provisions, I started immediately on the ascent. We made a rapid march, and passing over some subordinate mountain ranges, camped that night in a notch below the summit, near the edge of a precipice, which dropped sheer downward 100 or 200 feet.

Our camp was so elevated (3,650 feet), and the eastern precipice side of the notch so free from forest, that the sun, as it rose on the morning of the fourth, gleamed brightly in our faces, while all below was dark and robed in fog. We immediately addressed ourselves to the ascent, and early in the day reached the summit of the peak, which I shall hereafter term Snowy Mountain. The forest on the summit was in some places small and dwarfed, but was nevertheless too high to give a perfect view of the whole horizon.

A place being selected, the trees were chopped away by the guides, and the theodolite work commenced. As soon as the instrument was adjusted, the telescope was turned upon Mount Emmons, and the angle of depression, though slight, indicated that it was the lowest, after all due allowance for curvature of the earth and for refraction. The summit of Mount Marcy arose sharply in the north-east, and was selected as the zero of measurement; and, as the day was beautifully clear, the angular work proceeded steadily, save slight intermission for barometrical observations.

Bread, without water, made our lunch, and at dusk we hurried as best we could down from this lonely crag, to be soon overtaken by darkness, compelled to wrap our blankets round us, and, making the tree roots pillows, there pass the night. The following day, hungry enough, we reached Lewey lake again.

The altitude of Snowy Mountain, by barometer, is 3,859 feet above tide, which renders it almost positive that this unmapped mountain is indeed higher than the famous Mount Emmons. The synchronous observations of the assistant observer on barometer at the lake shore give for the height of Lewey lake 1,711 feet. This would make Snowy Mountain 2,148 feet above the lake.

Several reconnaissance maps having been completed and geodetic connection with the lake made, we passed, on the 6th, to Indian lake, the elevation of which, by barometer, is 1,669 feet.

The next undertaking was the exploration of the sources of Cedar river, about which much doubt existed. On one map a chain of ponds, which I had long known as the Cedar lakes (and which I had supposed were at the head-waters of the Cedar river), are shown as a part of the West Canada lakes or source of the West Canada creek, flowing westward. On another map, at this moment commonly sold to travelers of the wilderness, it is shown emptying into Moose river, under the name of Moose lake. These I knew to be mistakes, but it was important to prove them so.

Leaving Cedar river settlement on August 7th, we reached Cedar river falls the same day. The height of this station above tide is 2,098 feet. In the evening, altitudes of *Polaris* were taken with sextant and artificial horizon, for approximate determination of latitude. On the 8th, Moose lake was reached, at the head of Moose river. From this point a lofty mountain, hitherto nameless, and of about the same altitude as Snowy Mountain, is visible at the south. The guides, in compliment, called it by my name. Proceeding about six miles further we struck Cedar river again, having crossed the great bend, and the same evening, following up the river, reached the Cedar lakes, thus proving conclusively that they really discharged their waters to the Hudson river side of the watershed.

During this day's march through the forest we remarked, with wonder, that almost all the majestic spruce timber was either fallen and decaying or standing dead, so penetrated with dry rot and decay as to be crumbling to pieces. The same timber, only a few years since, was apparently sound and valuable. Now the lands on which they stand will probably not command ten cents an acre. This sudden decay of the forest is a most important matter to the owners of timber lands thereabouts, and deserves the attention of the botanist.

The night of August 8th was remarkable for an aurora borealis, which covered the whole dome of the heavens with a crimson canopy.

The morning of the 9th was devoted to topographical and barometrical work. The form of the Cedar lakes being approximately found by angles measured with sextant, by a forced march in the afternoon, we returned to Moose lake. The altitude of the Cedar lakes is 2,493 feet, and that of Moose lake 2,202 feet. Though the 10th was very sultry, we marched back to Cedar river falls, and the same evening, in a furious thunder-storm again reached Cedar river settlement.

The 11th was Sunday. One guide was paid off and returned alone, *via* Lewey lake, to Lake Pleasant. On the 12th, we proceeded to Round lake, where we encamped. The altitude of Round lake, by barometer, is 1,885 feet. The 13th opened stormily, but with an additional guide we struck into the woods to Long pond, a small and narrow sheet, whose elevation and position it was desirable to ascertain. Recent signs of bears were very abundant, the berries in the open glades affording them rich food. The lake, by barometer, is 1,924 feet, and the mountain near it has an altitude of 2,232 feet, both from tide. Soundings were taken in the lake and a reconnaissance map made. The sphagnum swamps in this neighborhood, though not very large, are remarkable for the beauty and depth of their velvety moss. Moving swiftly through forest and swamp, soaked with rain, we reached, late at night, a log hut occupied by a French or Canadian family.

On the 14th of August, rapid progress was made, and, by way of Puffer and Thirteenth ponds, reached the village of North River. By barometer the elevation of Puffer pond is 2,193 feet, and that of Thirteenth pond 1,652 feet, above tide-level.

The guides hitherto employed were here paid off and discharged. It has rarely been my fortune to employ better or more reliable men.

August 15th we ascended South Mountain and made angular observations and one reconnaissance map. The height of the mountain, by the large compensated aneroid barometer, is 1,917 feet. The same day, we drove rapidly to Johnsburgh, Warren county, and that night were at the foot of Crain's Mountain.

This mountain was thought, by the late Professor Emmons, to be an excellent station in case a triangulation of the mountains should ever be attempted, and I now designed making it the southerly corner of the great exterior quadrilateral of the survey. The morning of the 16th was cloudy, but with guide and packman I made the ascent of the mountain. Owing to a severe storm, which continued all day, we were only able to make a barometrical measurement, from which the altitude of the summit has been computed at 3,252 feet; and owing either to the exposure of the storm or the roughness of the climb, had the mortification next morning to find that the barometers were all out of order. Their repair, and other reasons, necessitated our return, and we reached Albany on the following day. The barometers were taken to New York, where they were fortunate in receiving the personal attention of Mr. James Green, instrument maker to the Smithsonian Institute.

The preparations for the further progress of the survey consumed some six or seven days.

The barometers and other instruments having been placed in complete order, the necessary camp equipage, heavy blankets, rubber coats, etc., provided, we were prepared for the second expedition into the wilderness, which was to include the most arduous as well as the most important work of the survey.

It was proposed to make theodolite stations on the summits of two of the prominent mountains on the west shore of Lake Champlain, near Crown Point, and from each to take, as *zero*, the apex of the government light-house on that point; by that means connecting the stations with the United States hydrographical survey of the lake. As the positions of the light-houses on the lake have been determined with astronomical precision, they form an invaluable basis for work of this character. It was now intended to advance the triangulation westward from this point into the wilderness, and connect it with the angles already measured.

Reaching Port Henry, near Crown Point, on August 27th, arrangements were made for conveyance, and on the following day we proceeded toward Bulwagga Mountain, and selected, as the first of the stations, a summit lying a mile or two westward and known as Bald Mountain. The mountain to the northward, in the town of Moriah, known as Bald Peak, was selected as the second station. The Bald Mountain, from which the forest had long since been burned, afforded extraordinary facilities for the work of triangulation. As the altitudes were to be taken with mountain barometer, one assistant, with barometer, was detached and returned to the lake shore, as a near lower station, with orders to take observations at intervals of five minutes during the continuance of our party upon the mountain. Meanwhile, procuring a man to carry the theodolite, we ascended the mountain, which was steep and fenced with rock ledges and ghastly with crumbling trunks of burned trees. The summit gained, the first labor was to chop down and clear away a growth of young trees that obscured the view in one direction. The theodolite was then placed and adjusted, and the whole circle (clamped at zero), turned till the cross-hairs of the telescope stood with precision on the very apex of the distant light-house. The circle was now carefully clamped and the vernier plate being released, the telescope was turned upon the mountain summits westward, and angle after angle was carefully measured and recorded. The sky was clear and favorable, and the weather, which below had been extremely warm, was here cool and pleasant. Meanwhile, an assistant had placed the mountain barometer, and sheltering it from the sun with a poncho thrown over a tripod of poles, took careful observations.

Late in the afternoon, it became evident that another day would be required upon the summit, and the guide was accordingly dispatched for provisions and blankets. We continued at our duties until the sun slowly sank behind the mountains, the valleys filling with shadows, and Lake Champlain, from a glittering sea, was turned to a drear and gloomy waste. Darkness was soon upon us, and after a long and toilsome descent among the rocks and ledges, where it was almost impossible to see the way, the guide was met, returning with aid of lantern.

Camp was made beside a small stream flowing at the foot of the mountain, and the bright fire burning and plentiful provisions made our late labors trifling. Wrapped in blankets, the fire glowing at our feet, we passed the night, with no other roof between us and the stars than the slight, swaying foliage of the trees.

The night was cold, but the morning of the 29th opened brightly, and was propitious for the survey. Again climbing the mountain, we resumed the occupation of the previous day, and in addition to the regular work I was able to take the angular direction of Mount Mansfield and the Camel's Hump in the Green Mountains. Reconnaissance maps of topography were secured, and we were able to descend and reach a farm-house, some miles distant, before evening, having auspiciously opened the work on the eastern angle. The barometrical observations of the first day indicate that this mountain has an altitude of 2,278 feet. The height of Lake Champlain above tide, as indicated by the barometrical observations taken there and compared with the records of the Dudley Observatory, is ninety-one feet.

August 30th opened with a storm; the rain descended heavily, and while looking upon the low, gloomy clouds and fog with unpleasant forebodings, we could not but congratulate ourselves upon the completion of the triangulation work at this station. Packing up our instruments, we took seats in a rude wagon, and, amidst pouring rain and spattering mud, reached Port Henry again.

The light-house at Crown Point was next visited, and angular readings taken from the turret. It is an important station, as from its well established geographical position, the latitude and longitude of stations connected with it (and it is proposed with other light-houses), by this triangulation, will be known with more precision than by any astronomical method practicable in the field.

On the 31st of August, the place of assistant Prescott was taken by Mr. James, and we immediately proceeded to Mineville, Essex county, in the neighborhood of Bald Peak, which had been selected as the second of the lake-shore mountain stations.

The morning of September 1st was bright, the thick clouds which for several days past had been drifting between us and the mountain prospect had vanished, and we hastened to avail ourselves of so unusually favorable a day. The Bald Peak, like the Bald Mountain, our previous station, had been, at some distant period, deprived of its forest by fire; so long since, indeed, that large evergreen trees had grown near the summit. Those which obstructed the view were cut away.

As this was one of the five more important stations, the eastern angle, or corner of the great exterior quadrilateral of the survey, a copper bolt (No. 5) was securely fastened in the rock, and will show to future surveyors the position of the theodolite. The day was superb and nearly cloudless, and knowing the fickleness of mountain weather all possible dispatch was made; and at sunset, although exhausted, we had the satisfaction of closing our field-books upon completed work. Mountain after mountain had been brought under the field of the telescope, and the horizontal angles, so carefully measured, exceeded 60, nearly every one of which served to locate the direction of separate rocky peaks, many of which we had yet to climb, often with no sign to guide us through the trackless woods.

The usual barometrical altitudes were taken, and show for Bald Peak an altitude of 2,083 feet above tide; signal staff and flag were placed at the theodolite station.

On the following day (September 2d) we returned to Port Henry, and the same evening, by steamer on Lake Champlain, arrived at Plattsburgh. On the 3d, we reached Wilmington village at the foot of Whiteface Mountain, which I had selected as the northern corner of the great quadrilateral, which, it may be remarked, encloses the most mountainous and rugged portion of the wilderness.

Leaving an assistant at Wilmington as observer on barometer at lower station, we climbed the mountain, and shortly after dark reached "Rustic Lodge," on Whiteface; a log shanty now occupying my camping ground of 1869. The night was wintry, and the morning of the 4th showed the forest whitened with snow and ice. The altitude of Rustic Lodge, as taken with barometer, is 4,080 feet.

We were early upon the summit of Whiteface and had the instruments up and adjusted. The day was most unfavorable for triangulation. Heavy clouds drifted around and below us, hiding everything. But, after a few dismal hours of waiting, the snow-white vapor lifted and suddenly we saw the rugged mountain crests, dark passes, blue gleaming lakes, and sparkling ponds. Nevertheless, the clouds still hung around the central Adirondack peaks, and the summit of Mount Marcy was long invisible. The constant drift of small clouds over the higher summits made the triangulation a slow and tedious labor, with more time fretted away in waiting than consumed in work. Two days were thus passed upon the summit.

At length all the angles had been measured; the Gothics, Marcy, McIntyre, Seward, Morris, and St. Regis Mountains, with all the numerous summits intermediate in view, in the circuit of the horizon, had been located; even the corners and points of lakes, and the position of the prominent rude buildings of the backwoods clearings far below, in the shadow of the deep valleys, were mathematically noted. Two signal flags were placed upon the summit and complete reconnaissance maps made; and two days' continuous duplicate readings of the mercurial mountain barometer, one set taken on the summit and one at the foot of the mountain, afforded better and more complete data for the determination of the height of Whiteface than any previously secured.

Whiteface first appears in print as having an elevation of 2,686 feet. This great error was corrected by the geological survey, and its height as given in the State Natural History is 4,900 feet above tide. My measurement confirms this result, and makes the height of the mountain 4,918 English feet above the sea.

We reached Wilmington, at the foot of Whiteface, in the afternoon of September 6th, and the same night, after a long and tedious drive, arrived at Lake Placid.

The seventh was devoted to topography and barometer work in the neighborhood of Lake Placid (which by barometer is 1,954 feet above tide), and in preparation for the more difficult labors of the survey. We were now again about to enter the great forest, having to make all further progress among the mountains on foot, all the baggage and heavy instruments being carried upon the backs of men. Provisions also, though plain and compact, formed a very considerable and weighty portion of the porterage.

The eighth of September was Sunday. On the ninth, after barometrical work in the neighborhood of North Elba (from which the altitude of that place has been computed at 1,635 feet), with three packmen carrying our heavier material, we crossed the Ausable river, and, entering the woods, took the trail for the Indian Pass. We camped that evening beside the brook along which I descended from the summit of Mount McIntyre in 1871, and building a shanty of boughs, passed a comfortable night. The altitude of this camp was 2,197 feet.

The morning of the tenth found us early upon the trail, and at the northern portal of the Indian Pass. Here a new camp was hastily made, and sending an assistant, with one guide, over the pass to the Hudson river side of the mountain, with orders to take barometrical observations at the south foot of Wallface Mountain precipice (valley), I took with me the other guides, and leaving the trail, proceeded to follow the main branch of the Ausable to its source. We were in hopes of finding some little lakes, known as "Scott's ponds" which, though doubted by some who had been unable to find them—Mr. Scott, their discoverer, having only seen them in winter, as level, snow-covered openings in the forest—were said to exist upon the top of Wallface, and which were probably the highest sources of the Ausable river. After a toilsome climb up the steep gorge of the river, wetted by spray of many an unnamed waterfall, ascending slippery ledges by aid of rope-like roots, we reached less difficult ground, where the stream divided into a number of smaller brooks. These streams had probably been the means of bewildering previous searchers for the ponds; lack of woodcraft leading them to waste time in exploring the source of all the numerous brooks. Pushing forward we passed the clear, cold, spring-like streams, following, without hesitation, the more tepid and discolored water of one branch which tasted like that derived from a pond or bog. Advancing in this manner, I caught the first glimpse of open water, which proved to be the largest of these high mountain ponds. It was small and apparently shallow. Several brooks enter it; one coming from two level moss-swamps which, in winter, had also probably the appearance of ponds. The altitude, by barometer, was found to be 3,054 feet, or higher than either Lakes Colden or Avalanche.

Leaving the pond, we passed to the western side of Wallface, where the brooks trend to the Raquette, through Cold river, but finding nothing of importance returned, and wandering through the marshy forest, hazy with thick, bewildering masses of cold, driving clouds, had the fortune to stumble upon another lake, whose shores it is probable had never been previously visited by man. It was a wild, unearthly place, and to the subdued, muttered words of our guides, came the sudden snort of a deer as he fled from our approach.

In the afternoon we reached the summit of Wallface Mountain, measured it, observation for observation with the station in the abyss at the foot of the precipice, where the assistant was busily engaged. Afterward, descending to the verge of the cliff, observations were made to ascertain the greatest height of that tremendous monument and record of dynamical geology. The altitude of Wallface Mountain was found to be 3,856 feet, and the height of Wallface precipice 1,319 feet. One reconnaissance map was made. Moving with celerity we were able to reach our camp again, at the north portal of the pass, shortly after dark. This was the first of a series of movements in which the labor of several days was pressed into one, and in which the wilderness was shown to be traversable to skillful woodsmen by night as well as day.

Next morning (September 11th) the whole party entered the Indian Pass, and after altitude observations at its center, which give for its elevation 2,901 feet, we passed beneath the dizzy crags, on the verge of which we had stood the previous day, and the same afternoon reached the deserted iron-works at Adirondack village. The day, as usual, had been one of storm and rain.

A slight delay was here necessary to enable us to replenish our supply of provisions from the slender stock of the single family residing in this lonely valley.

As the next station in the mountains was not more than seven miles distant, we took what provisions could be had, and at mid-day on the twelfth departed, notwithstanding the continuance of stormy weather; for I thought it best that we should be near our central station (Mount Marcy), in order to take advantage of the first clear weather, if we should be so fortunate as to have any.

Reaching Lake Colden, a little after dark, we encamped on the north shore of the Opalescent river, which, during the night, swollen by the heavy rain, became a furious torrent. The party was accommodated in bark wigwams, each of which afforded shelter for two persons.

The next day, the storm still continued unabated, and our chief occupation was to keep the apparatus from damage by water which soaked the floor, and dripped through the bark roof of the wigwams. A guide was sent back to the deserted iron-works for more provisions, for which we had made arrangements (for we contemplated making this point a depot of supplies), and another guide was employed in cutting down a large cedar tree, and hewing it into the shape of a canoe or dug-out for use in the mapping of Lake Colden, on whose waters no boat had hitherto floated.

The morning of the 14th was also stormy, but, upon the return of the man detached for provisions, immediate preparations were made for the ascent of Mount Marcy. Baggage was reduced to a minimum, provision for the party for one day only being carried.

We were early upon the trail, but, with the heavy theodolite and fragile barometers, made a slow march. The weather continued so unfavorable, and consequently the probability of our being able to accomplish the work was so slight, that even the guides, who had now acquired an interest in the survey, appeared discouraged. As hour after hour we ascended the foaming, rock-girt Opalescent river toward its source, the weather became colder and the thick clouds more disheartening.

It is not necessary to descant upon the climb. It was late afternoon, when, drenched with rain or cloud, that despite rubber covering had penetrated our clothing, we stood shivering in the gray, icy mist that swept furiously over the summit of Mount Marcy. Benumbed with cold and unable to see for more than a few rods around, at the entreaties of the guides I reluctantly ordered an immediate descent, which was made upon the opposite or eastern side of the mountain. About a mile from the summit we found a level spot where water could be had, and decided to camp. Upon attempting to put up the tent, we found our fingers so stiffened by cold that we could not button the canvas together, and the guides, after chopping some of the dwarfed timber for firewood, gave up in despair, and declared that we would "freeze to death" if we stayed there that night. Tent, baggage, and instruments were again shouldered, and we descended the slippery rocks down and across the great slide on Marcy, toward the spot, two miles distant, where I had encamped last year, and where we hoped to find the bark huts still standing. Meanwhile, the rain did not cease to fall, and it was dusk when, trembling from fatigue and exposure, we stumbled into the old camp in Panther Gorge.

The courage of our guides now returned. The timber was here large and good, and soon the echoing sound of chopping was heard, and the white chips flew from the trunks of the dead, dry, spruce trees. Huge logs of spruce and hard wood were quickly roaring and blazing, and we steaming before the fire in our soaked clothing.

All were so exhausted that, directly after supper, we wrapped our heavy army blankets round us, and fell asleep.

In the middle of the night, the penetrating cold aroused us, and shouting for the guides to renew the fire, I saw with delight that the long storm had broken, for the sky was clear and the stars sparkled in the blue firmament. With the warmth of the fire came slumber again, only broken by daylight.

The morning of September 15th showed us that during the night we had received a visitor. Signs of panther had been numerous, but the new comer was a noble deer hound, who had evidently, in following his prey into this most deserted portion of the wilderness, been lost. He was only too glad to join himself to human company. Our low stock of provisions made him an unwelcome visitor, but his evident timidity among strangers, and his determination in following our track as we again ascended Mount Marcy, won him friends.

The sun, which we had missed for so many days, now shone brilliantly over a cloudless landscape. Before leaving the timber, a small tree was cut for signal flag-staff, besides some stouter ones for props.

The summit of the peak was early attained, and the barometrical work immediately commenced. The theodolite was probably the first ever placed upon Mount Marcy. The day was so clear and favorable, so absolutely cloudless, as to be surprising; it seemed as though specially made for the work at hand. Thankful to the all-seeing Providence for this assistance, we did our best to take advantage of it, and the triangulation proceeded without an instant being taken for rest or refreshment during the day.

At night, by observations of *Polaris* and *Alioth,* the true astronomical meridian was laid out, and the declination ("variation") of the magnetic needle determined. Though we kindled a beacon fire and burned magnesium ribbon, there was no visible response from the other signal stations, and the attempt at measuring the great angles by this means was consequently a failure. The mean of the barometrical observations taken this day indicate for Mount Marcy an altitude of 5,333 feet.

The following morning (September 16th), work was continued until eleven o'clock, when a severe storm setting in, the tent was struck, and camp broken up. Taking with me one guide, I descended the south side of Mount Marcy, with the intention of climbing and barometrically measuring Skylight Mountain and Gray Peak, and to visit a little lake lying in the chasm between the mountains.

The rest of the party returned by trail to Lake Colden, where a series of barometrical measurements were immediately taken by the assistant, at short, appointed intervals during my absence. For ourselves, the cloud was so dense that we could see nothing a hundred yards distant, yet we were able to reach the Gray Peak and measure it. About four P.M., we stood on the shores of the little lake, in a deplorable plight, our boots full of water and clothing torn and dripping. The altitude of the Gray Peak, by aneroid, was found to be 4,917 feet. This little lake, by the mercurial (Green) barometer, has an altitude computed at 4,293 feet above tide. The little pond was a red-letter point in this survey, for we found it, as I had long surmised, not flowing to the Ausable, as has been represented, but to the Hudson river—an inaccuracy of the maps, which is perhaps the best proof that we were the first to ever really visit it.

Lakes Colden and Avalanche have been known, and still are known, as the highest lake sources of the Hudson river, being placed, respectively, at 2,851 and 2,900 feet above the sea. This pond, with its elevation of 4,293 feet, will be interesting to the physical geographer. It is, apparently, the *summit water* of the State, and the loftiest known and true *high* pond-source of the Hudson river.

Wet and chilled, we were forced to abandon for the time the attempt on Skylight Mountain; there was little chance also of valuable results being obtained in such a storm. Following the outlet of *Summit Water*, we made a hazardous descent through the ravine of Feldspar brook, reaching the shores of the Opalescent river about dark. The trail hence to Lake Colden, fair enough by daylight, proved full of stumbling blocks by night, and occasionally we plunged into the crevices amid the rocks, with a suddenness that threatened to break our limbs or fracture the barometer. We reached camp, however, without any accident.

September 17th opened with storm, and we determined to complete the canoe, or "dug-out," map Lake Colden, and make soundings. Barometrical observations were taken by the assistant at the lake shore, while I gave my attention to theodoliting, by observation of the summits of Mounts McIntyre and Colden, connecting points on the lake, with the primary triangulation. The canoe was finished by nightfall, but required some slight touches before launching. The stray hound, which still remained with us, here made an onslaught upon the provisions, devouring all the pork. A guide was sent for a fresh supply, and was directed to lead the dog out and leave him. The hound, however, escaped on the way, and, running a deer to water, returned to our camp.

On the 18th, the guide sent out for provisions returned about noon, and the storm clearing off, late as it was, we started to ascend Mount Colden. This dangerous climb was one of the adventures of the expedition. It is the mountain from which sped the avalanche of 1869, that temporarily severed Avalanche lake, and is a rugged mass of rock, with precipice piled upon precipice. We were able to make the ascent, measure it barometrically, and secure several topographical or reconnaissance maps before dark. Of the dangers of the descent, finished at a quarter to eleven at night, I will not speak.

The following day, which was one of rain and heavy clouds, I launched and tested the canoe—named the *Discovery*—being the first boat of any kind placed on Lake Colden, and was surprised at the shallowness of the lake. The boat was then transported to Avalanche lake, on which also no boat of any kind had ever floated, and I had the pleasure of the first sail upon that gloomy water. The canoe, though narrow, carried three men with ease—and more when balanced with out-riggers—and it enabled me to make soundings in different parts of the lake, and to examine the geological structure of the cliff walls, which fall directly into the water. This, with barometrical leveling, engaged us to so late an hour that we had again to stumble along the trail in the dark, back to camp at Lake Colden. The canoe remains at Avalanche lake, and will render the Avalanche pass more convenient to travelers.

The 20th of September showed no abatement of the stormy weather, and as our provisions were again nearly exhausted, and the time which I had allotted for work in the neighborhood had passed, camp was broken up. With one guide I determined to descend the Opalescent river, and ascertain its course from Lake Colden downward.

Accordingly, I sent the rest back by the trail to the old iron-works, by way of Calamity pond (elevation 2,560 feet), and taking all the provision—which was only sufficient for two meals, started. We were immediately separated from our companions and committed ourselves to the woods, during the whole morning continuing to follow the Opalescent downward. The clouds hung so very low that the summits of the mountain stations, and indeed of the inferior ridges, were invisible. The cold also increased and the wet bushes, from which the yellow, faded autumn leaves were now fast falling, gave a mournful appearance to the forest. At lunch we consumed half of our supply of food, reserving the remainder as a precaution, in case we should not be able, as intended, to cross the mountains and reach the old iron-works that night. The woods here seemed peculiarly wild, traces of game became abundant, and in one place we came upon the bones and fragments of a deer, which had been killed by a panther and torn to pieces.

Late in the afternoon we left the river and climbed the flanks of the mountains to the west. The clouds were so dense in the valley that nothing could be distinguished; but, compelled to hasten, we took our course by compass and pushed directly over the mountain ridges toward the Hudson. In this way, we became entangled in an almost impenetrable mass of fallen timber, a "wind-slash," which probably extended over more than a thousand acres. Here, in clambering and crawling amidst the dead forest, which, crumbling and decayed, was a perfect chevaux-de-frise, after an hour or more of exhausting labor (the fog rising thick around us), we were compelled to acknowledge that we were lost. About dark, after crossing numerous hills and ridges, we succeeded in extricating ourselves from the slash. Below us was an almost precipitate steep of dark spruce woods. Seeing that we should have to camp, we descended and hastily searched for water. A rill was at length found, and the guide casting off his pack hurriedly proceeded to cut wood for the night. Our food all disappeared at supper, and we slept—one on either side of the fire,—on spruce boughs cast on the wet ground. Some wild creatures came around us at night, but we were too tired to pay attention to them.

The 21st opened with brilliant sunshine, yet as no well-known mountain peak was visible, we were as much lost as on the previous day. Breakfastless, we resumed our march, and after working our way through fire-slash, through swamp, and through water, reached the Hudson and the old iron-works.

Here the guides, dissatisfied with the severity of the labor, demanded their discharge and asked increased pay; nor could they be persuaded to proceed further, exhibiting their torn clothing and soleless, gaping boots, as evidences of their inability. They were, accordingly, discharged, and returned on Monday, *via* the Indian Pass, to North Elba.

On Monday and Tuesday (September 23d and 24th), topography work was done in the neighborhood of the deserted iron-works and Lake Sandford; repairs and preparations were also made for the further progress of the survey, two sub-expeditions having to be made from this point; one to Mount Santanoni and one to Mount Seward.

On the 25th, we proceeded to Tahawus settlement, about ten miles distant, and secured packmen for the sub-expeditions.

Starting from Tahawus on the following morning, we reached the iron-works about noon on our way to Mount Santanoni, which was to be one of the triangulation stations. In the evening, we made a brush camp and passed a comfortable night. Next day (27th) we were early traversing the woods (there was no trail nor were there choppings on the trees for guidance), and following a small stream which came from the lofty crest, continued to ascend. The open character of the gorge we climbed, enabled me to apply my method of approximate measurement, by barometer and level, of inferior mountains to several summits, as hereafter more particularly described, from which the height of Andrew Mountain is found to be 3,180 feet, and North River Mountain 3,722 feet.

We reached the summit of Santanoni about mid-day. Singularly enough, the weather, which for a day or two past had been threatening, was now moderately fair, and permitted the angular observations to be made very complete. Mount Marcy, so often shrouded in the clouds, stood grandly out, a sharp, gray cone. The positions of various lakes and their islands were determined, and especially the lower end of Long lake, which, like a great river, lay stretched before us in the west. Late in the afternoon, the work was stopped by heavy clouds, but not until the necessary angles had been measured, the barometrical observations (showing its height to be 4,607 feet) finished, and five reconnaissance maps of topography completed. The sun was setting as we left the crest and forced our way down through the dwarf balsam and spruce trees on the flanks of the mountain. We had left all our heavy baggage cached a mile from the summit, beside the gorge up which we had climbed. For sake of food, camp-fire, and blankets we hurried down in search of the gorge, and in about an hour found it, and commenced its descent just at dark. At length, very tired, we found our supplies, and by the light of a torch the guides cut night wood and built a hut of balsam boughs, the sound of the ax echoing desolately in the dark forest.

During the night, the clouds disappeared, the stars shone out and a furious, cold wind swept over the woods.

Next morning (September 28th) we made a forced march, passing the camp of two days previous, and the same evening reached the old iron-works.

The next sub-expedition was to Mount Seward. It was advisable that this important mountain should be made a triangulation station, and I was also desirous of remeasuring it, having now an assistant with barometer stationed at the iron-works, who would take synchronous readings at that place as a near lower station. My ascent of

Mount Seward in 1870 had been made from Long lake, eastward, up to Cold river. We were now above the sources of that stream, and to reach the mountain's foot must descend Cold river, westward. The guides knew nothing of that portion of the wilderness, and placed upon my shoulders the responsibility, in addition to my scientific labors, of *guiding* them.

The 29th was very stormy, but in the afternoon we proceeded to the Preston ponds, at the head of Cold river, and encamped.

On the 13th, though it was still cloudy, we started early, and, by boat, reached the outlet of the ponds. Here one guide shouldered the theodolite-knapsack and tripod, and the other the provision pack, and we proceeded down the river. There was nothing to guide us besides the stream and the compass-direction of the mountain, and the clouds grew thicker and more lowering, so that we could not even distinguish the foot-hills. Crossing the river a few miles below the ponds, where a stream entered it on the north side, we ascended the ridge, in order to see whether anything could be distinguished. Having climbed a tree, I suddenly noticed, in a valley below, a lake (unknown to the maps), which I remembered having seen from one of the ridges of Mount Seward in 1870. Supposing that we might have a glimpse of the mountain from the open shore of the lake, we went to it, but only gained a view of the lake and its surroundings. I named it White-cedar pond, for the abundant growth of that tree upon its shores. We were compelled to diverge a quarter of a mile to reach the outlet, a small stream, and pressed on in the direction in which we thought Mount Seward lay. Presently commencing to ascend, we followed up a small brook, and continued to climb the mountain-side till we were lost in the clouds, and the general murkiness preceding night warned us to encamp.

Surprised at the apparent elevation of our resting place, I took barometrical observations, which indicated that the altitude was 2,951 feet, which was rather surprising, as we could not yet have reached the slopes of Mount Seward, and must, therefore, be upon the mountain eastward of it. This we called "Camp Somewhere," and went quietly to sleep.

October first was as cloudy as the previous day, and, without knowing anything of our whereabouts (the denseness of the fog or cloud preventing our seeing even the forest forty rods up or down the slope), we concluded to keep climbing till we found at least the summit of the mountain on which we were. Hour after hour we continued slowly to ascend, and still the summit was not reached. A barometrical observation showed remarkable altitude, and told me that we must either be upon the slopes of Mount Seward or of Ragged Mountain, the only high summits in this neighborhood. It did not seem as though we had gone far enough to reach Mount Seward, and I concluded that we must be upon the other, which, from the wild sort of precipice-climbing we had now to make, we thought had been justly named "Ragged." The thick, surrounding mist now began to brighten, and at length opened a vast view below of gaudy autumn woods, stretching away southward like a boundless sea. Then the clouds drifted from around us, and, rolling rapidly away, disclosed the superb mountain picture; showed us that we were indeed near the top of Ragged Mountain, and that there, darkly towering above the deep Ouluska Pass (the home or *place of shadows* of the Indians), arose the black crest of Mount Seward. It was unmistakable. An involuntary "hurrah!" arose, and we pushed on for the summit of Ragged, for we had no idea of losing the results of our labor. We were soon on the top and gazing down on Ampersand pond and the Saranac lakes, away to the north. Observation with the mountain-barometer on the spot gave Ragged Mountain an altitude of 4,126 feet. This was the "Mount Seward" of those who had previously attempted the ascent. It was this mountain, also, and not the rear of Wallface, that I had seen in 1870, at the time of my first ascent of Mount Seward, forming the eastern wall of the Ouluska Pass, as we had indeed noticed in 1871 from Mount McIntyre.

To reach Mount Seward, it was necessary to descend into the pass; and, as with difficulty we found a practicable place among the cliffs, we became more and more impressed with the grandeur of this gloomy gorge, so well named the "place of shadows." It is much deeper than the northern portal of the Indian pass, and having precipices on both sides, has a gloomier and more chasm-like appearance. Reaching the bottom, we lunched beside a rill, and the barometrical height of the center of the pass was taken, since computed at 3,050 feet. As the elevation of Ragged Mountain is 4,126 feet, and as Mount Seward upon the other side rises still higher, it is probable that the Ouluska Pass is more than a 1,000 feet in depth. It is filled with forest, and the ledges on its cliffs are green with moss and stunted trees.

Signs of the panther were frequent, and it seemed that this remote place must be their favorite resort and home.

The summit of Mount Seward, the very spot which I had reached two years previously, was attained at about two P.M., and the theodolite and barometer were immediately placed. The clouds, however, settling around the mountain peaks, prevented triangulation; yet, in addition to the barometrical observations, I found time to obtain reconnaissance maps. Though waiting till night, the clouds only grew thicker and colder, and at dark we hastily made camp in a ravine just east of the summit. The night was very dark and cold, and we constructed a hut of thick, evergreen boughs, facing the camp-fire. The boughs were piled on the roof and sides of the shanty till they were a foot or more deep, and the heat of the fire warmed the open front. It was late when we enwrapped ourselves in blankets, but our sleep was sound, and I reluctantly opened my eyes, at the exclamations of the guides, to see large flakes of snow thickly falling out of the dark, frozen cloud, in which we were, sparkling into the light of the fire. Drawing our feet in from the snow, we slept again, only awakening with the gray of morning.

October 2d showed the summit of Mount Seward whitened with snow. Another series of barometrical observations were taken, and soon the temperature fell to + 32° Fahrenheit (or zero centigrade), so that the reduction to freezing point correction for these barometrical observations could have been omitted. The temperature fell even lower; the mean of thermometer this day being + 32.22° Fahrenheit. The height of Mount Seward, as computed from these observations, is 4,348 feet above tide. The instruments employed in this measurement were far superior to those used in 1870, and it is my opinion that the results are therefore more nearly accurate. My previous conclusions (Report on the Measurement of Mount Seward, Twenty-fourth Annual Report of the New York State Museum of Natural History, 1870), are, therefore, remarkably confirmed. The height of 5,100 feet, attributed to Mount Seward by Professor Emmons, of the State Geological Survey, is thus proved to be in error some 600 or 700 feet.

At eight A.M., as there was no abatement of the storm, the cold growing intense, I reluctantly ordered the descent. Being short of provisions, and all anxious to return, we made almost reckless speed, yet did not reach Cold river till near mid-day. We struck it many miles below where it had been left two days previously. Though we followed it up stream for hours, with all possible rapidity and without stopping to rest, we came to no place where we had previously been, and at length were shut off from the river by high canon walls, through which the deep, clear-green stream flowed sullenly below. We have named this the *Canon of Cold river.*

We were compelled to encamp another night, but next day (October 3d) reached the iron-works. The height of Lake Henderson was taken this day barometrically and has been computed at 1,838 feet.

It was now late in the season and much remained to be done in other quarters. We accordingly proceeded directly to the settlement at Tahawus or Lower Works, and on the morning of the fourth, by team, reached Rich lake, where boats and another guide were secured. The same night, we camped upon the shores of Long pond, being upon our way to Long lake, *via* the Catlin waters.

On October 5th, Long lake was reached, and the settlement midway upon it. The guides were here paid off and discharged, returning by boat and carry as they had come.

The 6th morning proving unusually bright and clear, with an assistant and a guide carrying the theodolite, I ascended Owl's Head Mountain and made the usual observations. This mountain is the westernmost corner of the great quadrilateral, and the spot where the theodolite was placed is indicated by a copper bolt sunk in the rock of the peak.

The barometrical altitude was taken by the assistant, with hourly observations by myself. The height as computed is 2,789 feet above tide in the Hudson river. It is interesting to compare this result with the measurement of the same mountain by Professor Benedict in 1839, with syphon barometer, which indicated an altitude 2,701 feet. The difference is not great, when we consider the circumstances. The mountain has an irregular summit, and our stations may not have been the same.

The 7th was stormy, but the absolutely necessary portion of the work had now been nearly completed. The relative positions of the great mountain landmarks, and of numberless intermediate points, had been fixed by the triangulation. It was now becoming wintry in this region, and it was almost impossible to get guides to visit the cold mountain summits. The assistant was accordingly sent out with the heavy instruments and baggage, and returned to Albany.

I remained to complete a hydrographic reconnaissance of Long lake, designing afterward to proceed westward to the Beaver river waters, taking the altitude of lakes by barometer and making such geodetic connection as might be possible.

October 8th was stormy; on the ninth, progress was made on the form of Long lake with sextant; the reconnaissance from the settlement to near the outlet being completed.

On the 11th, with two guides, I started westward across the wilderness. One of the guides accompanied me but one day to assist upon a long carry. We reached Little Tupper's lake at dusk, and were hospitably received by a trapper camping on its shore. Barometrical observations were taken, and the altitude of the lake is computed at 1,715 feet.

From Little Tupper's, on the twelfth, we passed by way of Round pond, etc., to Tupper's lake, which is partially in St. Lawrence county. Barometrical observations were taken which indicate for the lake an altitude of 1,504 feet.

October 13th was Sunday, and was stormy. On Monday we proceeded with our light boat up Bog river, by the nine carries, or portages, to the Chain ponds on that river. The guide knew nothing of this portion of the wilderness, and henceforward advanced according to my directions. It was now really the Adirondack winter; snow had fallen at intervals during the day, and this night, despite the roaring fire, we shivered in our blankets. Daylight on the 15th showed the ground covered with snow, and the evergreen forest gracefully drooping under the weight of feathery crystals. The altitude of the Chain ponds by barometer is 1,707 feet. About mid-day we reached Mud lake, long thought to be the head of Bog river. The barometrical observations taken here give the height of Mud lake and the elevated plateau on which it lies at 1,737 feet. The rest of the day was passed in a toilsome portage to Bog river pond; the boat being carried by the guide, and the instruments and baggage by myself. The distance has been called three miles. It certainly seemed longer, as in snow and slush, over hill and through swamp, we forced our way. Camp was made between Bog pond and Clear pond.

October 16th, after devoting some time to an examination of Bog river pond, we carried to Clear pond and thence to Harrington pond, crossing the divide of this portion of the watershed, and reached the streams which flow into Smith's lake and from the head-waters of Beaver river.

On the 17th, it was my design to make a triangulation station on the summit of Smith's Ledge or mountain, on the west shore of Smith's lake, and this was the first bright and clear day that we had in more than a week. It was but a short distance from our camp to the ledge, and I was able to measure the horizontal angles between many of our major mountain stations, so that by a construction of the three-point problem, the angular position of this ledge, as measured by theodolite, from those mountains, could be verified, and the lake below and surrounding topography projected upon the map with direct reference to the base of Lake Champlain, more than seventy miles distant. The elevation of Smith's lake above tide has been computed from the barometrical observations at 1,738 feet. The height of the ledge or mountain above the lake may be placed at 498 feet.

Barometrical observations at Charlie pond, on the route to Little Tupper's lake, give its elevation above tide at 1,686 feet, making it 52 feet lower than Smith's lake.

It is to be remarked that if, at any future time, it should become necessary to have a greatly increased supply of water for the Hudson river or canals, even these distant lakes and rivers can be made tributary. The water of Smith's lake and of the lakes and streams emptying into it could be turned by a dam and canal into Charlie pond, which empties into Little Tupper's lake; by corresponding treatment, the waters of the latter could be led into Stony pond, which by the Slim pond empties into Long lake, and then by the dam and canal, long since proposed by Professor Benedict, led to the head-waters of the Hudson, nearly doubling the upper watershed of that noble river. In view of the proposed Champlain ship canal, this source of water supply may be of interest, but though the expenditure to render it available would be trifling, the consequential damages to mill owners in the settlements, on the lower waters of the streams thus diverted, would be considerable.

In leaving the wilderness, I proceeded down Beaver river, and from Lowville reached Albany.

In November, late as was the season, it was thought advisable to attempt the completion of the angular measurements from the one or two stations which remained unvisited. As soon as the disease (epizootic) among the horses—which had rendered travel beyond railroads almost impossible—had abated, work was recommenced. The lateral had been left till the more difficult work, in the interior of the wilderness, had been accomplished. Crain's Mountain, in Warren county, which had been selected and ascended for this purpose, had proved unfavorable, and Mount Moxon or Maxham, north-eastward of it, had been selected as its substitute.

November 14th found me in the neighborhood of Mount Maxham, with theodolite, barometer, etc. On the morning of the 15th, accompanied by a guide carrying the theodolite, and a volunteer assistant, we set out for the mountain, some five miles distant. The snow in the woods made the walking uncomfortable, but about noon we reached the foot, and after a short rest, commenced to scale the precipitous front. At this time, it was slippery with snow and hung with icicles, and consequently dangerous. After laboriously approaching the summit, we found ourselves in a cul-de-sac on the face of the cliff—the rocks overhanging—and were compelled to descend a distance and try another ledge, where, happily, we were more fortunate, and attained the crest. The theodolite was placed and angular measurements made, but the intense cold (+ 25° Fahrenheit, or 7° below zero centigrade), with the sweeping wind, prevented complete work. A reconnaissance map was made, and from the barometrical observations taken I have computed the height of this station at 2,479 feet.

It was after 3 P.M. when we left the summit, and so dangerous was the descent that it was nearly sunset when we reached the foot of the precipice. It was the intention to have proceeded from this station to Ticonderoga, where another triangulation station would have been made on the summit of Mount Defiance; but the horse disease— which had ceased in the cities—was here at its height. It was almost impossible to procure conveyance, and the survey was brought to a summary conclusion.

**General Summary**

Hypsometry

The great number of observations taken with mountain barometers, etc., have rendered the publication of the whole of the records unadvisable, some 8,500 readings of the different instruments having been taken, the field books forming two considerable volumes.

The mean of the barometer and thermometer at the more important stations is all for which there is space, and is attached hereto, condensed and tabulated.

For the more important mountains, etc., observations synchronous with those taken on the summit were made at near lower stations of established altitude. In the computation of all the altitudes, however, the observations at upper stations have been directly compared with the records of the truly wonderful and invaluable automatic instruments of the Dudley Observatory. It is my impression that this survey is the first in which the recording barometer, working day and night with mechanical precision, has been made the principal lower station, or station of record and correction. The position of the Observatory, directly south of the wilderness, has made it a most valuable station for corrections in hypsometric work in that region. The barometer at the Observatory is 170 feet above tide in the Hudson river.

Professor Hough has ably shown (Annals Dudley Observatory, vol. ii., pp. 234, 235) that the maxima and minima of atmospheric pressure occur contemporaneously along the same longitude, and also that the "local disturbance (viz., within the radius of one mile) may at any instant amount to + / − 0.02 of an inch."

The field observations during this season corroborate in a remarkable manner these important conclusions, and seem to prove that for ordinary engineering purposes—or purposes of exploration at least—such a lower station, though distant, is sufficient. Only during sudden storms is there danger of great error, and that measurement is to be the most valued in which there is the least indication of local disturbance. I have reason to believe that altitude observations taken upon mountain summits are more reliable than those taken in the valleys.

The almost simultaneous rise and fall of the barometer at the Dudley Observatory, and at some of our stations in the heart of the forest, are truly remarkable, and have made it probable that upon the same meridian, in fair, settled weather, if the time of observation were given by telegraph, so as to be absolutely synchronous, the barometrical curves would be very similar. The value of the barometer in leveling must neither be under nor over estimated. Our measurement of Mount Marcy, the mean of 72 observations, indicates that its altitude is 5,333 feet above tide. Professor Benedict, with syphon barometer, more than thirty years ago, found for it an altitude of 5,337 feet. It is remarkable that after so long a period, other observers, with different instruments, and with a far distant southerly station for corrections, should come so nearly to the same conclusion.

The careful re-measurement of Mount Seward, made this season, gives for its altitude 4,348 feet, being about 100 feet less than my measurement of 1870. The instruments used in this last measurement were superior to those formerly employed, and the observations more numerous. The summit observations, as compared with those taken at Adirondack village, make no material difference. The height of 5,100 feet, attributed to the mountain in the geological survey, is therefore clearly an error. The barometrical observations on Mount Santanoni, this season, indicate another error on the part of Professor Emmons, who attributes a height of 5,000 feet to that mountain. My measurement makes it 4,607 feet, or nearly 400 feet less than the previous estimate, and is, probably, the first recorded actual measurement of the mountain.

Among the most important results in the hypsometry of the survey this season is the measurement by barometer of the height of several inferior mountains, which were not ascended; a thing which will at first, perhaps, appear impossible. The method, I believe, originated with myself, and, simple as it is, seems never to have been even previously thought of. It is applicable only to mountains inferior in height, and should only be applied to summits which are not greatly distant.

In ascending a loftier mountain, the course of a gorge or slide should be followed, where the opening through the forest will admit of a view of the surrounding country. When a height is reached upon the mountain side, apparently at a level with that of the inferior summit, whose height is desired, sights should be taken with spirit-level, and the mountain ascended or descended till the *apparent* altitude of the other mountain is found. The barometer should now be placed and observations taken in the usual manner. The distance of the mountain should be determined by telemeter or otherwise, and the proper correction for curvature of the earth and for refraction afterward applied. An excellent opportunity for testing the value of this method was afforded in the case of Ragged Mountain, which is overlooked by Mount Seward. Ragged Mountain was first measured directly by barometer placed upon its summit, and its height found to be 4,126.81 English feet. The same day it was again measured from a point on Mount Seward, carefully found by level, and though readings of barometers and thermometers at the Dudley Observatory and at the station were different from those in its *direct* measurement, pressure and temperature having changed in the interval, the computed altitude was 4,126.41 feet; which, with a correction for curvature of the earth and refraction of + .572 of a foot, indicates the height of Ragged Mountain, by this method of combined spirit-level and barometer, at 4,126.98 feet, or about 17/100 of a foot higher than the measurement as made on the summit. This is an extraordinary result, and is surely exceptional, but it is nevertheless interesting. The method will save the topographer, working in a wilderness region, the toil of ascending all the small summits in order to ascertain their height, and in this way a great many inferior heights, which would not be otherwise taken, will be made known.

In military engineering, the simplicity and value of this method make it of importance; for by means of it, the height of places and a knowledge of the commanding summits within an enemy's lines, may be readily determined by an observer upon the opposite mountain sides, with barometer, pocket-level, and, perhaps, a telemeter.

In the table of barometrical results the mountains thus measured are italicized, Andrew and North River mountains being the only other summits recorded. The stations marked with an asterisk (*), it is believed, have been first measured during this survey. It is undoubtedly the most extensive series of barometrical measurements ever made in that region.

The computations have been made by myself, and again and again repeated to insure accuracy. They were made by the adaptation of La Place's formula to English measures, as tabulated and given in the meteorological tables of the Smithsonian Institute, by Professor Guyot.

I take this occasion to tender my thanks to Professor George W. Hough for the meteorological date with which he has furnished me. In the invention of the recording barometer he has rendered a service to science which is only beginning to be appreciated. While advancing the work of astronomical discovery, meteorology has been placed upon a higher basis; for the records of the Dudley Observatory have rendered more practically valuable the mysteries of the invisible atmosphere.

The recording barometer will, I have faith, be yet generally made the standard in hypsometry. If, in the course of a barometrical survey of the Adirondack region, superior instruments of this class, or the meteorographs of Professor G. W. Hough, were placed at different

| Date. | STATION. | Field Observations. | | | Dudley Observatory. | | | Altitude above tide, Eng. feet. |
|---|---|---|---|---|---|---|---|---|
| | | Barometer. | Attd. Ther-mometer, Fahrenheit. | Temperature of air, Fahrenheit. | Barometer thirty-two degrees. | Temperature of air, Fahrenheit. | Hourly change, B ± | |
| 1872. July 27 | Wellstown (— 10 feet) | 28.959 | 67.5 | 68.0 | 29.710 | 75.53 | −.002 | 980.53 |
| July 28 | Rift Hill (An.)* | 27.886 | (R .32°) | 80.53 | 29.816 | 76.86 | −.004 | 2,104.70 |
| July 28 | Burnt Mountain (An.)* | 27.885 | (R .32°) | 77.00 | 29.863 | 76.17 | −.010 | 2,085.16 |
| July 30 | Lake Pleasant (An.)* | 28.340 | (R .32°) | 76.0 | 29.769 | 72.0 | −.010 | 1,578.92 |
| July 30 | Holmes Hill (An.)* | 27.870 | (R .32°) | 76.0 | 29.788 | 76.75 | .0 | 2,085.50 |
| July 31 | Speculator Mountain * | 26.985 | 59.96 | 60.18 | 29.786 | 65.57 | −.008 | 3,004.97 |
| Aug. 1 | Jessup's River bridge * | 28.311 | 73.83 | 76.66 | 29.778 | 73.64 | −.006 | 1,727.52 |
| Aug. 1 | Mason Lake * | 28.155 | 65.0 | 65.0 | 29.758 | 73.28 | .0 | 1,824.02 |
| Aug. 4 | Camp on Snowy Mountain * | 26.401 | 47.50 | 47.66 | 29.850 | 66.8 | +.016 | 3,650.96 |
| Aug. 4 | Snowy Mountain *. | 26.330 | 62.0 | 59.2 | 29.938 | 71.96 | .0 | 3,859.95 |
| Aug. 4 | Lewey lake (synca.) * | 28.448 | 67.1 | 64.6 | 29.938 | 71.96 | .0 | 1,692.06 |
| Aug. 4 | Lewey lake (all day) * | 28.441 | 68.6 | 66.35 | 29.931 | 72.69 | +.002 | 1,711.73 |
| Aug. 4 | { Snowy Mountain direct * { with Lewey lake and tide | 26.330 28.448 | 62.0 67.1 | 59.2 84.6 | | | | 3,867.20 |
| Aug. 5 | Lewey lake * | 28.607 | 83.25 | 81.37 | 30.044 | 77.04 | −.018 | 1,721.42 |
| | Mean altitude Lewey lake | | | | | | | 1,701.93 |
| 1870. Oct. 10 | Blue Mountain (Mount Emmons) +100 feet* | 26.449 | 55.37 | 54.87 | 29.716 | 62.8 | −.026 | 3,595.93 |
| 1872. Aug. 6 | Indian lake * | 28.551 | 80.71 | 79.0 | 29.939 | 78.92 | −.012 | 1,669.34 |
| Aug. 7 | Cedar River settlement * | 28.534 | 68.9 | 67.9 | 29.975 | 76.45 | .0 | 1,670.11 |
| Aug. 8 | Cedar River Falls * | 28.091 | 61.64 | 67.42 | 29.959 | 77.31 | +.010 | 2,088.69 |
| Aug. 9 | Cedar lakes * | 27.744 | 81.58 | 81.0 | 29.863 | 85.74 | +.012 | 2,493.40 |
| Aug. 10 | Moose lake * | 27.943 | 82.22 | 81.31 | 29.853 | 81.15 | −.016 | 2,302.81 |
| Aug. 13 | Round lake * | 28.158 | 71.5 | 71.16 | 29.792 | 76.50 | +.002 | 1,885.97 |
| Aug. 13 | Long pond * | 28.114 | 79.57 | 76.71 | 29.746 | 80.16 | −.017 | 1,924.56 |
| Aug. 13 | Long Pond Mountain * | 27.724 | 70.5 | 68.5 | 29.697 | 76.91 | −.008 | 2,232.45 |
| Aug. 14 | Puffer pond * | 27.785 | 72.5 | 72.74 | 29.700 | 80.85 | −.022 | 2,193.25 |
| Aug. 14 | Thirteenth pond * | 28.260 | 71.1 | 70.1 | 29.658 | 77.23 | +.002 | 1,692.37 |
| Aug. 15 | South Mountain (An.) * | 28.042 | (R .32°) | 79.75 | 29.779 | 83.05 | −.006 | 1,917.07 |
| Aug. 16 | Crain's Mountain * | 26.918 | 61.4 | 60.4 | 29.924 | 75.78 | −.014 | 3,252.77 |
| Aug. 28 | Lake Champlain * | 27.697 | 60.0 | 60.67 | 29.784 | 75.14 | −.005 | 2,278.59 |
| Aug. 28 | { Bald Mountain *. { with Lake Champlain | 29.965 | 68.7 60.0 | 66.0 56.67 | 29.784 | 71.14 | −.005 | 91.40 2,265.95 |
| Aug. 29 | Bald Mountain * | 29.965 | 68.7 | 66.0 | | | | |
| Aug. 31 | Mineville * | 28.401 | 66.24 | 64.39 | 29.691 | 68.5 | −.005 | 2,313.00 |
| Sept. 1 | Bald Peak (Moriah) | 27.603 | 60.6 | 61.68 | 29.540 | 61.68 | #.022 | 1,337.75 |
| Sept. 4 | Rustic Lodge (Whiteface) * | 27.877 | 56.79 | 63.54 | 29.747 | 67.33 | +.001 | 2,083.66 |
| Sept. 4 | Wilmington village (synca.) * | 28.966 | 54.18 | 54.09 | 29.859 | 56.87 | +.001 | 1,053.50 |

**TABLE OF BAROMETRICAL MEASUREMENTS. — (Condensed).**

*Table of Barometric Measurements*

stations on the borders of the region; at Crown Point, Plattsburgh, Ogdensburgh, Lowville, Utica, and centrally at Adirondack village, and their records compared with observations taken at different points in the wilderness, most interesting results might be expected. It is not too much to say that the mean of such a series of comparisons would indicate the altitude of interior stations with as great accuracy as is economically possible.

In the interests of meteorology and advanced science, I cannot too strongly urge the erection by the State of a small stone hut or hospice, near the summit of Mount Marcy, to afford shelter, from sudden, severe and dangerous storms, to scientific observers. It would be of great interest to determine the maximum and minimum temperature, etc., by recording instruments left at such a station during the winter. The knowledge that such a protection against storm existed, would induce more tourists to visit the summit, and well repay the small expenditure, by bringing thousands of dollars into the State annually, which would otherwise be elsewhere expended.

Triangulation

A sketch, showing the condition of the principal triangles measured and the extent of the country which they cover in the different counties, is annexed. [The sketch is not included in the illustrations.] There are few ill conditioned angles. The region within the limits of the primary lines is covered with a network of inferior angles, which are omitted in this sketch.

Commencing at Crown Point, the angles advanced westward show the means by which geodetic connection has been made with Lake Champlain. A few additional angles should be measured to complete the great quadrilateral and perfect the connection with the lake. Comparatively few of the mountains have been found properly placed upon the existing maps; and it has even been made probable that some of the old county or town lines are improperly located. It has been rumored that the northern boundary of the State—being the boundary between the United States and Canada—is one point six miles from its true location. These are matters of importance and demand attention. The time is not far distant when a *precise* triangulation and geographical survey of the whole State will be required.

If, in the course of future surveys in this region, a base-line of verification be required, the frozen surface of Long lake—a true water-level—is recommended. Copper bolts, sunk in the rock at the water edge in summer, during the progress of work, would show the exact points sighted to, from the mountain summits—Mounts Seward and Santanoni; and it would then only be necessary to visit the lake when frozen and measure the base. An idea of the feasibility of this operation may be obtained by an examination of the triangulation sketch.

Topography

The reconnaissance maps of topography, made during the season, are ninety-eight in number. The mountains visible, and their several peaks, are as properly placed upon them as time and weather permitted; and the extensions of their ridges developed by horizontal contour lines, afterward filled in with vertical hatchings. The course of numerous streams and rivers, wherever advisable and possible, appear upon these maps, together with many lakes or ponds, whose forms or location required correction. These maps supply the place of plane table work, and will be used in locating the topography upon the large final map.

A specimen of a portion of a reconnaissance map, showing a mountainous region in Warren county, is annexed. [The map is not included in the illustrations.]

Upon the map-sketch of triangulation will be found a blue line, which indicates approximately the position of the summit of the watershed of the Hudson, or the divide between its sources and the waters which flow to the St. Lawrence river. This is a matter of interest in connection with the canals and general water supply. It may also be of value in the determination of the area of forest which it is necessary to preserve in order to protect from evaporation the springs and streams which are the sources of the Hudson.

Conclusion

The results of the survey are numerous and interesting. The vastness and wildness of the region are the better appreciated when, at this late day, we are able to find within it mountains from 3,000 to 4,000 feet in height, nameless, unascended and unmeasured. The incorrectness of the existing maps is understood, when we discover that the famous Blue Mountain or Mount Emmons is not 4,000 feet high (as represented), and that it is apparently inferior to the lofty neighboring summit known as Snowy Mountain, which rises to an altitude of 3,859 feet, where on the maps is shown a blank.

Again, while geographers have expatiated upon the great elevation (for this region) of the lakes Colden and Avalanche, in Essex county, a little more than 2,700 feet above the sea, they have gone blindly on, unaware that far in the south portion of the woods, the Cedar lakes—from whose shores the snows of winter depart slowly—lie, on the great and most elevated plateau of the wilderness, at an elevation of 2,493 feet; not flowing to the St. Lawrence, as represented upon their maps, but to the Hudson river.

As a matter of technical geographical interest, the discovery of the true highest pond-source of the Hudson river is, perhaps, more interesting. Far above the chilly waters of Lake Avalanche, at an elevation of 4,293 feet, is *Summit Water*, a minute, unpretending tear of the clouds—as it were—a lonely pool, shivering in the breezes of the mountains, and sending its limpid surplus through Feldspar brook to the Opalescent river, the well-spring of the Hudson.

But I may not enlarge upon these subjects. In the hasty journal of the survey, and in the tabular statements of altitudes taken by mountain barometer, will be found a great number of new results.

Many mountains still remain barometrically unmeasured, though their altitude may be trigonometrically computed. Mount Dix and Mount McIntyre, though they have been previously ascended, are among the number unmeasured. The appropriateness of the new names Mount Redfield, Mount Street, and Mount Adams given to summits hitherto unnamed, will be appreciated by those acquainted with the written history of the region.

It is now a question of political importance whether the section covered by this survey should not be preserved, in its present primitive condition, as a forest-farm and source of timber supply for our buildings and our ships. The deprivation of a State of its timber is a grave error in political economy, and at this time when the western States of the Union, feeling their deficiency, are laboriously planting forests, it behooves us to see to the preservation of those with which we are spontaneously blessed.

The question of water supply, also, is intimately connected with this proposition. I have elsewhere expressed my opinion that within one hundred years the cold, healthful living waters of the wilderness—the home of the brook trout, a fish that cannot exist in an impure stream—will be required for the domestic water supply of the cities of the Hudson river valley. With the exception of the Croton watershed, which, however, has its limits of supply, almost all the available water falling into the Hudson below Albany is the surface drainage of a settled and well farmed region, inferior in quality, often charged with the deleterious products of paper-mills and factories; being, in short, from watersheds over which the public has no control. It is not possible to protect from defilement the waters flowing through a settled country. Every storm washes the fields and carries to the streams, in solution, the strength of the manures of the agriculturist and much dissolved mineral matter derived from the plowed soil of the fields. The trees also are cut away to the very water's edge, and the shallow streams, lacking the volume and depth, which, in great rivers, renders the exposure of the surface of the water to the sun a mere superficial and immaterial matter, now, heated and evaporating, become nauseous and slimy with a growth of decaying vegetable organisms. The streams of the wilderness, on the contrary, are sheltered from the sun by the thick overhanging foliage of the forest. The more extensive underlying rocks of the region being generally gneissoid, contain little soluble matter; and the pure water from the clouds, after gaining carbonic acid by exposure to the air in the breezy lakes, comes brightly foaming over many a picturesque rapid and waterfall to the Hudson and the sea. A stone dam thrown across the Hudson above its junction with the Schroon, while securing water free from deleterious substances, would afford the head of water necessary for aqueduct purposes; the superfluous waters of the river escaping at the center of the dam, through a flume, would be sufficient for the purposes of the lumberman or the "river driver." The Sacondaga river above Northville is pure and of great value, and could be treated in the same manner.

The great expense attending this project is the aqueduct, which, if extended to New York city, would be more than 200 miles in length. When we consider, however, the Roman aqueducts (the *Aqua Maria,* 60 miles in length, built 145 years before Christ, and the numerous other aqueducts, some of which are in use to this day; the aqueduct of the inferior town, *Citiva Vecchia,* 23 miles in length; in Provence, that which supplied Nismes, crossing deep valleys at a height of 188 feet, conducting the water for a distance of 25 miles), the aqueduct proposed will not appear chimerical.

In Scotland, the city of Glasgow is supplied with water brought from Loch Katrine, distant 26 miles; furnishing 19,000,000 gallons a day. This aqueduct was completed in 1858.

In France, a covered conduit, 80 miles in length, conveys to Paris 8,000,000 gallons of pure spring water, daily, from the head of the Dhuis, in Champagne; and progress is being made upon the Vanne aqueduct, 104 miles in length; estimated to yield 22,000,000 gallons a day.

In England, the water furnished London being inferior in quality, a new source of supply, from the head-waters of the River Severn in North Wales, distant 173 miles, has been suggested. The cost of the aqueduct is estimated at about $43,000,000.

All these works are undertaken for the sake of procuring *pure water,* for, though each of the cities above mentioned has a river flowing past it, from which water could be obtained by steam pumps, the people of those cities are not satisfied, and demand such a *pure* supply as will secure them from cholera and other epidemics.

If the present ratio of increase of population continues, the Hudson river valley must eventually contain one long, marginal city, extending from the Mohawk river to New York. The Adirondack Wilderness is the only watershed which will afford a sufficient supply of pure water for such a population as will then exist.

In this country, the Croton aqueduct, 38 miles in length, has shown the practicability and value of this method of supply. Allowing that 150 miles of the proposed Adirondack aqueduct be built at the expense of the cities of New York and Brooklyn, and 50 miles at the expense of Albany and Troy, we have the major portion of the work complete; while 10 other towns, each worthy of an aqueduct 10 miles in length, would render their aid to the enterprise. Although this source of water-supply cannot, for various reasons, be made immediately available, yet, unless action be taken at this time, and the forests protecting and purifying the waters be themselves protected, there will be no opportunity in the future to accomplish this great work.

Such vast enterprises are of slow progress. If this aqueduct were commenced in these days, long before its completion the failing water-supply, would rouse the people to a clamorous demand that it be finished. For the present, the protection of the forest is all that is required, and unless this be done we shall incur the merited scorn of posterity.

In consideration of the hardships and exposure experienced in this exploration, it may be proper to remark that not a particle of alcoholic or fermented liquor of any kind—even for medicinal purposes—was used, carried, or permitted to be used or carried by any member of the party. It was a rule against which some of the men employed murmured, but they were only able to break it surreptitiously. The result has been subordination, steady work, health, and success.

The survey has now progressed far toward completion. The measurement of additional angles, with some other work, is contemplated during the coming season. Accompanying the report will be found the map-sketches of primary triangulation and reconnaissance, therein referred to.

All of which is respectfully submitted.

VERPLANCK COLVIN

ALBANY, *March 10th*, 1873.

# Excerpts from the Seventh Report on the Survey of the Adirondack Region of New York 1875—1879

## Report

*[Pages 4–10: General summary of geological, botanical, and other information, including current events pertaining to the Adirondacks]*

*To the Honorable the Legislature of the State of New York:*
In accordance with law, I have the honor to submit, accompanied with maps and illustrations, the following

## Report

The progress of the work, since the last communication was laid before the Legislature, has been extremely satisfactory. A complete reorganization of the different departments of the survey has been effected, and an improved system of work suited to the additional labors imposed, devised, and put to practical test in the field, affording—notwithstanding the limited means at command—the most important and permanent results.

The topographical character of the survey has been made complete in all respects, as will be readily seen by an inspection of the details of work, and reports from the different departments hereto appended; while in addition to the exploration and topographical reconnaissance of the wild interior, and the trigonometrical measurements therein heretofore made, I am now conducting a general geodetic survey of

*Above the Clouds: Signal on the Summit of Mount Marcy*

the whole of the region known as the Adirondack district of New York, including also the bordering settlements.

The natural limits of this great topographical area are sharply defined. Geographically, its boundaries are Lake Champlain, the St. Lawrence, the Mohawk, and the Black rivers, into one or the other of which the mountain streams of the wilderness finally pour their waters. Geologically considered, the limits are almost identical with the geographical, and may be briefly said to be the outer line of the great central area of azoic or metamorphic rocks (*granitic, feldspathic or crystalline*), which give so marked a character to Adirondack scenery. Botanically the borders of the wilderness region are indicated by the termination of the great forests of spruce, Canadian fir, beech, and yellow birch, and vast peat mosses; while zoologically it may be designated as the region of wild game, or—more accurately, at the present day—defined as that portion of northern New York, contained within a line uniting those points along the borders of the great forest, where men still at times trap the black bear, (*Ursus americanus*). This last limit is much better marked than would at first thought seem possible, and follows very nearly the limits of the primitive rock.

Each of these natural limits, when traced upon the ground, gives a very irregular figure not unlike a great contour line, surrounding the wilderness region, and owing to the rectangular form of maps, in order to properly enclose this very irregular area, and to show its relation to and connection with the remainder of the State, it is necessary to bring within the lines of latitude and longitude, which form the outer limits of the map, a great portion of the settled districts.

This is important in order that the approaches to the forest may be seen, so that those using the maps may be enabled to recognize points on the margin with which they are familiar, to get a general idea of directions and of distances; in the language of the topographer, to orient themselves.

In carrying the field work of the survey out into those portions of the settlements within the map area (where the most glaring mistakes on old maps rendered such additional work absolutely necessary), I have been amazed to discover that the same monstrous errors which have prevailed on all the maps of the wilderness are even surpassed in the maps still in use, of these border lands. It is at first sight a little difficult to understand why this should be so, but upon careful examination, I reach the following conclusions: these maps have been copied the one after the other from the old original compass survey notes, with occasionally later but imperfect surveys, made without any unity of design or systematic method for obtaining accuracy. Maps which might have sufficed a century ago, when few traversed the region, have in this manner, to a certain extent, been reproduced whenever there seemed to be a demand for maps, and the public, knowing of no better material, have been satisfied with what they could thus obtain. The old survey department of the State has always had more the character of a land office and an office of record than that of general surveys, and has never been permitted to enter upon topographical work. In consequence, up to the time of the initiation of this survey, there had been no attempt to make a proper geodetic survey of New York, and it has thus become my privilege to make the first trigonometrical survey of any portion of the State, ever authorized by the Legislature.

The Adirondack Survey has now been in progress under the authority of the State government for seven years. Beginning in 1872 with the smallest of appropriations, its work has been steadily advanced as far as the means admitted, from year to year, until at length the great mass of the highest mountains of the State—the immovable landmarks of the past and of the future—have been covered with an intricate network of triangles, and thousands of miles of distances measured, so that from the astronomical and trigonometrical work, we now find for the first time the true positions of thousands of places within our State, that were not known before. Thus are obtained the latitudes and longitudes, which enable us to prove the exact distances of our monuments and stations from Paris, London, or Washington, or any geodetically determined position on the surface of our globe.

It is my task in this report to show the progress of the work to the present date; to explain the methods, the results aimed at, and the work accomplished. The difficulties encountered, and the methods employed to overcome them, are also shown. The former will explain the laborious nature of the work; a knowledge of the latter may aid other engineers when placed amid similar obstacles.

Five years have elapsed since the Legislature has required a report from this department, though the financial reports have been regularly rendered, with vouchers, to the comptroller, and during this interval—despite the smallness of appropriations—the amount of work has been so great that to embrace a sketch of it within the present report, so as at the same time to give an adequate idea of the whole, is a task of difficulty.

During the years that have passed, I have been enabled not only to extend the survey, but to study the growth of settlements throughout the region, so as to obtain an insight into the probable ultimate character of the development of the country; to which attention must be paid by our State administration in order to properly aid and forward this growth where it has found a place in natural channels leading toward permanent results.

It is for such reasons that memoranda relative to the settlement and causes of settlement of these wild lands have been made, to the extent also of including some account of the industries which are at present most active in effecting changes throughout the region.

While to the political economist these matters are of the first and most vital importance, to the lover of nature and of the wilderness, the progress of settlement, and the extension of civilization into the primeval forests, is recognized only with regret. To the explorer, also, it is pleasanter to imagine the wild mountain crest, or mirrored lake which he was first to reach, remaining as unvisited, in all its aspects as unchanged as when he first beheld it.

Viewed from the standpoint of my own explorations, the rapidity with which certain changes take place in the opening up to travel of the wild corners of the wilderness has about it something almost startling.

A few summers since, I stood for the first time on the cool, mossy shore of the mountain springlet lake, Tear of the Clouds. Almost hidden between the gigantic mountain domes of Marcy, Skylight, and the Gray Peak, this lovely pool lifted on its granite pedestal toward heaven, the loftiest water-mirror of the stars; beseeching, not in vain, from each low drifting cloud some tribute for the sources of the Hudson; fresh, new, unvisited, save by wild beasts that drank; it was a gem more pure and more delightful to the eye than the most precious jewel.

It is still almost as wild and quite as beautiful; but close behind our exploring footsteps came the "blazed-line," marked with axe upon the trees; the trail, soon trodden into mire; the bark shanty, picturesque enough, but soon surrounded by a grove of stumps; while Skylight, so recently the untrodden summit, with its barrier of dwarf forest, is now from this new pass by a new trail an ascent of only so many minutes.

True, by the discovery of this pass two thousand feet of clambering had been saved to those desiring to cross the range, the old trail and its miseries thrown aside and Marcy made easily accessible. But the first romance is gone forever.

And so, glancing over the field of former labors, I find following in the footsteps of my explorations the blazed-line and the trail; then the ubiquitous tourist, determined to see all that has been recorded as worth seeing. Where first comes one—the next year there are ten—the year after full a hundred. The woods are thronged; bark and log huts prove insufficient; hotels spring up as though by magic, and the air resounds with laughter, song, and jollity. The wild trails, once jammed with logs, are cut clear by the axes of the guides, and ladies clamber to the summits of those once untrodden peaks. The genius of change has possession of the land; we cannot control it. When we study the necessities of our people, we would not control it if we could.

This change—this new revelation of fresh, exhilarating mountain summer life—is having too important and beneficial an influence upon society at present, not to demand the sympathy of government. To the wealthy dwellers of cities, debilitated by a tainted atmosphere, the breezes and the mountain springs bring life, while the free, joyous exercises of their children in these summer homes, lay for them the foundations of continued health. Their wealth and refinement distributed among the mountains, raises at once the thrifty inhabitants of the settlements to competence and enlarged ideas of the outer world.

But while these changes have opened to travel many of the most interesting nooks among our mountains, they have only rendered more marked, by contrast, the wildness of the remainder, and the unvisited wilderness centres or cores are still left in all their sylvan purity.

The bear and deer, though somewhat reduced in numbers, still haunt these remote places; panther still roam untrammeled, and the wolf alone—persecuted by the trap and poison—begins to be relatively scarce.

Therefore, save to the hermits of the forest, whose semi-savage life cannot always be maintained, these changes are rather changes for the better, and no unselfish person will for a moment regret that his once solitary pleasures are now shared in by the many. The sportsman has still a thousand unfrequented recesses—if he will seek them—where he may travel unmolested.

Though the waters of the Raquette now flash responsive to the oars and paddles of ten boats, where once they saw but one; and though its shores, once rendered less desolate by even the howl of wolf, are now dotted with the summer cabins of the new dispensation, the panther and the bear still visit it; the deer, alas, still driven by the hounds, seek a false safety in its waters, and to my own knowledge (the summer song and camp-fire long departed), in mid-winter the wolf does not disdain to travel on its ice.

Though a wee steamer now ploughs the waters of the Saranac, the huge lake trout—*salmonidæ*—still leap at evening from the surface; deer still drink at its shores, and but a few months since the little steamer had its first adventure, chasing a party of four bears that were swimming in the lake.

Though at the St. Regis lakes, the hotel has the character of a Saratoga, deer are still shot within sight of the croquet lawn, and a few miles' travel on foot or by canoe suffices to place the sportsman in the midst of the haunts of wild habitants of the forest, and if the howl of wolves be less frequent, he may rely upon the solemn voices of the owls to soothe his slumbers.

Where in 1870 and '73, the small bark shanty of our hunter guide stood solitary—our only shelter—near the sand beaches of Blue Mountain lake, now stand here and there the comfortable woodland hotels, with semi-rustic grounds, and bright Concord coaches, drawn by sleek "four" or "six-in-hands," lend color to the scene. Yet the boat-canoes that cluster on the sand beach, mutely but eloquently, tell of the sweet nooks and corners which may be reached in them, not only on these lakes, but on more distant waters.

And so elsewhere; a thousand new resorts are found. At Keene Flats; at Lake Pleasant; on the Fulton Chain; on Cedar river—so lately the loneliest of places—; on Smith's lake and Little Tupper's, Meacham lake and Chateaugay, new resorts have grown into existence, possibilities and probabilities have become facts accomplished: the future is not dark nor much obscured.

The region is already the summer home of untold thousands—a public pleasure ground—a wilderness park to all intents and purposes; safe from human savages, and without a harmful serpent within its borders.

Already private clubs have separated large areas. The moose (*Alce Americanus* Jardine), by importation from Maine and Nova Scotia, have been restored to the grounds of the Adirondack club, near Lake Sandford, within the shadow of Mount Marcy, and the lakes restocked with choicest fish. So elsewhere in the forest the task of preservation is beginning, and only the luckless bears, wolves, and panthers, etc., hiding from the uproar of invading civilization, find themselves without protection.

With this brief sketch of the character of the changes that have taken place in our wilderness region since the last narrative report was rendered, sufficient to explain the new conditions by which the work is to a certain extent influenced, I turn to the details of the work of the survey.

*[Pages 86–93: Excerpts from Colvin's journal concerning the Great Range in the High Peaks]*

*October 9th.* Set out with two guides for the exploration of the region to the north-eastward of Marcy, including the Gothic mountains. Ascended the valley of John's brook, a wild rapid mountain stream, shut in by gloomy mountain ranges, and rendered more wild by the dense forest of black spruce, which extended on either side up the steep mountain slopes into the dull gray canopy of cloud. An hour or two before sunset the guides unslung their knapsacks beside a tributary brook that descended from the lofty peak to the northward, known as Slide Mountain, which we proposed to ascend and measure upon the morrow. A comfortable camp was built, thatched, and carpeted with dense layers of soft balsam boughs, and while the guides made the forest echo to the blows of their axes, I ascended a slight prominence near by, which commanded a view of the valley, and proceeded to note the salient topographical features.

The mountains to the northward were hidden by the evergreen covered ridges and knolls, the range upon the side of which we were encamped, but southward and eastward the clouds had disappeared and a serrate ridge of peaks was seen, among which—easily recognized by the fearful precipices that scarred its side—arose the highest peak of the Gothic mountains, wildest and most rugged of the Adirondacks. Far above, reared apparently against the blue vault of heaven, the sharp snowy peak stood glowing in the last rays of the autumnal sunset, then—as I sketched—the pure white upon its crest turned to pale pink and crimson, slowly fading into the gray gloom of evening. Descending, I returned to the camp and beside the crackling fire made a hearty repast. Soon, wrapped in our heavy blankets, we dropped asleep, soothed by the glorious fire at our feet.

The morning of the 10th opened drearily. Lowering clouds had settled far down into the valley, and the prospect was any thing but cheering. Made an early breakfast and set out for Slide Mountain deferring the ascent of the Gothics till next day. Having left our supplies at camp, the guides carrying the instruments, carefully packed, we climbed rapidly, notwithstanding the discouraging appearance of the clouds. Now following the banks of a brook, now climbing through dense woods again to descend into the deep ravine bed of the lesser brook—here only a rill—upward over boulders of gray *hypersthene,* sometimes blackened with exposure to the weather; tramping in the soft, fresh, clayey gravel of some fresh slide—in which the recent tracks of a deer were seen, where he had jumped from the bank above—we saw at length through the cold drifting fog, forming the under surface of the clouds, the black slippery slope of rock from which the peak obtains the name of Slide Mountain. Clambering up to the edge of the cloud we seated ourselves upon great blocks of fallen rock, and drearily waited for the drizzly storm and cold vapor to pass away. Sweeping through the dark spires of the balsams and spruces, the clouds drifted by, hour after hour, and at length, disheartened and chilled, we descended and returned to camp, dispirited, but not discouraged as it was determined to make this ascent again at some future time.

A cold frosty night was followed by another stormy morning, but the barometer which last night stood at 27.450 was now rising, and I determined to ascend the Gothic mountains. By the time that breakfast and packing had been finished, the clouds cleared away from the mountains to the eastward—showing the peaks, however, all capped with snow. We set out at once, following the stream, which for a while flowed through a more level portion of the valley. Reaching at length the forks of the brook, we crossed at a gravelly beach and following at first the left bank of the brook, soon left the stream and commenced to ascend through a forest quite free from underbrush. The clouds now gathered again and soon flakes of snow commenced thickly to descend. Suddenly a deer, startled by our approach, leaped to its feet and fled through the forest. The woods became choked again with underbrush and fallen timber, black, mossy ledges began to show themselves above, and we climbed with difficulty, till an opening in the forest appeared immediately before us, and showed a long slope of naked rock trending steeply upward—narrowing in wild perspective amid ledges far above—and covered with a thin sparkling film of water.

With rejoicing we emerged from the tangled woods and following this "slide"—path of an avalanche—made our way slowly upward, cautiously over the slippery rock, laboriously up the dripping ledges;

the water of which, cold as ice, soon demonstrated that exploration was far from pleasant under such circumstances. With surprise I now noted that the rock beneath our feet was not the usual hypersthene or norian rock, characteristic of the high peaks of the Adirondack, but appeared to be the more ordinary gray gneiss so common along the borders of the wilderness. Could it be possible, that in the midst of the central group of hypersthene peaks an island (as it were), of the common gneissoid rock should appear? This was an interesting development, and I watched the rock as we ascended, and soon found the gneiss abounding in granular crystals of a course *almandine,* proving this to be the true garnetiferous gneiss, oddly appearing isolated in the midst of the norian rock. Further up on this slide I was astonished to find the hypersthene again, and where the ascent became precipitous, and the rock crumbling and decayed, the garnetiferous gneiss was again encountered; a singular and suggestive combination or association.

At the head of this slide we obtained a grand view of the valley from which we had ascended; and the clouds clearing away, we beheld the peak which we had assailed on the preceding day, now cloudless and for the moment bright in sunshine. A glance above showed us that we were far from attaining the summit of this range, while to our dismay we now discovered that the path of the slide had led us away from the highest peak of the Gothics, and that we were now near the summit of the Wolf-Jaws—two formidable peaks to the northward on the same range. I resolved to continue to the top of the nearest peak, and then follow the ridge southward so as to obtain a full knowledge of this portion of the range, and after a weary climb we at length reached the top. The summit of the first peak reached was covered with dense dwarf forest, and the ground white with frozen snow, showing no sign of footprint of any creature.

Following the ridge, we made our way as rapidly as possible toward the southward, and soon became involved in an almost impenetrable windslash of fallen timber; and in working around this impediment along the tops of precipices, grasping icy limbs and roots for support, made a perilous passage. Here one of the guides attempting to pass a dangerous point, was overbalanced by his heavy knapsack and for a moment hung suspended feet upward over the verge, but with prompt aid escaped with the loss of his bowie knife.

Reaching at last a level space just under the highest peak, and be-

*The Crest of the Gothics*

numbed by the cold, we hurried to build a fire before venturing further. After a hasty lunch in the snow, we resumed the climb, and soon reached the timber-line, and at length beheld the crest of the Gothics!

Before us an irregular cone of granite, capped with ice and snow, arose against a wintry sky. The dwarf timber crept timidly upward upon it in a few places, not too steep for root to find a foothold, and on either side the icy slopes leaped at once down into gloomy valleys. Beyond, irregularly grouped, the great peaks, grizzly with frost and snow—were gathered in grand magnificence, all strange and new— in wild sublimity. No sound save the shuddering hiss of the chilly blast as it swept over the fearful ridge of ice that must now be our pathway. With fingers benumbed with cold, I hastily sketched the wild landscape—the shivering guide holding the broad sheet on which I drew. Then with spikeless boots, and no alpenstock save the tripod of the instrument, we essayed the last ascent, the glary slopes of ice on either side, descending a thousand feet or more, threatened death as the penalty for a single slip.

At length the summit was attained, a small flat space on the solid rock, and the instrument quickly placed in position and a circle of observations taken. Deep in the basin to the eastward lay a dark, narrow pool—black as ebony between its even darker walls of rock— the lower Au Sable lake; further south the Upper lake, like a bright jewel set in the gorgeous autumnal forest; and southward, still other ponds and lakes; while to the westward and northward a portion of the Saranac waters, and the bright surface of Lake Placid showed themselves, and above or beyond them, all the black, frost-crested

mountain billows—revealed from this new station in strangely different contour—with new passes, new gorges, and new chasms. It was
nearly 4 P.M., when we attained the summit, and the angular measurements and topographical work required every moment; so that
darkness was upon us when shivering and almost frozen by the cold
wind having a temperature of 22° Fahrenheit (− 5.°6 Centigrade), we
started on along the icy ridge to seek some means of descending. We
were struck with horror. On every side yawned icy precipices, showing more grim and dreadful in the fast increasing darkness; and the
elder guide attempting to pass along below the crest, where some
ice-clad stems of the Labrador tea (*Ledum latifolium*) alone offered assistance to the hand, was suddenly suspended over the edge of a
cliff—where, a thousand feet below, the clouds were drifting—and
rescued himself by the sheer strength of his muscular arms.

Down a sharp ridge into a sag between the peaks we made our
way southward, till at length, following the sunken *dyke* or gorge
worn in this angle of the mountains, we reached precipitous rocks,
barely descendible in safety. Down these the guides dropped or low-
ered their packs and knapsacks, step by step, ourselves following as
best we might, till at length, reaching a little shelf on the face of the
mountain, further descent appeared, in the gathering darkness, impossible, and we determined to camp in the little cluster of trees this
oasis afforded. A rough shelter of evergreen boughs was quickly im-
provised, and the ledge made home-like by the warmth and light of
the camp-fire; a scanty repast was soon finished, and wearied with
the labors of the day, wrapped in blankets we dropped into profound
slumber. In the midst of the night a crash like some strange thunder
awakened us. The moon now shone bright, and we started up to see a
vast mass of ice, detached from the cliffs above, go dashing down into
the abyss below. Again and again these dread disturbers of our slumbers swept down with sudden and fearful noise. At length the warm
breath of the south wind thawed the ice and snow upon the trees
around us—and we slept again.

*October 12th.* Awoke this morning overheated by the combined influence of a fierce fire and heavy blanket. It has turned cold again,
however, and the frost crystals float in the air. Water taken from a
little fall near our camp became congealed in a few moments beside
the fire! Recommencing the descent as soon as our frugal breakfast
was finished, we found a route which, though difficult, enabled us

slowly to make our way down into the great circular gorge—a mountain walled amphitheatre—from which Basin Mountain takes its name. Rejoicing that we had not attempted to descend further the preceding evening, we toiled downward—for our camp seemed to have been the only spot available upon the mountain's side. Descending an icy ravine, we at length lost sight of the grizzly front of Basin Mountain and the Saddle-back, and reached an upland forest glade where the ground was covered with the fresh tracks of deer, while in one spot the recent signs of bear were noticed. Hurrying on our journey—being short of provisions and anxious to reach the upper Au Sable lake that evening—our march was between a walk and a run, until a sudden and dangerous fall of one of the party admonished us to go more carefully. From this upper "basin" a steep descent led down—and obliged by a cliff to diverge, we took to the bed of the stream—and found a difficult descent. Now we began to leave the dark spruce forest behind us, and, more fresh signs of bear and deer were seen, the hardwood or deciduous forest was reached, and a little later we struck a brook flowing to the Au Sable in many a sparkling cascade and rapid. Here we came suddenly upon a high fall where the whole body of the stream leaped down in foam. Another branch of the stream now joined, and we hurried on, and at length, thoroughly wearied, reached our old trail over Bartlett Mountain now disused—the first trail which we had seen since starting for the Gothic—and soon reached the shores of the Upper Au Sable.

Being out of provisions, I determined to return with the guides to Keene, and take the opportunity to examine the progress of the leveling party; accordingly, though late, we passed the lower lake and by a forced march, via the Au Sable pass, reached Keene again the same evening, having been moving rapidly since early dawn, making the last four miles in one hour and a half over a wretched trail, treacherous with mud and roots of trees. The results of this expedition had been extremely satisfactory, for notwithstanding the severe exposure, most valuable reconnaissance maps and topographical sketches had been obtained, the arrangement and location of the mountain ranges and valleys to the northward of Marcy with the streams and the contour, and geological character of the Gothic mountains had now for the first time been ascertained.

*October 13th.* Found the leveling party already at the head of Keene Valley, and placed my old veteran guide with them to aid in selecting the best route for their work. Kept with them and watched and directed the work personally. The difficulties increased as we ascended from the valley into the densely wooded route to the Au Sable pass, and a large amount of chopping and brushing had to be done. The old guide proved invaluable, having come provided with a famous brush hook which swept away leaves or boughs intervening in the line of sight of the leveling instrument, much of the brush being beyond reach of the axe. The mud and moisture of the trail were fearful, exciting the growls of the party, and late in the afternoon we diverged into the bed of Gill brook and made better progress, stopping at 5:45 P.M. at a beautiful little cascade in the stream, the Artist's Falls, where the water pours in a clear sheet over a sloping rock into a crystal pool, to glide brightly away amid the great boulders below. Left a bench-mark (No. 62) on the rock—determining its altitude to be 1937.947 feet above tide-level—and marched back to quarters at head of Keene Valley.

*October 14th.* Sent forward the provisions for the party to the Au Sable lakes, ordering them to be carried in by the pack load to the future base of supplies. Remained with the leveling party until afternoon, when I went forward to the lower lake with one of the guides, and found our camp already prepared near a spring on the western side of the outlet. Rejoined the leveling party in the afternoon, being anxious to urge the work forward, as all indications pointed to an early and severe winter; which might soon prevent our reaching the high peak that had served as our station of reference in the past, making the precise determination of its altitude so important.

Our camp to-night is filled with the smoke of the fire, driven in by the wind gusts of cold wind from the stormy lake.

*October 15th.* The leveling party was out early at its work, being still on the muddy trail below the lower lake. Taking one guide, I made a reconnaissance down the river as far as a beaver meadow, where a low notch was known to extend to the trail, and it was thought might enable us to avoid ascending a high ridge which the trail climbs just before the lake is reached. Found the notch and explored it, reaching the trail where the leveling party was at work. Concluded that it was best to continue along the trail, as the notch was very densely wooded, and the banks of the river above difficult to work along. Urged forward the work and at 2 P.M. had surmounted the hill, descended, and made a bench-mark on a great rock at the east end of the sand beach of the lower Au Sable lake; whose dark waves reached away southward between the black mountain walls rising canyon-like, more than 2000 feet above its surface. After a hasty lunch, we resumed the work and, touching on the water level to connect it with the line, proceeded to run the levels along the shore of the lake with difficulty over the great masses of rock at the foot of the cliffs, measuring the distances and testing the line as heretofore, and reached at night a point about half way up the lower lake, and nearly 34 miles along the line from our datum on Lake Champlain, having occupied 432 stations with the instrument, and permanently located 65 important bench-marks. The guides having, by my orders, changed camp to the upper lake, we made a night march through the pass, and by canoe upon the Upper Au Sable reached the old trapping cabin where we had camped in 1873, again made cheerful to a weary company by a comfortable fire and a savory supper.

The 16th was stormy. Rain fell with little intermission throughout the whole day and we remained in camp. In the afternoon the guides took their hound and endeavored to drive a deer into the lake, but the dog did not return, and at dark, we drew in from the drizzling storm without, and at an early hour turned in to sleep.

*[Pages 156–70: Excerpts from Colvin's journal, including a description of a panther shot in the Adirondacks]*

## 1877

The work requiring attention during 1877 was as follows:

The exploration for future signal stations, by means of which to extend the survey into the western portion of the Adirondack region;

The measurement of subsidiary base-lines on the ice in order to locate certain lakes, and by that means connect the land-lines with the triangulation:

The construction of new and substantial "tower signals" in the place of the light, movable ones; so that, instead of moving the signal when a station was occupied, it would be only necessary to set up the instrument beneath it; the pillars of the "tower" being so placed as not to interfere with the lines of sight. By means of the ring bolts leaded into the drill holes in the rock of the peaks it was now possible to so secure these signals by iron as to render them practically rigid and immovable. It was the experience of 1876, which showed that this form of signal was the only one which would remain permanent during the continuance of the work.

The completion of the line of levels which formed the basis of all the altitudes throughout the region was urgently called for. An interval of about 70 miles remained uncompleted between the terminus of the first line from tide at Keene, and the nearest bench-mark on the line run near the Beaver river.

The extension of the triangulation and general topographical work, as far as the means admitted.

*February 13th* found me at the settlement on Moose river, westward of the Fulton chain. A weary journey through a cold and dark but starlight night had brought me to this point. The snow was deep, but the whole party was provided with snow shoes; and wrapped in heavy woolens and fur, we defied a temperature which the thermometer showed to be 13° below zero Fahrenheit, or—25° Centigrade. Under foot the hard dry snow crunched with a crisp metallic sound, and the bright stars in the dark black vault of heaven gave promise of the clear atmosphere so much desired.

*February 14th* brought us by afternoon to the foot of the stillwater, below the chain of lakes; but only halting for a brief repast, we placed our luggage and instruments upon the hand sleds and resumed our journey eastward. The bright sunlight gleamed on the wintry shores of Moose river, and the smooth ice of the stream formed a noble avenue, on either side of which the stately trees wore the inimitable ornaments of frost-work and wreaths of snow, which nature gave to grace this highway of the wilderness. The ice was without snow; for the water had penetrated to the surface and converted all to ice: and the march was easy. About sunset we reached the First lake, and crossing it, and the narrow point separating it from the Second, continued our strange journey; the distant shores of the lake growing dim, and the mountain ranges looming up dark and gloomy against the fading light; then the stars came out again, only to pale before a magnificent display of the zodiacal light, which showed itself with sharper outline as twilight deepened. The sharp "crinkling" of the runners of the large hand-sleds—drawn by the guides—the bright glow westward in the zodiac, and the glories of stars and milky-way overhead, made this a memorable night march.

At the head of the Third lake we put on our snow-shoes, and entering the woods, commenced the winter equivalent of a portage. All hands drew at the sleds; or held them back, or steadied them on steep inclines, or grasped them to prevent their overturning in deep soft snow beyond the snow-shoe path trampled to bear them. Thus we reached the Fourth lake and, discarding our snow-shoes, once more resumed our march. Late in the night we made our camp at the cabin of the chief guide; a comfortable shelter in the pine grove, on the southern shore of the lake.

*February 15th.* Provisions were packed and at early dawn we set out for Seventh lake mountain; the broad but elevated summit lying to the southward of the lake, from which it takes its name. Ascending the Fourth lake on the ice, we left the shore near the upper end of the lake, and the guides slinging their knapsacks we started in a southerly direction over a wild forest region deep with snow. The height which we designed to climb lay far beyond a series of lesser ridges, broken by steep ravines and hollows; and we marched slowly, the keen, cold atmosphere penetrating even through the heavy clothing. The day was still; a pale sunshine gleamed through the leafless forest, and the guides assured me that we should obtain a superb view from the summit.

Now we commenced to ascend, but the slope was gradual, if not easy, and the brush and fallen timber so deeply covered by the snow that the ascent by snow-shoe was far from difficult, though the snow was in some places seven feet in depth. Gradually we attained a greater elevation, and a cold, though slight wind breathed through the open forest; and about noon we stood upon the northern end of the crest of this broad mountain.

The leafless trees interposed but little between us and the view; and below we could see the white expanses of the frozen lakes, most of them old and familiar friends, but now strangely changed and interesting from this new station, from apparent changes of form the clearer revelation which this commanding height afforded. Other ice-bound waters also made their appearance, some of which seemed to be new to us, while elsewhere on every hand to the dim distant horizon extended the billowy mountains over the unbroken sea of wilderness. Chill and silent, though bathed in the cold glories of the winter's sun, it was a dreary, even a terrible landscape for any but woodmen to contemplate; yet to us it was as beautiful as a scene of summer verdure, enwrapped in hazy warmth. The deep blue of the winter sky above was equaled in pure beauty by the snowy mantling of the earth below, richly arabasqued with trees, whose purplish brown trunks and leafless limbs intermingled in strange tracery; deep in contrast with dark evergreens or gloomy rocks. Here and there, in the distance, looming up against the clouds, we saw the great peaks of the Adirondacks.

A careful study of the ground showed that this would be an extremely useful station, could it be occupied; but the great flat summit was densely covered with hardwood timber, and of so large an area as practically to prohibit its adoption as a station.

Passing to the southern portion of the crest we obtained a view over the wild region of the south branch of Moose river, and here the guides found the carcass of a deer killed some time since by a panther, whose deep trail was but partially filled by fresh snow. Descending the southern slope of Seventh lake mountain, we reached a stream flowing to the south branch, now ice-bound, and here with aid of axe where the ice was thinnest, cut an opening and obtained fresh water, most delightful after the melted snow or "smoke-water" that we had been compelled to drink. Crossing this stream, we again commenced to ascend, and about nightfall reached the crest of a high ridge, having had glimpses of the distant signal stations during the day, and having selected an important primary station, which would certainly afford the triangulation and entrance into this district. Here on this elevated ridge the guides proposed to encamp; but longing for spring water rather than melted snow, I urged, though weary, a further march. Proceeding, we soon commenced to descend; but the mountain became precipitous and difficult for snow-shoes. By jumping down ledges into the deep snow—a process in which we had obtained experience—we reached an open forest plateau on the mountain, where we were surprised to find a "deer-yard." Here the deep snow was tramped down by deer into a broad central level area, from which numerous irregular paths led in many directions through to forest or dense growth of saplings; the tender tops of which formed the browse or food of the animal. It was impossible to estimate the number of deer which had occupied this yard, as they had fled at our approach, plunging into the deep snow below. The ground of this central area resembled a sheep-yard in winter, the forms of the deer being plainly discernible in the beds of snow, in which they had slept, on every side.

Here we were startled by the sight of the fresh tracks of a panther or cougar, which evidently made his home in this abode of plenty; and shortly thereafter we found the body of a deer freshly killed, and shockingly torn and mutilated. The guides were now all excitement, and followed the cougar's trail eagerly. In less than 30 minutes, a shout announced that he had been encountered, and rushing forward to the southern front of the plateau I came upon the monstrous creature, coolly defiant, standing at the brow of a precipice on some dead timber, little more than 20 feet from where I stood. Quickly loading the rifle, I sent a bullet through his brain, and as the smoke lifted, saw him struggling in the fearful convulsions of death, till finally precipitated over the cliffs he disappeared from sight in the depths below.

By this time it was night, and after long search to the westward, we found a place where the cliffs could be descended, and made our way into the bottom of the valley, where we dug a space in the snow, and with the aid of a huge fire were comfortably encamped, notwithstanding the severity of the night, the temperature standing far below zero, Fahrenheit, beyond the radiance of the fire.

*February 16th.* Arose early and breakfasted on frozen venison *pemmican*, after which we climbed to the foot of the cliffs, and found the panther dead, the blood congealed upon the mouth and around the bullet hole in his head. The body had frozen during the night, so that it was difficult to remove the skin. The animal disemboweled, and the viscera removed, the guides fastened a wythe around its neck and drew it after us on the snow, having first enveloped it in a deer's skin to save the fur. Marched westward through a notch and valley toward the *great plains*, which I had hoped might prove available for the measurement of a secondary base-line. Reached the "little plains" about noon, and found them to be rather irregular barrens or burnt lands, than plains, and unfavorable for such measurements. It was evident, however, that from some point in these plains, with the aid of the new triangulation station proposed in this section, it would be possible to properly locate the line between the great townships 3 and 4 of the Moose river tract, which was essential to the map work. Turned north-eastward, and crossing a branch of the south branch of Moose river, commenced to ascend a brook that seemed to offer a favorable route to the range northward. At nightfall camped in the snow near the summit of a lofty pass, which we designed to explore on the morrow. Dug another space in the snow for the camp, and on a knoll just above it built an enormous fire, the intense heat of which thawed the snow banks round, despite the below zero temperature. An hour after dark we retired to our couch of deep, soft beds of balsam sprays, and fell asleep fairly roasted by the fire, the *direct radiant heat* of which alone rendered slumber safe in this bivouac; above, the stars twinkled in a frozen atmosphere.

*February 17th.* We continued to ascend the gorge, and before noon had reached the summit, an easy pass hemmed in only by small cliffs and ledges, more picturesque than dreadful; the dark rock with its bright trimming of green and gray lichens affording color and life to the snowy scenery. The descent from this gorge, which we named the panther pass—having drawn the dead *cougar* through it with us—led down an easy incline covered with hardwood timber, till at length a frozen brook began to appear. We made excellent progress, and about noon entered a broad tamarack swamp, passing through which we reached the shores of Limekiln lake, on the creek of the same name, another affluent of the South Branch. The deposit of lime occurs in the stream below the lake, and is of the primary or metamorphic series. The icy lake was bright with sunshine, but a fierce wind swept its surface and drove the snow in wild eddies, sometimes culminating in whirlwinds that moved before the gale in strange, spectral fashion up the lake. Now the clouds of drifting snow enveloped us, so that it was impossible to see; then the wind dying away, the sun shone upon us again as we marched slowly across the icy barren, its forest shores deep with snow and desolate.

No track or trail of fox or wolf was seen; no sign of living thing; no sound save the hiss of the snow crystals driven before the wind along the ice; even the sudden white fog or smoke rising from the distant forest made the scene still more wild; for it was not the smoke from hunter's camp, but dry snow caught by sudden blast and carried in icy spray before the gale. Penetrated by cold, we hastened our march, and reaching the northern shore climbed over the deep drifts into the forest. Here the guides built a fire and prepared dinner, the fire soon thawing out a cavern in the snow. Meanwhile, I completed the map of the lake and secured a sketch of the topography to the south and east. The summit of the high peak which we had climbed two days before, was visible in the east, and this lake could therefore be located by a subsidiary base-line. This was important, as my search had shown that the statutory boundary of the counties of Hamilton and Her-

*Tertiary Triangulation: Sub-Base-Line,*
*Measured on the Ice of Raquette Lake, Feb. 1877*

kimer would pass very near, if not directly across, this lake. Yet it could not be located until the line had been run out and the new signal station built on the summit of the broad, flat peak at the east. This was clearly impossible for the present, no mountain work being practicable.

Another problem was also solved. The open, smooth surface of the lake was undoubtedly to be attributed to the wind which swept it clear of the snow, driving it into the forests on either side, where, near the shores, great drifts accumulated. This again in its turn solved another mystery; the cause of the death of all the lower limbs of the cedars (arbor-vitæ) growing along the lake shores. This had been observed in summer, and was unaccountable. Now it was evident that the deep snow drifts buried these limbs, and in some unfavorable season, becoming compact and icy, had killed the enclosed evergreen foliage.

Resuming our journey, we crossed the ridges to the northward of Limekiln, and reaching the shores of the Fourth lake, gladly unstrapped our snow-shoes, and made our way to camp upon the ice.

*February 18th* was spent in preparations for the expedition to the

Raquette, where I proposed to measure several of the subsidiary base-lines upon the ice, connecting the lakes with the mountain signals. Sleds were repaired, snow-shoes mended, and provisions packed. In the afternoon, I placed the transit over the copper bolt at the station on Pine Point and took a series of observations, to the Mount St. Louis signal, and magnetic readings, purposing to obtain the direction of the true meridian the same evening by astronomical observation. It was after 9 P.M. when the western elongation of the star Polaris was observed, and as the temperature was almost zero Fahrenheit, the handling of the instrument was difficult.

The azimuth of the signal on Mount St. Louis from the true meridian was obtained with nicety, and will serve all the purposes of a meridian line at this station. It will hereafter be only necessary to set up a compass over the Pine Point copper bolt, and observe to the signal on Mount St. Louis, when the difference to the true azimuth will be the magnetic variation. I found the mean variation (declination) on this day to be 8° 32' 54" west from the true meridian. (Lat. 43° 44.'6; W. Long. 74° 53.'5.) Left the panther at this camp frozen solid.

*February 19th,* the baggage and instruments were packed upon the light Indian sleds, and we started eastward on the ice; the guides, drawing their sleds and carrying their snow-shoes, to use on the marches in the forest between the lakes. At this inlet of the Fourth we resumed our snow-shoes, and drawing the sleds ashore, soon found the difference between the easy drawing on the ice and the deep snow. By tramping with our snow-shoes in advance we managed to make a practicable sled-path, and passing the smaller lakes and por-tages, reached the broad ice sheet of the Seventh lake before noon. Here the snow-shoes were again discarded for the fur-lined moc-casins, and the Indian file for the easy open march on the ice; the lake stretching like a broad plain, white and pleasant in the sunshine, to the eastward where the stately pine forest, richly green, descended to the shore.

Crossing the inlet sand beach, deep with snow, we reached the river—the inlet—and continued our march. The ice of the river was not smooth and bare like that of wind-swept lakes, but covered with snow, yet not deep enough to render snow-shoes necessary, and of-fered us an easy foot path through the forest. Here we came upon the fresh trail of a huge wolf. The foot-prints were as large as those of a panther. Crossing the forest, we reached at noon the Eighth lake, where we sought our camp of the preceding fall and lunched within its shelter.

Again advancing, the Eighth lake, also, spread its open plain of ice before us; but at the eastern end we once more strapped on our snow-shoes and turning our backs upon the waters of the Moose river, soon crossed the divide and struck the frozen rills, whose ridden waters journeyed on beneath, to join the Raquette and the far St. Lawrence. A weary journey down the shores of the Brown-tract inlet followed. Through alder swamps and laurel that held up the light deep snow to let the snow-shoes sink and dive into its depth, on treacherous ice of spring holes in the marshes—through the dense shade of snow-hung tamaracks, we made our way; and at evening saw before us the broad ice sheet of Lake Raquette, like a sea of frosted crystal, broken here and there by islands; purple tinted in the twilight, all still, lonely, remote, and quiet as the blue sky overhead.

A long march over the ice brought us to the camp of our old trapper guide on Osprey island. It was silent and deserted, and had, evidently, not been visited for a long time. The other camps were also found to be vacant. Crossing the island, a faint shout in the distance attracted our attention. Hoping that this might prove to be our trapper guide, we marched that way, and soon perceived some hunters slowly making their way along the ice near the shore, drawing heavily-laden sleds. Proceeded with them to their camp on the South bay, and met the chief of the party; hunter and explorer in many lands, who courteously and hospitably detained us as his guests for the night. Soon huge trout, taken that day, through holes cut in the thick ice of the lake, were cooking on the fire; the skill of voyager and traveler producing a sumptuous repast; and, after an evening of interesting conversation, we enjoyed the repose which a march of 20 miles on snow-shoes and frozen lakes made grateful.

*February 20th.* The morning broke clear and bright; and I hastened to avail myself of the opportunity for measurement. Bidding adieu to our new friends, we marched on the ice to the westward part of the South bay, and commenced the search for suitable stations, for the termini of a subsidiary base-line. We now longed for swifter conveyance than our own weary limbs afforded; the great distances across the ice, the points which jutted out here and there, and the deep snow drifts at the shores made the search severe physical labor.

Points were at last found, from which a signal station was visible, and the measurement of the base-line was at once commenced. The steel ribbon was extended along the smooth level surface of the ice, and brought taut, by a uniform pull with spring balance attached to one handle. The alignment was made by transit, and the measurement was executed carefully and skillfully. When completed, this line was found to be more than 6,600 feet in length; which, while admirable for the lake survey work, was too short a base to serve for the connection of the lake with the distant signal station.

The measurement and verification of this line completed, in the afternoon I put to practical test a method of leveling by water surface, which I had long contemplated. Bench-marks were selected at the North bay, the East inlet, and South bay of Raquette, and permanently located; and at a concerted time the level of the water from holes cut in the ice was taken at the stations six miles distant, and referred to the stone datums, which were carefully marked. Thus in an instant, the bench-marks at opposite ends of the lake had their relative value determined: which obtained by the ordinary process of leveling along a shore line of 40 miles would have been a slow and expensive process. Now the water, protected by the ice from the influence of the wind, served as the instrument, an immense water level, having its readings taken at points many miles distant.

At evening, marching northward, we encamped on one of the islands, in what proved a most inhospitable place; the wild winter gale sweeping over the rocky isle with such violence as to almost extinguish our fire. A fearful night which none of the party will be apt to forget. The men fought the cold by stamping, and chopping by turns, snatching some sleep occasionally when the fire could be maintained. Many were the longings expressed for a "comfortable camp in the snow."

*February 21st.* Returned to the base-line and commenced the angular measurements, taking careful repetitions. About mid-day, our old trapper made his appearance, coming over the ice from the north, drawing his sled and accompanied by his hounds. At nightfall he conducted us to his winter camp on the island, where, in a cabin sunken in the ground, his ice-house in summer, we made a comfortable camp.

On the following morning, refreshed and rested, we made an early start, and marching northward over the ice, reached the outlet of the lake. Here we secured our show-shoes, and crossed the ridge to Great

Forked lake; which I proposed also to connect with the triangulation by a subsidiary base. Measured the base-line on the ice of the long, singular southern bay or "fork" of the lake, and re-measured it with equal care, as a verification of the work. This done, the transit which had been used in aligning the base-line stakes, was employed to repeat the angles from both ends of the line to the distant mountain signal, where the star-like stan-helio glittered against a bright winter sky. Altitudes of the sun were also taken for time and azimuth; and late in the afternoon we started to return to our camp on Raquette. Noticed near the shores of Forked lake the fresh foot-prints of a wolf, supposed to be the same whose trail was seen near the Eighth lake, as the tracks are of the same huge dimensions. He is evidently watching and waiting for somebody or something, but shows his wisdom in keeping out of rifle range. Near the shore of Forked lake, I collected a peculiar kind of tree lichen (*usnea*), which when tasted was found to be nearly as pungent as pepper. As we marched back over the broad icy plain of Raquette, I was enabled to select a favorable location for the measurement of the most important of these subsidiary base-lines, which would not only serve to connect this large lake with the triangulation, but serve, also, as a base of verification and extension in the secondary and tertiary work. The line proposed to be measured would extend from the southern end of the lake, northward nearly half its length, as far as the points or headlands of the lake permitted; and from both extremities I hoped to be able to observe to the signal on Mount Emmons, and to other peaks. Reached our semi-subterranean camp at dark, and retired early, hoping for successful work upon the morrow.

*February 23d* opened propitiously. The intense cold had moderated, and when the glorious sun arose glittering in bright yellow light over snow and ice and forest, lighting even the dark mountain ranges with cheerful brilliancy, we were already merrily marching southward on the ice sheet, joyous in anticipation of a favorable day.

Reaching the South bay, I made search for a station for the southern extremity of this base-line. Attempting to pass from the open ice up the shore to a small elevation, only a few hundred feet distant, we soon had cause to regret having left our snow-shoes at camp; and floundering through snow up to our shoulders, soon found a *journey* of 200 feet in this deep snow a fierce, exhaustive struggle of an hour, in which hidden brush, logs, and cavities beneath served as additional obstacles in the way of advance. It was a revelation of the value of the snow-shoe, sufficiently practical to be long remembered. We could now understand the story which a guide narrated of a hunter, long years since, entrapped at the Eighth lake by a sudden fall of deep snow, late in autumn, starving to death there for lack of snow-shoes on which to make his escape.

After much search, a favorable station was found near the shore; the snow dug away, the instrument set up and adjusted, and the northern terminus being also selected on a great rock near Indian Point, the careful alignment and staking out of the base was proceeded with. Tall pickets were cut and set regularly at brief intervals in a right line toward the northern station, and while one of the guides chopped away timber on a projecting point to the eastward, which obscured the view of Mount Emmons, two of the assistants proceeded to make the first careful measurement of this base-line. Nicely aligned and brought taut along the smooth surface of the ice, by uniform pull upon the spring-balance handle, the work proceeded, and at nightfall the first measurement had been completed, together with the angular observations at the southern terminus of the base; which by this measurement was found to be 14,573 feet in length, uncorrected for temperature, and the elevation above tide. At dark we marched back to our island camp.

*February 24th* we were to discover that of the scanty provisions barely enough remained for a single meal! We were a long day's march from our nearest base of supplies, and had still the verification re-measurement and angular observations at the north end of the Raquette base to complete. One counseled a retreat to the Fourth lake camp before hunger should weaken us. As I glanced at the quiet face and white hair of the old trapper-guide, it occurred to me that this experienced hermit of the forest might offer some expedient by which we might at least delay our retreat until the work was done. Pointing to his tall ice chisel I asked him whether trout could not be taken through the ice, and obtained an answering intimation that such things had been done. Bestirring himself he gathered the long-disused implements of fishery, and throwing on his sled his lines, axes, and the ice chisel, whose handle resembled a beam, he disappeared upon his quest, while we, with empty haversacks, so far as food of any kind was concerned, started for the north end of the base-line.

Before commencing the re-measurement and verification of the base, the instrument was placed and the angular measurements made between the signal on Emmons and the south base. This completed, I proceeded personally to supervise and aid in the measurement of the base-line, observing also the temperature, which varied from + 30° to + 32° Fahrenheit. So busy were we with this work, that we scarcely had time to think of hunger or realize the lack of food, but at night-fall, as we moved wearily across the ice, began to feel both curiosity and anxiety to know how our old trapper had succeeded in his quest for game, for on his success depended the feeding of a hungry party.

As we drew near the island we saw faintly in the twilight far away upon the ice, a figure slowly coming, and we strained our eyes to see, at length, our faithful fisherman indeed, his sled deeply laden with huge frozen lake trout, and his face lit with quiet good humor at the *vivas* which his success excited. The quality of the fish we soon pro-ceeded to put to the test. Having no oil or fat in which to fry them, we were forced to boil them, sans salt or pepper, and made a most hearty meal upon *clear fish and nothing else*, save frequent libations of cold water. This was, indeed, surveying under difficulties, but our work was now completed, and I had been fully justified in remaining to execute it by the success of our fisherman in procuring food for the party.

A meal of boiled fish, without salt, or pepper, or fat, or bread, or potatoes, or any accompaniment, however, is a very singular dish for very hungry men.

*February 25th.* After fortifying ourselves for the journey by a break-fast of boiled fish again, we set out upon our return. Though our moccasins were worn by walking on the ice, and our feet blistered by marching, we moved rapidly, now ascending the Brown-tract inlet, crossed again to the Moose river waters, and after a weary march from lake to lake down the Fulton chain, striking the head of the Seventh lake at noon, reached our camp on the Fourth at 3 P.M.; a rapid march of 19 miles, having crossed the forest between the lakes on snow-shoes.

*February 28th.* A reconnaissance was made of several hills and ele-vated ranges near Boonville, in the hope of being able to select the stations by which the triangulation could be brought out of the wil-derness and a base of verification measured. The result of the search was unsatisfactory, for the eastern horizon was filled with the endless mass of subordinate forest-covered mountains, shapeless, nameless, unrecognizable, disheartening to look upon. From one point, however, I imagined that the telescope showed the signal on Mount St. Louis, and a station was here located for future reference in the work.

On the following day I returned to Albany, bringing with me the frozen body of the panther, which was placed in the rotunda of the State house for inspection by the legislature then in session.

Official duties prevented me again entering the field until May, when a special investigation in barometric hypsometry was made, the results of which are hereafter discussed. The question proposed for examination was, what were the actual fluctuations of the atmosphere at near stations of the same altitude? Taking with me six assistants, I proceeded (May 12th) to make a practical test, which I felt sure would show how far the barometer could be relied upon in affording differences of elevation between stations quite near together.

In the first place a line of levels was carefully run and datums established at distances of 1,000 feet apart, where stakes were driven so as to be precisely at the same height. At each one of these stakes an assistant with barometer, hygrometers, etc., was then placed, and regular observations were taken synchronously every 10 minutes.

At the close of this work, I commenced the reduction and comparison of the sets of observations, obtaining the most interesting results. *It was evident that even at distances of only 1,000 feet the times of maxima and minima were not contemporaneous, but that numerous irregular fluctuations were liable to occur even between stations so nearly associated.*

This demonstration of an important element in barometric height measurements is hereafter discussed. It renders apparent the difficulties surrounding the semi-meteorological work of the survey.

The appropriation this year for the survey was the smallest which had so far been made, and rendered it impossible to undertake work upon a large scale, yet at the same time afforded me a desirable interval for reconnaissance, and the execution of special measurements, and study of the land lines and general features of the country which had become absolutely necessary.

During July I gave my personal attention to the building of substantial signals at a large number of stations, and organized, instructed, and disciplined several parties of signal men in the construction of the large "tower signals"; which, though expensive, I had found to be really economical, by their permanency.

While this work was in progress, I determined again to attempt the repetition of the angles at Marcy between Mount Emmons and Snowy Mountain which, despite two expeditions, we had failed in obtaining in 1876. I hoped also to be able to obtain observations to the signal on Mount St. Louis, which would close that triangle with increased precision.

*August 2d* found me at Beede's at the head of Keene valley, and guides and supplies being ready, we proceeded the next day to the Upper Au Sable lake, reaching the old camp in the Lake Tear pass on the afternoon of the day following. The old camp was quite broken down by snow and storm; but the skillful guides quickly constructed a new and picturesque cabin or open camp, logged on three sides and covered with thick spruce bark; and at nightfall we were comfortably housed.

The next day was Sunday, and it was our good fortune to have religious services conducted by a reverend friend who accompanied us. The guides ranged logs for seats, and under a bright sky in this remote but sheltered forest glade, deep-carpeted with rich green mosses and rare ferns, arose the mingled voices, offering thanks for all the blessings that we had received.

The calm day of rest passed, night came and went again, and with morning, preparations were made for the cutting of timber for the permanent signal on Mount Marcy. These had to be procured a thousand feet below the summit, the dwarf timber on the upper ridges being worthless for this purpose. While the guides were busy with their axes, I climbed the mountain and set up the instrument. The day was reasonably clear, and some observations were obtained, but I looked in vain for the two signals in the far southwest. Why dwell, however, upon the labors of each day?

Nearly a week passed of constant, anxious watching, and yet those distant signals failed to appear. Bright and sparkling gleamed the signals on Bald Peak and Hurricane, and elsewhere; but where I watched, longing for the least sign or glimmer, no sign appeared; and the mountain ridges of Moose river, even, were mingled, and lost, in the dim obscurity of the horizon.

The length of the triangle sides—the further station being 60 miles distant—was not excessive, but the angle of depression from this elevated peak threw the lower summit St. Louis against the mass of similar ridges so as to render the signal undistinguishable. It was clearly necessary to arrange a new system of triangles by which to reach this section by shorter sights.

*[Pages 187–98: Excerpts from Colvin's journal, including the search for the true division line between the Brown tract and the Totten and Crossfield purchase]*

## 1878

The necessary work of preliminary exploration and reconnaissance had now been nearly completed. The important points to be located, and the means by which most of them could be reached whether by triangulation or measured lines, had been ascertained.

The work which now remained to be done was not the less laborious or less important because less exciting or less adventurous.

The slow, minute, piece by piece measurements, were now to be extended out into the settlements throughout the whole region under survey, until the distant and disconnected land-lines of the past— irregularly scattered, no one knew just how upon the surface of the earth—were tied together, joined and connected for all time, by the precise work of the triangulation which I personally executed.

The details of the reorganization of the work, the system adopted, and the general results, have been already given (pages 38 to 61); it is only necessary to briefly describe some of the section of country traversed this season, the special difficulties encountered in the work, with a brief mention of notable phenomena observed which seen worthy of preservation.

In May the work of organization was commenced, and was continued through the month of June; a vast amount of journeying to and fro, of discussion, and correspondence being completed.

Using every effort to place the parties in the field, by the 1st of June, one permanent meteorological station had been established, and the signal parties sent out to traverse the eastern portion of the region, preparing for the triangulation. By July 6th, the work for the subordinate parties had been cut out, and an assistant was dispatched from Albany with orders to proceed to Lyon Mountain, Clinton county, and commence the clearing for a station on that summit.

The leveling division, and the assistants connected with the middle and south-western divisions were directed to meet me on the 8th of

July at Lowville, Lewis county, where other assistants and surveyors were also directed to rendezvous. Estimating that I should be able to place these parties immediately in the field (and by proceeding with them to the interior, see them fairly started with their work so as to insure their working accurately), I directed the assistants and employees connected with the north-eastern division of the local work to rendezvous at Plattsburgh on Monday, July 29th, myself designing to be at Ticonderoga on the 27th, to organize the south-western division, and proceed thence to Plattsburgh on the 29th to meet the party to be assembled there. These divisions organized and fully under way, I proposed to take up the search for a new base-line, designing to occupy some stations of the U.S. Coast Survey near Plattsburgh, so as to use one of their tested trianglesides from which to develop my new triangulation over the north-eastern section. This accomplished, I should proceed to execute personally the triangulation, with all the necessary geodetic work, directing also, from my field head-quarters, the operations of the subordinate surveys of rivers, roads, land-lines, and other measurements, by which the old survey-lines and new data would alike be connected with the triangulation, rendering all of permanent value. The leveling, meteorological observations and signal work was to be done by the assistants under my immediate direction, while the subordinate road and river work would be placed in charge of the contract surveyors with full instructions for its execution.

*July 8th.* I left Albany for Lowville, Lewis county, which was the rendezvous appointed for the assemblage of two parties; one charged with connecting the ancient lines in the Beaver river region with our measurements and monuments, and the other with the extension of the regular work of leveling. On the 9th, we reached Beaver lake, where the whole party was assembled, the supplies having been brought by team. Here the leveling party was detached with orders to continue the line of levels from Beaver lake westward to the canal datum at Lowville, making permanent bench-marks along the line.

On the following day, despite a severe storm we reached South Branch, at a point about 35 miles from Lowville. A depot of supplies was made, and on the 11th we took the field to commence the search for the *true* division line between the Brown tract and the Totten and Crossfield purchase.

The aged forest surveyor, who more than 20 years before had seen the marks and had followed a portion of the line, was now to verify its accurate restoration, and commenced his search under my direction, while the baggage of the party was conveyed down the Beaver to a trail leading northward to the Red Horse chain, near which the line was supposed to be located. Landing at the carry, the guides and packmen proceeded to transport the supplies over the portage, and passing Burnt lake and Deep pond, we reached Salmon lake the same afternoon.

Here we were rejoined by the aged surveyor who, greatly fatigued, alarmed us by the statement that, notwithstanding the most anxious search, he had been unable to find the line. Fire had years since swept over the section where he had hoped to discover it, and the old marked trees were gone—a dense second growth of maples and aspen now covering the rocky soil, having grown since the fire.

Learning from the guides of localities where the old timber had not been burnt, parties were sent out, but failed to find any sign of the line.

The morning of the 12th was pleasant, and after the old surveyor had with great earnestness—though fruitlessly—searched the old timber of a tamarack swamp for the line, I resolved to adopt another course and see whether matters could be expedited. Examining the old field-notes, it was found that the line was recorded to have crossed a lake—marked as "Hawk lake"—somewhere, as I judged, over the mountains to the westward. As the old forest fires had not, probably, penetrated there, it seemed to me that on or near the shores of that lake the old trees might be found, still carrying the marks of the first compass surveyors.

Computing the bearing of the lake, I assembled the party, and cutting down the baggage to a minimum, each man carrying a knapsack, we set out in search of the lake. We immediately commenced to ascend a mountain, where in the dense thickets the summer heat was intense, and reaching the crest, looked out through the timber on the bright surface of Salmon lake. Then turning, we descended, and through wind-slashes, dense timber, and open forests, ascending and descending, we reached at noon, the summit of a mountain, where from a fallen tree lodged so as to serve as a projecting platform, I was able to look out over an extremely wild country. In the sea of woods before us sparkled the waters of two lakes, with which neither myself nor any of the guides were acquainted. This was not surprising, as this was to a great extent unexplored territory; and we might reasonably expect many more discoveries of such waters.

*Exploration: Middle Western Division,*
*Hawk Lake from the South Shore, July 1878*

Descending this mountain, a deep valley was seen to the left, and leading the party in that direction, I soon had the pleasure of standing upon the shores of a charming lake, whose bright green bordering of forest was reflected in the placid surface. The stately evergreens descended to the shores and gave grace and dignity to the scenery; while rocky points projecting into the clear water, and marshy bays, rich with lilies and soft herbage, offered luxuriant feeding ground for deer, whose delicate foot-prints were seen along the shores. Above rose undulating hills, the dark slopes of which found partial reflection in the forest pool.

Satisfied from the form and the peculiar projecting points, that this was the Hawk lake of the ancient survey, we unslung knapsacks near a spring on the southern slope and partook of lunch. This finished we commenced the search for the ancient line, which, to our delight, was at length discovered on the northern shore, on dead and crumbling timber.

Descending the outlet for nearly two miles, I failed to find any other lake, but satisfied myself to which river system the lake belonged. Later still I proceeded alone to the upper end of the lake, and

*Exploration: Camp of the Mid-Western Division on Hawk Lake*

was not surprised to find a line of marked trees extending eastward, for I had begun to suspect that this was the Emerald lake, noted in 1873.

Returning to the spring, the guides proceeded to construct the camp, which would serve also as a depot for the shelter of supplies, as we advanced, upon the line. Bark was peeled from the stately trunks of the spruce trees, in broad sheets, almost as flexible as leather, and the frame-work of poles was quickly covered with a roof impervious to rain. The rich carpeting of moss, the graceful foliage of the evergreen forest, the quiet beauty of the lake beyond, with its silent margin of forest, in contrast with the bright gleam of the fire upon the aids resting after the labors of the day, formed a characteristic camp scene, and filled a blank leaf of my sketch-book. Soon the fragrant couch was spread, composed of soft balsam sprays, and we rested from our labors.

*July 13th.* I resolved to march the party to the northern terminus of the line to find, verify, and monument the important corner whence the line originated, and see the party regularly started working southward toward their base of supplies. Found the region obstructed with much fallen timber. This and the retracing of the line made progress slow and difficult; but at four o'clock in the afternoon we struck one of the smaller affluents of the Oswegatchie, a still stream flowing northward through a vast forest swamp. Here we were surprised and interested by finding the remains of a very ancient city of the beavers. This forest swamp had evidently once been the pond of a settlement of these intelligent creatures, but at an extremely remote period. The beaver houses were most singularly preserved as to form—though themselves decayed and gone—by the tree roots. In one spot, I noticed a tree apparently growing upon the top of a well-formed beaver house. An inspection showed that it was simply a dome of the tree's roots, which preserved as a *cast* the figure of the ancient habitation of the animal. Anxious to get on, we crossed the stream and made our way along its northern bank, traversing a deep swamp where dead trees with rocks and alder brush together made the march toilsome. Climbing and descending, passing deep ravines, night at length overtook us on the side of a marshy hollow, where the guides hoped by digging to find water. Bivouacked under the shade of a large tree, whose curved trunk seemed bent with the weight of foliage. A fire soon lit the dark glade and water was at length obtained, cupful by cupful, from a small cavity in the moss.

In the night before retiring, the camp was alarmed. A strange distant cry came from far away on our trail, and as there were wolves in this section, and but one rifle with the party, some of the novices looked serious. The cry was again and again repeated, each time more plainly, and at length we distinguished the voice of a man, and answering his shouts, one of the guides from Hawk lake bringing up supplies made his appearance, having had a severe experience amid the fallen forest in the dark.

Some idea of the roughness of the ground may be had from the fact that in going less than two miles of direct distance my pedometer recorded eight and three-fourth miles. For men carrying heavy packs of provisions, this fallen timber makes each day's march an exhausting climb. At Hawk lake, I had foreseen this difficulty, and had ordered the aids and guides to throw aside all baggage. Blankets, ponchos, coats, and every thing almost, except the instruments, axes, and provisions were left, and yet it was a weary company.

*July 14th* we continued our march northward toward the great corner which we had hoped to reach at night, but made slow progress over the fearful wind-slashes. The land is broken into ridges with few swamps. At 2:20 P.M., we reached Wolf lake, a strange body of water, of which the broad branch of the Oswegatchie that we here struck was claimed by our old surveyor to be the outlet. Searching up along the wide, marshy shores of the river for a place to cross, I found a rapid where we enabled to pass, and leaving the party to go forward on the line, with orders to build a camp near the west end of Wolf lake, I proceeded with one assistant along a sand ridge on the southern shore to make a reconnaissance. The further I proceeded along this ridge, the more I became interested in the odd form of the lake, which seemed to be made of two great bays, almost separated by the ridge on which I advanced. This ridge, by the way, was one of those singular, long narrow dunes, which had so interested and perplexed me in the Bog-river section. It was most singular. Open and picturesque with superb white pine trees here and there upon it, with numerous deer paths deeply stamped, leading through its carpeting of moss and whortleberry bushes, the beautiful lake on the one side and the shallow winding river on the other, made it far more entrancing than the choicest ramble of guarded park. Now I began to surmise that there were *two lakes*, and hurrying forward found that it was true,—the waters barely separated by the narrow ridge,—and that the river passed was not the outlet of Wolf lake at all, but came from a broad nameless sheet with low sandy shores.

This was an interesting discovery; and passing around the head of Wolf lake, I undertook to return along its opposite shore to where in the distance the faint smoke rising from the forest told that my party was encamped. This was soon found to be vastly different from the easy deer paths on the sand ridge; and wading along the shore, rather than traverse the fearful tangles of the fallen timber, a slow advance was made. In one of the wadings I suddenly entered a cold, heavy quicksand, and descended so suddenly that I had barely time to grasp some laurel bushes (*Kalmia angusti folia*) at the shore, and with difficulty escaped entire submergence and drowning. Got ashore at length and made my way to camp, rather late in the afternoon. Secured map sketches and some barometrical observations, and in attempting to get a station to observe the sun for time, was caught in a severe thunder storm.

*July 15th*, awakened by the report of a rifle apparently just beyond the camp, and presently two of the guides came lugging a fine deer which had been shot near by. The fog of morning was streaming through the trees, and breakfasting we hung up the venison beyond the reach of wolves, taking only a small portion with us, and marched northward again.

After crossing some ridges and one stream, we entered an open hard-wood forest; and here I observed in a moist place a deposit of marly clay, a rare thing in this region. What was most interesting, however, was the fact that this was a natural deer-lick, many places showing where the deer had licked the clay, possibly obtaining a trifle of potash, alumina, and iron, derived from sulphates from decomposing pyrites. This was the first and only natural deer-lick which I have ever observed in the Adirondacks. It was not remarkable in its appearance, and other than a hunter's eye would have noticed merely the shapely foot-prints in the clay, and not the inconspicuous smooth spots licked by the tongues of the deer.

Proceeding northward we reached at length a broad branch of the little Oswegatchie, flowing through a large swamp; the stream abounded with speckled trout, and a handsome string was easily caught with coarse tackle from where we forded it. Passing this swamp, we ascended and descended along ridges, and occasional moist swales, still following the old line, sometimes only discernible under the moss on mouldering trunks of fallen trees. At 5 P.M. the men called a halt, being fairly unable to travel farther that day, and could not be persuaded to go on, though I now estimated that we were within a mile of the sought-for corner. Built a camp, and at dark retired to profound slumber.

*July 16th,* making an early start and leaving our packs at the camp—for I judged that we should reach the corner to-day—we traced the line northward still, but with great difficulty; for many of the marks were not only a century old, but the trees themselves prostrate and decayed. We now came out on the banks of a large branch of the Oswegatchie; a rapid stream flowing amid huge boulders of a reddish quartzite. Here the line was obscure, and we crept through a dense windslash. Now it crossed a brook, then ascended a hill, and I hurried in advance, as the corner must be near. Entering a level, partly swampy, the line ceased, and as I looked again, some singular hollows, sunken places and contortions in the bark of the surrounding trees caught my eyes. They were evidently ancient witness trees, blazed on one side only, each blaze pointing toward the centre of the glade in which I stood. A glance showed a crumbling stake, having three small stones, moss-covered, at its foot. It was the long sought-for corner, the great pivotal point on which all the land titles of nearly 5,000,000 of acres depended. In a few moments, the rest of the party had joined me, and the old surveyor recognized the stake by which he had replaced the mouldering fragments of the original corner post!

The shouts of the party showed their joy at reaching the end of an exhausting journey; and during a brief rest and lunch, their several duties were explained, together with the method to be pursued in restoring the ancient line, so as to make it permanent, and render it available as a topographical base-line with which to connect the lake and mountain work in that section.

A ponderous boulder of brownish quartzite, of regular form, was selected as the monument with which to mark the corner, and was rolled with great labor to the station by the sturdy guides. Before it was set in place, four stout stakes were driven opposite each other, having the crumbling corner stake at the middle so that when a fine linen line was drawn from stake to stake—adjusted around copper tacks driven in the tops of the stakes—the intersection of the lines covered the centre of the great corner. Then the lines was removed, and in the open space between the stakes the cavity was dug in which the monument, nearly a quarter of a ton of massive everlasting flint was imbedded solidly; and the fine lines of linen once more brought taut from stake to stake, again showed by their intersection where the drill hole should be sunk which would mark the centre of the station. Alas, drills blunted and splintered upon that monument of flint, but by slow and persevering drilling, the centre was at length made. Then the nickel-plated copper bolt, being heated red hot, was run in with melted lead, and the great southern corner of the largest county of the State, St. Lawrence, (and of all the great land patents of the north,) was for the first time marked with a stone monument. With eager hands, the men brought other stone and heaped them, till a pyramid was made over the monument, around a central post of wood standing above it, and the instrument being placed, the re-measurement and restoration of the line commenced. The light ribbon of steel was aligned and brought taut by spring balance, and the sharp-shod ranging pole with its level showed the first "chain's length" of the new measurement. Meanwhile, the aids dug stone to add to the pyramid, and carved in the huge granite boulders near at hand, deep sunken arrows pointing at the monument; whose directions intersecting would show the centre, even should the monument be gone.

At evening, wearied enough, we marched back to our last camp, where a frugal, scanty supper of hard tack and salt pork, with a last remnant of the venison brought from Wolf lake, appeased our hunger.

*July 17th.* I watched and guided the party during this, the first day of their continuous measurements; directed the axeman who chopped the passage through the forest and slashes of wind-felled timber; instructed the chain-men; saw that the stations for future reference in our lake explorations were set at regular intervals of 500 feet, and that every rill or stream or marsh, hill or hollow encountered was located by the topographer; in every way instructing and explaining how the work should be done, in order to secure the required results.

The appointments made for the organization of the rest of the survey work now claimed my attention; while the failure of provisions, occasioned by the unexpected length of time which it had taken us to march here from Beaver river, rendered it important to hurry forward supplies; for there was but one meal remaining for the party. Giving them my final instructions, I took with me one guide, and without a particle of provisions, we set out on the return along the line, determined to make in a two day's march the distance, which it had taken the party six days to come in over. We relied for food upon meeting on our way the packmen coming in along the line with provisions, either that day or the next.

With light and rapid steps we traced the line back again, more by the bent or broken twigs, foot-prints, and occasional newly marked trees than by the old line, and reaching Wolf at noon, halted for five minutes to rest and drink from the mossy rill near the camp. It was near 4 P.M. when, having passed our bivouac of the 13th, we saw the packmen with provisions approaching upon the other side of a ravine, at the bottom of which we joined them, and, obtaining some hard tack and pork from their packs, made our lunch. Directing them to march northward as far as they could that night, to join the party on the following day if possible, I started on again, and at dark reached Hawk lake and our camp of July 12th. There we rested for the night.

*July 19th.* We reached Beaver river and Stillwater, by way of Salmon lake, at evening. On the 20th, I overtook the leveling party, now more than two-thirds of the way from Beaver lake to the Black river. Inspecting their work and furnishing the assistant with additional funds, I hurried to Lowville, and the same night reached Albany by rail.

Office work required my attention until the 26th, when I proceeded to Ticonderoga to select signal stations southward from that point, and to have a conference with the surveyor whom I had instructed with the measurements for the connection of the road and land-lines in that section with my triangulation. On the 27th, I returned to Albany again and on the 29th proceeded to Plattsburgh on Lake Champlain, where, on the same evening, the river and signal parties had assembled.

The arrangements for the field work of the triangulation (which I proposed, as heretofore, to execute personally) were, in all the details, carefully systematized, so as to secure constant and regular work, without interfering with my general control and management of the detached parties engaged on local work.

The signal corps was thoroughly organized; the signal men being carefully trained and competent; all of them being, also, thorough woodsmen, accustomed to forest life, rapid marches, and vigorous work. The work was divided into the preparation of stations, and the building of signals; the different classes of work being done by different parties. Where the stations were to be on summits requiring much clearing and preliminary work, advance parties of pioneers were sent to prepare the stations. These pioneers were followed by the regular signal party when the station was reported ready for occupation.

As my head-quarters during the middle portion of the season would be far back from the settlements, in inaccessible portions of the wilderness, the advance or pioneer parties were directed to prepare log houses at the more important of these stations, for the shelter of my personal party, and instruments. These log camps had to be made in a substantial manner when located near mountain crests, in order to secure them from the terrific gales sweeping those summits, which, even in the more sheltered valleys below, frequently prostrated the forest in winrows before their irresistible violence.

The pioneers had also to clear trails and prepare a passage through the tangled forest for the heavily burdened porters and packmen carrying the heavy instruments upward to the stations; these trails being subsequently kept clear by the guides engaged in bringing in provisions for the camp.

On the evening of the 29th, I received the report of the signal party
of work and expenditures, and on July 30th, having settled their
accounts to date, I placed Assistant Manning in charge of the party
and directed him to proceed to Lyon Mountain to relieve the assistant whose term had expired, and to supervise the construction of the
log-house head-quarters upon that summit. He was furnished with
mountain barometer, thermometers, hygrometers, etc., for taking the
necessary meteorological observations, and set out immediately with
his party by special conveyance up the Saranac valley to the foot of
the mountain.

The same morning, the party organized for the survey of the Saranac river assembled, and the work commenced.

Beginning at the north monument of the U.S. Coast Survey base-
line, at Plattsburgh, the transit line was started which was to extend
to the head of the river, for the purpose of accurately locating this
important stream in connection with the lines of the great land patents in the counties of Clinton, Franklin, and Essex. Carefully explaining the manner in which the work was to be executed; the
necessity of rigid accuracy in both transit and chain work in order to
secure the desired results, together with the particular method of repetition of angles to be followed, and the necessity of marking every
station with stone so as to insure a permanent line for future use in
the plane table and other work, I remained with the party all day, and
at evening felt sure that my instructions were understood by every
member of the party.

Work on this division being well under way, the tents, transportation supplies, and funds provided them, I returned on the following
day to Albany.

Here important dispatches were received from the other divisions.
I learned of the labors—almost starvation—of the party engaged in
retracing the ancient line north of Beaver river. Of the lakes discovered and measured to, from their chained line; of the discovery of
other ancient lines almost extinct, and of the placing of heavy granite
monuments in the place of the crumbling stumps. I learned also of
the difficulties met with in arranging for the work on the south-east-
ern and north-western divisions; of the difficulty of finding some
lines, and of the illness of the engineer in another section preventing
work.

The arrangement of the work of these parties, and the examination

*North Eastern Division: River Survey Party*

and settlement of their accounts required constant attention until August 8th, when the accounts were filed with the comptroller, and the funds procured for the continuance of work.

*August 12th,* all arrangements having been made, and the improvements in the stand for the huge 20-inch theodolite completed, I proceeded, with one assistant, to Plattsburgh, where I was joined by the remainder of my personal party.

On the 13th, I ascended the Saranac river and inspected the work of the river survey party. Along the route, each of the transit stations had been carefully marked in accordance with the instructions, on stone with drill-hole and number. About five miles from Lake Champlain, the first of the tertiary signals had been built, and at noon I came up with the "chainmen," carefully measuring their way with the delicate steel ribbon nicely aligned, leveled, and stretched by the spring balance handles.

After a critical examination of the field-books and the general progress of the work of the party, I proceeded with them to their camp, near a pleasant grove through which a fine stream of clear cold water ran southward to the river. The busy party, active and interested in their work; the bright tents under one of which—a light fly—

the cook spread their repast near where the camp-fire crackled merrily; the contented horse picketed near by cropping the fresh herbage;
the murmur of the stream; together formed a camp scene of unusual
interest.

Having selected the station for one of the tertiary signals, and issued further instructions to the assistant in charge of the party, I returned to Plattsburgh.

PART FOUR

# Albany Institute Lectures

But what a strange and wonderful winter habitation have these mountain dwellers. The peak's appearance at a distance is now that of a vast snow cone or dome uprearing itself against the dark blue vault of heaven. Black ledges here and there show themselves in deep, sharp contrast with the spotless mantling around, and dark evergreen forests slope upward from the gloomy depths of the gorges; breaking, as the ledges are reached, into long, upward trending curves or belts of timber that struggle up the cliffs, diminishing and dwarfing till the timber-line is reached. From the icy summit we behold a very different view. We stand upon the highest land in New York, the centre of an icy citadel! Frozen clouds drift slowly and wearily below. Away to the south and west in billows and billows of dazzling silver, they extend to where the horizon joins with them in mingled brilliancy. The sun sinks slowly westward. Behind us on each mountain-side the deepening shadows of other mountains climb. The gorges begin to fill with unutterable gloom; and now the sinking sun shakes from itself for one moment the haze and mist, and covers our mountain with a burst of glory that makes it seem transfigured. All the frost wreathed forest on the sun-side slopes, bursts into sparkling light, each tree a weird Christmas tree, adorned with wonderful and fantastic frost-work as though the frozen clouds had midst their limbs become entangled and, settling, enwrapped them all in silver fleece. The sun descends amidst the clouds; each white mountain peak beams with faintest crimson— then all is gray and chill and night.

— VERPLANCK COLVIN
The Winter Fauna of Mount Marcy, 1876

# Narrative of a Bear Hunt in the Adirondacks

*[Read before the Albany Institute, Jan. 18, 1870.]*

*Gentlemen of the Institute:* I have been requested by our secretary to give a statement of a recent hunt in the Adirondack Wilderness of northern New York, during which I was so fortunate as to kill a large and very splendid specimen of the American black bear, after two days chase upon snow-shoes.

The comparative scarcity of the animal, the dangers and fatigues incurred in its pursuit, would render it seldom an object of the chase but for its value to the hunter and trapper, and as a trophy.

On Friday the 31st of December 1869, while deer hunting on show-shoes with David Sturgis of Lake Pleasant, Hamilton county, in the direction of Jessups or Indian River, we struck the trail of a large bear. It was of the black species and, according to naturalists and hunters, should at this season have been hybernating. The bear had passed during the previous night, and we immediately determined to pursue him, being willing to undergo the fatigue on the mere possibility of success. Besides, we had each our theory in relation to the habits of the bear, which the successful result of this chase would settle. In the Adirondack Wilderness, hunters generally hold to the opinion that bears, when adult and prime, cannot be run down by man; and that just previous to the first deep snow of winter they suddenly disappear and are not seen again till spring. Those killed in that region are generally shot in traps in which they have been caught; or, when accidentally met with, shot on sight if the hunter happen to be prepared.

Reprinted from *Transactions of the Albany Institute, Vol. VI.* Albany: J. Munsell, 82 State Street, 1870.

When we discovered the trail, we immediately abandoned all thoughts of deer hunting and commenced the pursuit of the bear. Sturgis was armed with a Ballard breech-loading carbine, I carried a Spencer repeating rifle [with seven shots in the magazine and one in the barrel] besides bowie-knife and revolver.

I will not tire you with the details of the first days chase; but will merely remark that the bear would go out of his road to walk the prostrate trees, and when approaching a stream, which had a precipitous bank, he would make directly towards it for a quarter of a mile to the only log spanning it. He did not hunt wood or deer-mice or other small game, which he could easily have taken, and which swarmed in some localities; but where beech-nuts were found, he turned up the deep snow and the earth in search of them. He did not descend to the valleys to re-ascend the mountains, but continued along the ridges, from mountain to mountain, in a south-easterly direction with an evident and reasoning purpose which was surprising. He waded into spring-holes, and followed in their beds the little slush and snow-filled streams; whereby I judged him to be fat and heated by traveling, for he loved to wallow like a pig, and came out on the snow dripping with muddy water. In this he resembled the raccoon, another plantigrade, whose generic name of *lotor* is obtained from his habit of playing in the water, even though it be icy cold.

The course taken by the bear was such as to return us toward the settlements, and to bring us by evening to a road, by following which for two miles the hotel of Mr. Sturgis could be reached. Before arriving at the road, I had the misfortune, while sliding down hill on snow-shoes, to be precipitated from the edge of a little cliff some 10 or 12 feet, snapping the heel rivet of one snow-shoe and tearing loose the foot straps of the other; filling my gun muzzle with snow and slightly wounding my left thigh, on which I fell. Sturgis had far outstripped me when I reached the road; and, being dinnerless and lame, and night approaching, I took the way to the hotel.

Sturgis had already arrived and lay upon a sofa perfectly exhausted; he declared that, trapper and moose hunter as he was, he had never been so tired. It appeared that he had followed the trail across the road into the swamp of the Cundjemonk river; across the river, through water a foot or so deep over the ice, and up an evergreen covered mountain known as Rift hill.

From where the Cundjemonk empties into the bay of the Sacondaga river, a mountain ridge follows the Cundjemonk two or three
miles, on the south-east side of that stream. This ridge has two summits separated by a little valley; at the south-west is Burnt mountain,
a bare and desolate rock; and at the north-east, up the Cundjemonk,
is the Rift hill, darkly green with hemlocks; its name derived from
a cleft or little pass that severs the summit; a cleft 20 or 25 feet
wide, perhaps an average depth of 20 feet, with perpendicular walls.
Around the summit of this mountain Sturgis chased the bear several
times, yet never caught sight of the animal. When he turned and ran
back on the trail, in order to outwit and meet the bear, he invariably
found that the bear had done the same, and "back-tracked" also.
Besides, the bear would perform the technical back-track; which is
stopping and walking backwards in the tracks already made, a considerable distance, and then leaping out clear of them to take another
course. This generally deceives the dog, but avails little with the skillful hunter.

From Rift hill he pursued the bear to the summit of Burnt Mountain, and round and round it, till at length, utterly fatigued and discouraged and night closing in, he abandoned the chase for the time.

On hearing his narrative, I formed a plan for the hunt of the following day. It was, that keeping together we should follow the trail,
and that the instant he commenced circling a mountain-top, as he had
previously done, Sturgis should continue in pursuit while I would
await the approach of the bear, who, finding a man following would
not expect another waiting on the trail for his return. If this worked as
I expected, it would put bruin between two fires; but, if he did not
circle a mountain summit, the hound, which we could put upon his
track on the morrow, would with his voice tell us the course he was
running, when I could cut across on the hypotenuse of the angle, and
perhaps head him off and get a shot at him. Sturgis would meanwhile
follow up—after the dog—and do his best to come within range and
end bruin's career.

This plan met with the warm approval of Mr. Sturgis.

That evening we were the butt of the trappers, who lounged into
the hotel to inquire our success. We had "attempted a thing impossible," it was a "wild goose chase," "a bear could not be hunted down
so." We determined to prove the contrary.

After mending snow-shoes, cleaning rifles, and preparing every thing for the morrow, we retired, thankful that the chase had brought us home to warm suppers and comfortable beds.

Aroused before daylight, I again took breakfast by the light of the candle, and as soon as we could see to follow the trail, we sallied. Sturgis led his hound "Patsey," and carried on his back a knapsack containing provisions for one week—a minimum—and a hatchet for shantying, for it was determined to pursue the animal to extremity. It was about three miles to where we would strike the trail and our course was down the Sacondaga on the ice, up the Cundjemonk to the base of Rift hill, which we then commenced to ascend. This mountain is so covered with cliffs, huge blocks of stone and boulders, wind-slashes of fallen trees and the like, as to slightly remind one of the Indian Pass; it was a fit retreat for the chased bear: here he would throw off the dog by climbing the boulders and walking logs across chasms. Here the crevices in the rocks afforded comfortable retreats for great numbers of porcupines, the snow was every where tracked up by them, trees barked and little paths beaten through the snow. I noticed that the track of a porcupine exactly resembled that of a small bear; having the plantigrade appearance.

At the foot of Rift hill, I separated from my companion, and, climbing the mountain, went at his request, over to a spot on the Burnt Mountain, where he thought the bear would come when chased. It was about a mile from the summit of Rift hill to this place, and, if neither the bear nor Sturgis came to me, I was to judge that the bear had left the mountain, and act accordingly.

On my way over to Burnt Mountain, I crossed the summit of Rift hill, through a recently deserted deer-yard that was there. I discovered by the signs, that the bear and Sturgis had passed through the previous evening and scattered them and, while examining the Rift, the cleft summit of the mountain—a geological phenomenon unaccountable to me—I noticed that near the deer-yard the bear had been four times. Through the Rift, along its edge, across and around it; seemingly through necessity from the conformation of the ground. This appeared to me by far the best place to await the bear, but, according to agreement, I proceeded to the summit of Burnt Mountain and there awaited much longer than I had promised.

It is unnecessary to state every incident and every move taken in the chase; I will take a few hours from my narrative.

I had stopped to sketch a beautiful lake and forest scene, for the chase seemed dull—I had heard nothing of it for some time—when, far away up the Cundjemonk, echoed the distant cry of the hound. If it came this way, Rift hill was much the better place to await; I hurried round the brow of Burnt Mountain into the valley and up Rift hill to a spot near the deer-yard, where from a stump which occupied the center of the glade, I commanded a position for many rods around. The Rift was about a rod to my right, and I could have a shot at anything passing through or around it; the only place where it might easily be crossed was near at hand.

In coming from Burnt Mountain, I had started a deer from his browse, where he was feeding on the long hanging lichen, *Usnea barbate*,—improperly moss,—depending from the dead branches of a fallen tree. As I was not prepared, he escaped, but in selecting my new stand I kept him in mind, remembering also that our hound being a deer hound might take to the chase of his usual quarry instead of the bear. I seated myself upon the stump and waited; now glancing toward the vacant deer-yard a few rods to my left, now at the great tracks of the bear in the snow at my feet.

It was noon when I took my new station and the sun bright and warm; snow birds, blue jays, and red squirrels chirped and frisked around. A quarter of an hour passed, then, miles away, I faintly heard the hound on the Pine Mountain, toward Oregon, up the Cundjemonk. Once, twice, three times and I heard the dog no more. I waited, listened; half an hour passed; three-quarters—it grew tiresome; I felt inclined to start up and be doing, but I had lost an elk the previous fall by leaving the runway before the dog came in and—I sat down again.

Another quarter of an hour. I was leaning drowsily forward, my rifle on my lap,—listening intently however—when I thought I heard a faint distant tramp far down the mountain.

I sat up. *Jump, Jump,* JUMP, JUMP, JUMP, JUMP, JUMP, *JUMP, JUMP, JUMP!* something came up the mountain on a long swinging canter. I heard it crash through the bushes, descend into the Rift and ascend, and, though hidden by some hemlocks, come directly towards me still at a canter. My rifle was at my shoulder and sighted, and I could not rest my left elbow on my breast for my heart thumped audibly. Another moment, and he would clear the bushes that screened him from view—No! he had stopped suddenly, and all was silent for one long minute. Then there was a slow, dubious whine, followed by a snuffing and snorts—*so peculiar, so wild*—that told me I was in the presence of the untamed savage, scarce five rods of the forest glade between him and me.

The snowy woods were bright as ever; the snow-birds still chirping and fluttering among the tall evergreens; could there be a bear behind those hemlocks where my rifle aimed?

Another whine, another series of snorts, having expression in them like articulate language. There was doubt, indecision, anger, surprise! hesitancy—he would be off! Aiming a little lower, I guessed his position behind the hemlocks, sighted carefully and fired.

With the explosion came a shrill scream of agony—human, though bestial—it almost unnerved me. No animal that I had shot before gave such a cry; had I mistaken? The expressions Oh! Oh! Oh! *Whew, whew, whew!* were as plainly uttered as ever by human voice, and in an agonized way that was distressing. I heard a sudden roll in the snow, then a tumble, and the animal pitched off the bluff; in a moment I was on the edge and beheld, about 10 or 15 feet down, a huge black bear—an immense fellow, biting and tearing at his bloody side. He saw me and turned, showing jaws replete with white teeth; the rifle passed to my shoulder and I fired again, but not before he leaped.

As he ran, following him closely, I fired once, twice, three times; each time he turned and showed his teeth I shot again, when he would take to flight again, scarcely seeming to be hindered by the bullets. Suddenly leaping about eight feet up to a log that ran to the opposite cliff of the rift, I saw him walking carefully yet nimbly, limping in his right fore paw, which was bloody, and it seemed to me that I must have touched him. Aiming, I fired again, and just as he reached the end of the log, I discharged my piece once more; but, as I fired, he leaped on the cliff top and ran—ran but three rods, when, with a deep groan, he pitched forward and fell headlong in a heap.

This was about quarter past one, January 1st, 1870.

Leaping down into the rift recklessly, for I now began to get excited, I dashed across it and up the opposite side; I know not how, I dared not descend there in returning. In a moment I was on the opposite side of the pass; no bear was to be seen!

Rushing forward, I slid suddenly down over the icy crust on my snow-shoes, into a hollow upon the dying bear! His eyes were glaring with a yellow light of rage, and seizing my right snow-shoe with one of his hind paws, his claws catching in the net work, he struck at me rapidly with his left front paw; the long, black hairy claws seemed to make the wind whistle past my face while his jaws, over the ivory teeth of which streamed blood from his throat, opened and shut with a sound like a steel trap. Bowie-knife and revolver were in my belt, but I had no ambition to try these romantic weapons. I jerked my snow-shoe from his claws and scrambled up, back; unstrapped the shoes, pulled forward for dernier resort the knife and pistol in my belt, then slipping another cartridge from the magazine into the rifle, stepped down again and held the muzzle near his breast.

He was now quiet, save his watchful, restless, glaring yellow eye, heaving sides, and the deep grumbling rattle in his throat at every breath; for he was choked with blood and, besides the thick clots around his mouth, each second a great, red bubble rose from his nostrils and burst. I watched him,—with the rifle at his breast,—so full of life I thought he might be shamming; but he was dying.

I now shouted for my companion, and at length received an answering cry from far down the mountain. It may not have been many minutes, but it seemed to me half an hour ere he came within speaking distance. I called to him that I had killed the bear; breathlessly he climbed, pulling himself up by the saplings and trees; he was wild with excitement. Breathlessly he leaned against a tree, and surveyed the prize—then shouted: "You have killed the biggest bear in Hamilton county!" breathed hard a moment and continued, "many New Yorkers, whom I have guided, would have given a thousand dollars to have killed that bear!" and was beside himself.

Soon, the hound came limping in, his feet cut by the crust and bleeding. Like a staunch dog, as he was, he had held to the track, and came in slowly now, wagging his tail, he knew it was all over, and his poor skinned feet did ache so on the cold snow. I led him to the bear and, lifting him, laid him on the warm furred body. He took it kindly and fell to licking his feet, so sore and bleeding.

Meanwhile, I commenced sketching; and Sturgis, after looking the bear all over, discovered that my last bullet had entered the skull near the ear and had shattered the bone in pieces. Twisting a young black birch tree into a wythe, he knotted it around the neck of the bear—

three feet in circumference—and started to "snake him out" (phrase more expressive than elegant) down the mountain and along the rivers, three miles to the road and the house.

I remained a little while to sketch and to measure distances. Just beyond the hemlocks through which I fired the first shot, I saw some black hair on the snow, and taking it up found a bloody bullet wrapped in it, the lead indented and mashed, and fragments of bone inclosed. The first bullet had passed through his chest; yet he lived on! When that shot was fired I was distant from the bear four rods, four yards and one foot; being 24 lengths of my snow-shoes and a foot. The last shot, which pierced his brain, was fired at a range of about seven rods; at that distance, it is a matter of nicety, with a long-range rifle, to keep from overshooting, especially when added to the excitement the object is in rapid movement.

Hunters generally mention the fore shoulder as the proper place to aim at; for the head, they say, being always in rapid motion makes a poor mark. I fired five shots at this bear's right shoulder, and it was only at the last moment that I changed my aim to the head; with what effect I have already told. When skinned it was found that his right fore shoulder bone was broken; pierced in two places by bullets, while three other balls had entered and passed through his chest, yet so far up or forward as to escape the heart and lungs; cutting some arteries, however, from which he bled inwardly and very profusely. Heavy and large as the bullets were (three-quarters of an ounce) the muscles on his breast and shoulders were so thick and elastic that they closed in after the bullet; even a small pencil could not have been pressed into the wounds. The sixth and last bullet entered the skull a little below the right ear, penetrating the brain, and shattering the posterior portion of the cranium. This bullet was mashed and broken in three pieces, lodging in different parts of the brain; two of the fragments have been recovered and are retained as mementos. That he lived and offered resistance after this wound is worthy of the attention of naturalists, and bids the grizzly, the far famed *Ursus ferox*, look to his laurels. With this wound (besides the five bullets already received) brains and blood streaming out on the snow, he ran three rods—fell, yet was still fiercely ready for conflict.

I will not relate in detail what followed; how we dragged the bear out to the settlement on his glossy back; how long it took, how weary we were, how night was upon us when we reached the road. How we laughed as we thought of the surprise of croakers—not only at our return, but at our success—of the guides and hunters who had the previous day joked us on our "wild goose chase." At length we neared the hotel, but before we reached it the settlement had taken the alarm and was around us. We had our triumph. "It was a great feat; the first bear hunted down and killed in this manner, on snow-shoes in that region;" said those hardy northern hunters.

The bear weighed over 300 pounds before being disemboweled, and had bled so very profusely that he must have lost gallons of blood. He measured seven feet from hind claws to tip of nose; around the neck three feet; around the chest, inside the arms, four feet two inches; diameter of chest, from outside of shoulders, two feet. Length of hind foot ten inches; length of palm of fore paw eight inches; length of head one foot.

I had him opened carefully; and examined in detail the viscera, and judge that they weighed between 40 and 50 pounds, though they were not put upon the balance together, nor all of them weighed. The lungs were light colored and seemed uninjured, but had through and upon them clots of coagulated blood. The whole cavity above the diaphragm was filled with liquid blood to the amount of several quarts. The heart was very large, firm, and healthy and had not been touched by the bullets. It measured five inches in length, the greatest diameter being about four and a half inches; it resembled in shape the heart of a pig. Here it may be noted that there is a singular resemblance between the vital organs of these animals; but for the human-like arms, clawed paws and furred pelt, the likeness would be complete.

The liver was healthy in appearance, and both heart and liver when cooked were excellent eating. To the entrails were attached long strips of fat, yielding much oil when fried.

The stomach of the bear was to me an interesting study; I carefully examined its contents before venturing to eat any of the meat. First taking the size and shape, I proceeded to open it and found it filled with beech-nuts; nor could the most careful examination of the stomach's content evolve a trace of animal food. Had it been the stomach of a wolf, a fox, or a wild-cat, the minute teeth, small bone splinters, and rolls of hair of mice or squirrels and the like, would have been found; there was no trace of anything of this sort in the stomach of this bear. There might have been two quarts or more of freshly masti-cated beech-nuts in the stomach when first opened; these had to procure singly from beneath the deep snow, by digging it away with his paws and rooting like a hog. When started on the second day, he was 10 miles from where the trail was abandoned on the first day, and had rooted over about a quarter of an acre under the beech trees: with great labor, he had turned up the earth, discoloring the snow. Notwithstanding the numbers of small animals of the mice and squirrel kind, whose burrows abounded both through the snow and in the ground beneath, in no instance had this supposedly carnivorous beast stopped to dig them. From observations, at this time and previously, of the habits of the true black bear of our State, I am forced to the conclusion that he is not a carnivorous animal. The tusks and claws, carefully examined, will be found to be best suited to digging up roots, seeds, mast, and the like. The only carnivorous habit that I have observed in the *wild* bear, is that of eating the common black ant, and the grubs found beneath rocks and logs; omnivorous he may be, but strictly carnivorous he is not. His dental system, the number of tuberculous teeth in either jaw do not support it; as for his ferociousness, he is like any other animal, when wounded and cornered dangerous.

His eating flesh when kept in confinement or driven to it by starvation, is no proof of his carnivorous habits; two of the rodents, the beaver and musquash, have been known to devour flesh, and they have no carnivorous teeth. Baron Cuvier speaks of the bears; "almost frugiverous dentition" and states that they have "three large molars on each side in each jaw, altogether tuberculous." Tuberculous teeth are the posterior blunted ones.

The following seem to me facts: that bears are naturally strict vegetarians; that when the winter is mild and open, and beech-mast, etc., plentiful, they remain out during the entire winter and do not hybernate; that when they "den," they seldom resort to caverns, but select a shelter beneath a fallen tree or wind slash, where the deep snows cover and form their only blanketing; that even when strongest and most powerful they may be run down and destroyed by man. Abbe Dupratz speaks of their migrating during winters when there was a scarcity of food; our Adirondack Wilderness affords no space for the habit, if such habit they possess.

I have here the snow-shoes which I used during the hunt and which, as they are rather peculiar in their construction, may be of interest to the Institute. They differ materially from those made by our north woods' hunters; being longer and more pointed and fully netted, toe and heel, they support one better on the snow, and served me nobly throughout the chase, despite rough usage. They were made by the Indians of Maine from the raw hide of the *Cariboo* or American rein-deer, which is highly esteemed for the purpose. A light, thin string of this skin is as strong and durable as one much larger and heavier, made from the coarser deer or neat's hide. An Indian made *Cariboo* snow-shoe is a marvel to our white hunters, both from the material used and the skill displayed in the manufacture. There is a fault in the Indian snow-shoes however; though their length enables one to go forward rapidly, yet it is difficult to turn quickly on them; again, the toes being very pointed, one is apt while running to catch in the bushes or crusted snow and trip headlong. These faults are obviated by practice, when great distances may be traveled swiftly upon them through the dense forests.

Minute details, merely interesting to hunters, I have omitted. There remains the outline of the adventure and a few notes, perhaps of scientific interest.

# Portable Boats

*[Read before the Albany Institute, May 1, 1875]*

*Mr. President and Gentlemen of the Albany Institute:*
It affords me pleasure to accede to the wishes of the members of the Institute and others who have desired me to afford them an opportunity of examining the portable canvas boat or canoe which I invented, and which was used during a portion of my Adirondack explorations of the remoter lakes.

Before entering into an explanation of the character of this portable boat, it would seem appropriate here to give a brief account of the portable boats which have heretofore been used, so that the peculiarities of the one which I place before you this evening may be better understood, and the point wherein it differs from all boats heretofore used may be made evident. This distinguishing characteristic may be stated in brief, to be the fact that my boat has no frame carried with it; but, by a few bits of leather, etc., peculiarly contrived and placed within an exterior of water-proofed canvas, poles and boughs, cut in the forest or among the bushes on river or lake shore, are readily fastened within it as its temporary frame; a frame entirely inexpensive, and which may be thrown away when you start upon a carry or portage, so easily are they replaced. Thus I obtain a boat weighing a little over 10 pounds—all that has to be carried being the canvas exterior and its leathern attachments. My invention may therefore be called, with much propriety, *a boat without a frame!*

In reviewing history to trace the origin of portable boats, we are led far back beyond even the most ancient chronicles, and find some forms of them existing even in prehistoric times. Indeed, when we come to examine the causes which lead men to desire a light, portable boat, we will find that all the different available forms known to the

Reprinted from *Transactions of the Albany Institute, Vol. VIII.* Albany: J. Munsell, 1876.

world have been originated either among savages with the first dawning of civilization or—for here extremes meet—when civilization pushes out into the wilderness or among savages, where the narrow lanes of water and frequent landings and portages will not admit of larger craft.

Perhaps the first of portable boats was that which carried Moses in the bulrushes—but that cannot be determined.

The earliest form of water conveyance was probably the raft. A floating log may have saved some tired swimmer—a witless savage flying from murderous enemies—with yet wit enough to grasp the log, as a drowning man is popularly supposed to grasp the straw. The log which floats him he soon learns to guide. Another step—his leathern water bucket, left at the water side, he sees wafted off upon the tide, high and dry, which, if full of water, he knows would sink. He sees and thinks, and shortly turns shipbuilder. Whether he labors in vain to build a raw-hide boat, collapsed as soon as his foot is placed in it, who can tell: this much we know from archaeology, the earliest remains of boats found mingled with the remains of prehistoric races are "*dug-outs,*" hollowed logs, monstrous shaped things like horse-troughs, which served them to navigate the prehistoric waters.

The dug-out, however, as every one is probably aware, cannot be considered a portable boat. Even the light cypress dug-outs of Florida, beautiful in shape and finish, are hard to propel through the bayous against wind and tide, let alone their carrying. The boat of skins might, indeed, have been the earliest, the perishable character of its substance preventing its preservation in the cranogues with the other remains of more solid character.

The earliest form of portable boat of which history gives us any account is that which we might call the bull-boat, being made of neat's hide upon a light wicker-work but permanent frame. Herodotus says (Book 1, page 193): "The boats which come down the river"—meaning the Euphrates—"to Babylon are circular and made of skins. The frames which are of willow are cut in the country of the Armenians, above Assyria, and on these, which serve for hulls, a covering of skins is stretched outside, and thus the boats are made without stem or stern, quite round like a shield." This form, which seems to have existed even in prehistoric times, about the same in form in Egypt as in Britain, was known to the Romans as *curuca, carocium,* or

# UNITED STATES PATENT OFFICE.

VERPLANCK COLVIN, OF ALBANY, NEW YORK.

### IMPROVEMENT IN PORTABLE BOATS.

Specification forming part of Letters Patent No. **155,710,** dated October 6, 1874; application filed July 9, 1874.

*To all whom it may concern:*

Be it known that I, VERPLANCK COLVIN, of the city and county of Albany and State of New York, have invented a Portable Boat, or contrivance therefor, of which the following is a specification:

The object of my invention is to provide a portable boat, for which no permanent frame is necessary, it being so contrived-of flexible water-proof canvas (or its equivalent) that it may be rolled up and carried in trunk or knapsack, (this forming the boat exterior,) and when required for use in woodlands or wilderness, be readily framed with boughs and timber (cut in the first thicket or wood,) and bound and fastened suitably within the canvas boat exterior, by the means hereafter described.

I construct my boat exterior, preferably, of stout canvas, rendered water-proof by treatment with suitable substances, (pure rubber gum, dissolved paraffine, or a mixture of wax and tallow, being preferred.) The extremities are closed and water-proof, and the canoe-shape generally preferred. In this shape the boat is double-prowed. The two ends are bound exteriorly by their metal guards (V-shaped) riveted down, and forming cut-waters to each prow. Along the bottom of the boat from end to end are thongs or straps, or their equivalent, and along either of the sides are similar rows of thongs. The thongs or fastenings along the bottom are used to tie in and fasten down a keelson, which gives the length and stiffness to the whole boat, and which, in wilderness practice, is frequently a young tree, strong and straight, cleared of branches or knots. These thongs, at the same time, fasten at the middle certain ribs, made of boughs or their equivalents, said ribs forming the crossway frame-work of the boat, and answering the purposes of the knees or ribs of other boats or canoes. The thongs, &c., along the sides, are usually tied through holes, which, at suitable distances, are worked into the canvas at the margin, and serve to fasten down not only the gunwales, (which, in practice in a wilderness, are usually long poles properly trimmed,) but also the ends of

the ribs, or boughs which serve as ribs. The ends of the keelson and gunwales are joined or restrained and kept in position by the four metal contrivances called "framing-blocks," A A and B B of drawings. The elbow-shaped framing-block B receives at one opening the end of the horizontal keelson-pole, while the other opening (of B) receives the lower end of the vertical wooden prow-piece or upright. The triangular-shaped framing-block A receives at the lower side the upper end of the vertical wooden prow-piece or upright, above which are two horizontal openings (in A) which receive the ends of the gunwales. These openings are of various forms, as preferred, and the ends of the gunwales and keelson may be confined or fastened by screw or clamp, if desired. In practice, cross-bars of wood, L, are generally placed from gunwale to gunwale, and the form or trim of the boat may be governed by their length. The only portions carried in a wilderness are the four framing-blocks A A and B B, and the canvas boat exterior, as prepared, with its straps, thongs or cords, &c., and the exterior metal cut-waters on prow, as shown at C and C in Figure 1.

In the accompanying drawing, Fig. 1 is a representation of the canvas boat exterior, as rolled up and tied with cords for carrying. C and C are the metal cut-waters of the two ends, (the canvas having been folded in the middle, so that, in rolling up, the two ends will be brought together ou the outside.) The letters *d d d d d d* show some of the upper marginal thongs or straps used in binding down the gunwales.

Fig. 2 is an outline representation, in perspective, of one of the prows of such a boat, and shows the upper framing-block A, and the lower keelson-block B. The position of a cross-bar is shown at L.

Fig. 3 is a perspective view of the boat as framed, with poles and boughs A A and B B, at the respective extremities of the boat, being the framing-blocks; L L, two cross-bars; P, the prow-piece, and K the keelson, the direction of its continuation being shown by the dotted lines.

*Patent for Portable Boat*

*caribus,* and to the Celts as *corwig* or *curach.* Caesar describes those of the ancient Britons as having, in addition to the wicker-work, keels and gunwales of wood, permanent and substantial, though rather light boats for sea voyages, we would be apt to think. Yet, there are records of those early days—when men were men indeed—of the North sea daringly navigated, and the Irish channel crossed (a tedious voyage of seven days) in one of those leathern tubs! In England this form of portable boat has long since gone out of use, a few specimens gathered from the Highlands of Scotland remaining as trophies in archaeological museums; though latterly, some of modern construction have been used in so-called *coracle races* for fashionable

V. COLVIN.
Portable Boats.
No. 155,710.
Patented Oct. 6, 1874.
Fig. 1.
Fig. 2.
Gunwale
Gunwale
Rib
Rib
Bow Piece
Kelson
Fig. 3.
Attest:
Geo. D. Hill,
Mills Blake
Inventor:
Verplanck Colvin

amusement. It was, however, only in recent times that the coracle, as it is modernly called, disappeared generally in Scotland, where they had been long retained by the highland lumbermen for what our American lumbermen would call river driving—the loose timber being finally made up into rafts, and the bull-boat no longer needed. In Ireland the coracle is, however, still in use, and has been described as follows: "It is in shape oval, near three feet broad, and four feet long; a small keel runs from the head to the stern; a few ribs are placed across the keel, and a ring of pliable wood around the lip of the machine. The whole is covered with the rough hide of an ox or a horse; the seat is in the middle; it carries but one person, or, if a second goes into it, he stands behind the rower leaning on his shoulders. In float-

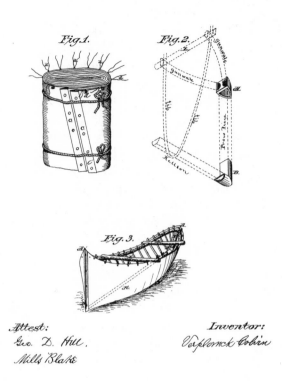

ing timber (lumbering) a rope is fixed to the float, and the rower holds it in one hand, and with the other manages the paddle. He keeps the float in deep water, and brings it to shore when he will. In returning home, he carries the machine on his shoulders, or on a horse." The frame is permanent.

England, to whom the "hearts of oak" of old, and iron ships to-day, afford subject of vast pride, would, perhaps, hardly feel elated in the contemplation of what a majestic fleet of bull-boats obeyed the orders of Queen Boadicea—the infant navy of Great Britain—the portable boat, suited to the wild and savage character of England at that early period.

Among our western Indians of the great plains, a sort of coracle was in use, made from the hide of the buffalo, strongly secured upon a firm frame. A boat, essentially the same as the coracle, is still in use in Thibet, and is described by Abbe Huc, in his travels in Tartary, etc., where he found it in use upon the river Bo-Thou. The interior was formed of ox-hides, strongly sewn together, and formed upon a frame-work of bamboo. It could be carried overland by its owner, but the frame was permanent.

Nearly allied to the bull-boat or coracle is the kayak, kajak, or kia of the Esquimaux—differently called in different dialects—an ocean vessel of the Arctic zone; how ancient we can hardly tell. Like the coracle, this boat is made so light that it is said "a man can carry his kia on his shoulders from the house to the water." The frame of the kia is permanent, and consists of whale-bone joined with fragments of the drift-wood which the ocean tosses upon those Arctic shores. Over the frame, the covering of seal-skin is tightly and securely fastened, the seal-skin being neatly and elegantly sewed together, the smooth thin covering being almost transparent, and showing indistinctly the limbs of its owner, who, sitting in the centre of his narrow, tube-like craft, with the seal-skin collar of the man-hole gathered and bound around his waist, his coat collar and sleeves also made waterproof, ventures out upon the stormy sea to secure his livelihood; daring with his harpoon and lance to battle with the walrus and narwhal, and to assert, in those wild boreal waters, the pre-eminence of man and mind.

The kia or kayak has an average length of 25 feet, with a width of perhaps 18 or 20 inches. It has no keel, and being so narrow requires skill in its management among the billows. The Esquimaux, however, with his double-paddle, not only navigates the icy seas with safety, with wonderful skill balancing and propelling himself with his paddle, but also manages to perform some feats which may be termed national and peculiar to those northern tribes. He regards it as a mere pastime to leap one kayak over another at sea, but with more caution approaches his *chef-d'oeuvre*. Throwing himself and canoe sideways violently on the water, with a strong, quick stroke of the paddle, he disappears under the surface to leap in sight again upon the other side—sometimes proceeding thus rapidly 15 or 20 times—the kayak serving as the axis of motion. Thus we perceive that even the dwellers amid icebergs have their pleasures and pastimes—wild and savage as the rude regions of their habitation, yet dependent upon the same emotions of the heart as those of more favored people.

It is stated of this boat that "The paddler is so tightly tied to the kia, that he is unable to change his position without assistance, or even to lift a heavy weight, such as a seal. In such a case, he asks assistance from a companion. The two kias are placed near each other, and paddles are laid from one to the other, so that for the time they are formed into a double canoe, which cannot be upset . . . . An inflated seal's bladder is always attached to the canoe. When the kia is not in use, it is taken out of the water, and rested in an inverse position upon the huts."

The Esquimaux have also another kind of boat of skins, which may be carried from place to place, but is so large as to hardly come within the limits of the portable. This is the woman's boat, called the oomiak, a large, clumsy, scow-like, straight sided ship, of raw hide, which conveys their baggage. A well made oomiak will carry a heavy burden. One is mentioned "measuring twenty-five feet in length, by eight in width, and three in depth," in which more than 20 Esquimaux were conveyed. This boat is occasionally fitted with a sail, and its general character renders it far from portable. Like the kayak, its frame is permanent, for indeed on those Arctic shores the material for boat-frames is not easily procured.

The canoes of the South Sea islanders, being generally intended for ocean voyages, and constructed of wood, lie beyond the bounds of our subject. Their wonderful double canoes, in which they venture far from land on the broad Pacific, are not portable, and even the light, small forms of canoes which they have, though they may be lifted and carried, are hardly more of a portable boat than the surf boats which the Sandwich islanders use in the exciting pastime of their tropic coast.

Nor are the bamboo rafts of the Chinese, boats in any true sense of the word. Like the catamaran of the East Indian coast, they are simply floats—excellent in their way—the catamaran being more safe than the ship's boat in the furious surf of Madras. This form of light raft is also used on the west coast of South America.

Among the Indians of South America we again meet with good examples of portable boats in their periaguas of the lighter construction; but one of the heavier kind which Columbus, on his fourth voyage to the New World, saw at the Guanaja islands, was hardly portable, though made from a single tree; being eight feet wide and propelled by 25 rowers. It had awnings, etc., and was supposed to have come from Yucatan.

Among the Patagonians, we find elegant examples of light boat construction, most singular and interesting forms being made by the inhabitants of Tierra del Fuego; but it is only among our own North American Indian tribes that we find what, to my mind, is the most beautiful and elegant of forms—the birch-bark canoe.

The Indian canoe probably owed its origin to the peculiar character of our northern regions, where myriads of small lakes, each almost if not entirely joining with the other, and streams and rivers, now foaming in rapids and now stretching in long reaches of still water, interposed a tangled net-work of impediments to the traveler without boat, and at the same time remained equally difficult to those whose boats could not readily be carried over the numerous portages necessary.

The origin of the birchen boat can not be traced. Wherever the canoe birch tree is found, the natives made from it their boats. How many millions worth of fur and peltry have these light canoes carried down from the heart of the wilderness to the trading posts of the whites, since the day when those frail boats clustered around the ship of Henry Hudson! How many white pioneers have, in these birch canoes, penetrated to the far west to lay the foundations of our modern empire!

It is superfluous to describe the Indian canoe, and it is hardly necessary to remark that its frame, like all those before mentioned, is permanent, and that the removal of the frame of an old canoe would amount to the destruction of the craft.

In our wilderness, the first substitute for the birch canoe was the light boat known as the bateau, well-suited for the transportation of military stores, and extensively used during the French and Indian and Revolutionary wars. Thus we find the savagery of civilization making the first improvements by substitution of the bateau for the boat of the savage, to aid in the successful prosecution of more savage war.

In the Adirondack region, at the close of the Revolutionary war, there were many white hunters and trappers who used the birch canoe in their voyages by lake or river. Few of these white trappers were able to build their own canoes, and as the Indians slowly disappeared from our northern wilderness, the white hunters were gradually thrown more and more upon their own resources for water craft. They commenced building provisional canoes from huge sheets of bark from the spruce tree. From a personal experience with this variety of craft, I cannot recommend it. The fresh spruce gum covers the inside in a disagreeably sticky way—your only satisfaction being that it is "pitched both without and within with pitch," in a manner which might have satisfied Noah. It is also frail and perhaps unsafe, its frame, of course, being as permanent as the boat itself.

The canoe, however, was the desideratum in a country like the Adirondack, where the traveler by water can scarcely proceed a dozen or half a dozen miles without carrying the boat and baggage over several miles of portages, and after many trials and years of patient labor, the Adirondack guides have produced, in their light boat-canoes, one of the most graceful, elegant, and portable of boats. Nevertheless, the ordinary Adirondack boat, 10 or 12 feet in length, weighs from 60 to 90 pounds, and in addition to the other baggage forms a heavy weight to be carried on the shoulders of one man through the forest, over carries or portages sometimes two or three miles in length.

During the last 10 years, I have had frequent occasion to use these boats in all their different forms. I have always entertained for them the greatest admiration, but have never liked to back one over a three-mile carry. Often my pity has been aroused at the sight of my guide, struggling through the forest and over the hills under his bulky burden, and often have I been annoyed in the course of wilderness exploration by the sudden discovery of a lake where none was supposed to exist, by finding myself without a boat in which to explore it; and oh! the slow and solemn times that I have experienced while endeavoring to pole along a raft!

After much reflection, I came to the conclusion that the first essential of a boat was its outside—the very cuticle, if firm enough, being sufficient. Further study and tests led me to select canvas as the best substance for the exterior, and that was many years before I placed this boat upon the Adirondack waters.

Now, portable boats of rubber were in use long ago, and canvas has also been employed in boat construction. Colonel, now General John C. Fremont, carried with him a rubber boat, and with it explored a portion of the Great Salt lake, perhaps the first navigation of that water by a white man. His boat, however, had a frame which it was necessary to carry with it, and withal leaked badly; it was used, I think, but once afterwards, when it was wrecked in navigating a rapid river. Dr. Kane, in his Arctic explorations, carried with him, also, a portable rubber boat, of the fate of which we only know that it was cut to pieces by a thievish Esquimau, who wanted the wooden frame within. This boat required its frame to be carried with it. In the army, canvas pontoons have been used, but these also require very heavy and substantial frames to be carried along, and old soldiers may remember how many men were detailed to bail them out. Captain Hall carried with him on his last ill-fated expedition in the Polaris, a canvas boat; but this, like all the others, had its heavy, cumbersome, and bulky frame. Paper boats, of fine construction, have been made in the neighboring city of Troy, and have proved good for racing purposes. It is almost unnecessary to state that they are permanent in character, and rigid and constant in frame. The Rob-Roy canoe, in which Mr. MacGregor explored so many of the waters of Europe, had a permanent frame. (The remarkable life-dress of Captain Beynton, cannot be considered a true boat, nor would it serve the purpose of one for ordinary use. Life preservers, cork jackets, and the valuable canvas life rafts, of tubes, now used on ships, cannot be termed boats, being properly called floats.) All these differ from my boat, for which it is not necessary to carry any frame in any region this side of Arctic and Ant-arctic circles. Even on our great western plains, I have not seen a stream, whether it be the Platte, the Cache La-Poudre, or the Smoky Hill or Republican forks of the Kaw, which had not along its banks sufficient brush or timber from which to construct all the frame that my boat requires. There is hardly an *arroyo* of the habitable west whose shores have not some margining of brush, sufficient for my boat frame.

The peculiarities, then, of the boat which I place before you to-night, are the means by which I so readily attach a frame within the canvas boat exterior.

The canoe exhibited is 12 feet long and four feet wide; the portion of the boat which is carried weighs 10 pounds eight ounces (leaving out the light leathern pieces which receive the corners of keelson and gunwales); and when compactly folded it occupies the space of less than 864 cubic inches, or less than half a cubic foot. It has carried, in a heavy storm, far from land, a burden of 700 pounds, and will proba-bly, in smooth water, convey a much greater burden. The prows, as seen, are guarded with brass cut-waters, riveted on. One great pecu-liarity of the boat is that no iron or steel is placed in it, and the sur-veyor using it in the reconnaissance of a lake will have no trouble with the local attraction of the needle. The name which I have given it is that of the Adirondack lake on which it was first practically put to the test.

Ampersand Pond! Glorious lake, silent and remote in the depths of the Adirondack forest. Walled in on the south by the dark, massive summits of Mount Seward—loneliest of peaks—and on the north by the ridge of Ampersand or Moose Mountain, while other peaks clus-tering, seem eager to shelter it from all view save that of the celestial orb of day that gilds the valley with its glory, and fills its wavelets with sparkling brilliancy. Well do I remember that day, when the guides, having tied in the light boughs, that we had cut a short while before, carried it down and placed it lightly on the water. Their merri-ment at the idea that "such a pork bag," as they called it, could float or carry anything, was scarcely concealed. But when the huge hound, after gazing at it with gravity, walked out upon the log beside which it floated, and soberly climbed in, they could not restrain their laugh-ter, but yet exclaimed, "Well, it looks just like a boat." And then I persuaded first one and then the other, to enter—the boat floating meanwhile like a feather, and with the dip of the paddles we were off, over the flashing waters, seeing each wavelet, as it rippled against the sides, flash in the morning sun.

How we traversed the lake over its deepest waters, with nothing between us and the water but the thin canvas; how, with sextant and compass used from the boat we had so lately occupied as bed or tent by turns, the figure of the lake was mapped; how in it we chased a deer, almost catching him as he leaped ashore, or how, shortly afterward, in pushing down into the outlet of the lake, we suddenly came upon a monstrous panther stretched at full length upon a log, watching for deer, permitting us to come within a rod or two ere he retreated, leaving us surprised and forgetful of our revolvers, I can not here expatiate upon.

Nor can I tell you of our more dangerous experience on the Lower Saranac lake, in cold and storm. A stormy, rainy day found us on the beach of Cold brook, an affluent of the Saranac river. Here we designed reconstructing our boat frame, the old one having been thrown away at the last camp. In a short space the guides had cut a young tamarack for the keelson, a couple of stout poles served as gunwales, while two dozen boughs, cut among the bushes at the brook side, formed the ribs. A couple of paddles were hewn from a white cedar near by. While one guide cooked dinner, another, with my aid, tied in the ribs of boughs, slipped in the keelson, and bound on the gunwales and cross pieces, and in an hour and a half from the time we struck the brook, we were gliding down stream, three men, 200 pounds of baggage and instruments, and the huge hound sedately standing toward the prow.

The navigation of the stream was easy. Out in the broader river the violent cold wind made our craft veer a little, and when, an hour later, we struck out into the broad Saranac lake, the white caps in the distance proclaimed a heavy sea. It was a wintry day. Snow lay upon the mountain tops, and when another hour passed, wild, black, foam-crested billows swept around us, and our craft rode safely, now high on the crest, now low in the trough, we felt, though chilled and shivering, when we floated up at Martin's in safety, that it was a triumph.

# The Winter Fauna of Mount Marcy

[Read before the Albany Institute at the Annual Meeting, Jan. 4, 1876.]

The fauna of an elevated mountain district is usually more or less peculiar and different from that of the surrounding lowlands, and the rule seems to hold that with increase of altitude and decrease of temperature a hardier and more boreal vegetation will be found, accompanied with animals common to colder and more northern regions. It is not so generally understood that the fauna peculiar to a given mountain section in summer often changes considerably at the approach of winter, many of the forest or mountain habitants departing to more hospitable regions. Not alone the migratory birds who flutter with fashionable elegance from the Adirondacks to Florida at the first rude blast of winter—having only as their home the free air, which is everywhere—but the less favored forest-dwellers, beasts of prey and beasts that are preyed upon, two great natural divisions of animated nature not used in technical classification, which, having no wings to bear them away, are fain to stay and take their chance to devour or be devoured.

Those who have a knowledge of the wilderness are aware that however wild a region may be, and however abundant the game, it is rare that any but the most skillful and stealthy hunter catches even a momentary glimpse of the creatures of the woods. In fact, thorough foresters readily detect the novice in woodcraft by his invariably expecting, upon entering the wilderness, to behold abundance of game—beasts and birds—in sylvan simplicity, unwarily parading themselves upon his view. The mere civilian, after exhausting marches through silent solitude, generally returns half in doubt whether he has really

Reprinted from *The Albany Institute of Useful Arts, Vol. IX.* Albany: J. Munsell, 1879.

visited the region of his fancies and day dreams—whether living thing really dwells in that region through which he has been conducted. Nevertheless, the only fault lies in his dreams, as the region of his fancy has no existence. Had he the skill of the still hunter, the crushed leaf, the twigs browsed by deer, the scratched tree bark, the broken branch, the trampled grass, the muddied water of the stream, and footprints only visible interpretable to the eye of skill, would have revealed a wonderful variety of life: telling the secrets of their modes of living, their food, their homes, pursuits, and their pursuers. It is easily seen that the accurate study of the habits of wild animals, undisturbed in their native haunts, is a study in which the man of science, unless skilled as a hunter, is at a discount. The true book of wild life is the open volume of tracks and trails spread over the whole wilderness and far more difficult than Greek to savans. This volume has written upon its broad pages the daily journal of savage society, telling of their deeds uninfluenced by human presence, the outgrowth of natural instincts. The nocturnal habits also of most of our wild animals, which, like the owl, sleep by day, and prowl by night, render it still more difficult to secure observations of their ways of life.

The summer woods give to us no such plainly written pages of this history as the winter's snow affords, for now though the night be dark, let there but be soft snow, and the footprints stand as records, plain as day. It is to some readings of these records in the snow, had this winter upon the slopes and summit of Mount Marcy, that I desire to call your attention.

Mount Marcy, or *Ta-ha-wus* (interpreted, "I cleave the clouds"), as it is said to have been called by the Indians, is unquestionably the highest of our mountains—over 5,400 feet in altitude above the sea. It rises sharply upward, a solid mass of rock, while huge ridges, each one a mountain, trending in different directions from its summit, support the central mass like giant buttresses. The summit is often lost amid, or soars above the clouds, and its slopes—below the bare, desolate, Alpine crest of rock—are densely covered with a stunted evergreen forest, rooted amid the crevices, the trees increasing in size and vigor as the altitude decreases. The deep valleys, descending between the mountain crests one and two thousand feet, thickly forest-covered on their slopes; the irregular plateau-like valleys north and south, and the little mossy nooks of level land upon its sides, are the haunts of its wild inhabitants, the fauna of the coldest, the most Alpine, and most desert portion of our territory.

Huge mountains tower upon every side, like captains encircling their chief. Whiteface far away, MacIntyre less distant, Mount Clinton and Mount Wright, Mount Haystack and Mount Skylight, Mount Colden and the Gothics, and far in the east Mount Dix, the Giant, and Macomb, and numberless others—the landmarks of the Adirondacks—show themselves.

This is a wild place for any living thing; let us see what creatures make their home here.

It is evident that he who is so fortunate as to first read the footprint writing on the snows of the slopes of Marcy, holds the key to a history of its fauna, and at the same time is permitted to be the first to ascertain the effects of the rigorous mountain climate upon the habits of the different species, as far as his observations go. The study of trails enables him to ascertain the approximate altitudes at which certain of our wild animals exist, and, in turn, by a careful classification of animals, he is enabled to show that within zones of different altitudes are found associated animals which belong to similar zones of cold, in higher latitudes. The flora of the Adirondack peaks has been studied; of the fauna of these mountain summits this is thought to be the first publication.

It may be mentioned that my presence among the mountains in the early portion of this winter, was occasioned by the work of the Adirondack survey, under the authority of the State, for which work appropriations had been made by the last Legislature, and that the constant duties of the survey permitted only the taking of natural history notes of such matters as came unsought before me. This paper, therefore, is only intended as a brief contribution to the winter history of our mountain fauna—preferable, perhaps, to a mere list of the species observed, which was all that I originally intended to present.

Winter may almost be said to have a perpetual lease of Mount Marcy. It is true that about the beginning of July, he finds his banks of snow badly broken by the sun's inroads—beyond his power to remedy—and so takes himself away to his cooler resort, gliding away to the south pole, which now demands his entire energies; but scarce two months will have elapsed before he will be back again.

If snow be the criterion, Mount Marcy has barely two true months of summer. The summit is often whitened with it as late as the beginning of July, and the first of September rarely passes without a premonitory, though temporary, covering of the crest with snow. It is safe to assume that the climactic winter of the summit commences at the latter portion of September or about the first of October, and ends in June.

Besides mentioning the different species, the presence of which have been determined, I shall call your attention briefly to the principal absentees—animals which once were or are now found in this locality in summer, but which were obviously absent during our stay, though with few exceptions, still met with in the warmer lowlands.

Studying the fauna in this manner, we find among the most important of the animals which have left a record of their presence by foot-prints in the snow—the panther, the *Felis concolor* of naturalists. This animal, the painter of the guides, the largest and most powerful of our Felidæ, is entirely carnivorous—an Ishmaelite among beasts. Immensely muscular, it is yet more remarkable for agility and swiftness of movement, and finds no difficulty in providing itself with game food. In the notch between Mount Marcy and Mount Skylight, one of the guides came upon large foot-prints in partially thawed snow, and following them up the slopes of Mount Marcy, through the dense, low timber, now ascending steeps, now traveling along snowy ridges, found in several places clear and unmistakable impressions, large, massive foot-prints of this mountain lion.

To myself the trail of this animal was far from unexpected. For years I had, summer after summer, remarked indications of their presence along the Opalescent river valley, and on the neighboring mountains, and less markedly, in the Panther gorge, once its undisturbed resort and home, for the *chat de montagne*, is here, as in Canada and the west, found true to its name, rendering it, veritably, the cat of the mountain. It is with regret that I must record that in the present instance his trail appeared to indicate that he was in the ignoble pursuit of rabbits! This could not be owing to necessity either, for deer in plenty were to be had in the valleys to the southward, and from indications observed during the summer, were not only frequently destroyed by panthers, but devoured with more haste than delicacy—flesh, hair, entrails, and skin being greedily eaten together. It may here be remarked that in accordance with the opinion of some of the guides, the panther, like others of our wild animals, is quite local in its habitation, the guides telling of one having a large and well marked foot-print, which for four or five years has resided upon a small mountain homestead of about 25 square miles, always returning after his occasional progresses to his more distant dominions. These long, direct journeys are also a strongly marked peculiarity of the panther. In the love of locality the panther shows a similarity to the common cat—*Felis domestica*—and leads us to surmise whether the strange affection which the latter creature exhibits for home rather than for an individual, is not the great, unextinguished wild trait of its character. Indications of the panther were also met with near Lake Tear of the Clouds, and other guides reported tracks seen near the Boreas. Where the exact habitation of this panther was we were unable to determine. Our advent must have annoyed him, for his trail was seen no more. Whether in the dark recesses among the rocks it found a home, or in some sunny glade with southern exposure, all sheltered from the chilly northern gales with dense evergreens, we do not know.

Next in importance to the panther in the list of species the trails of which were observed, is the gray or Canada lynx, the *peeshoo* or loup-cervier of the Indians—*Lyncus borealis* of De Kay, *Felis canadensis* of Richardson. Its large, bold foot-prints were observed on the southern slopes of Mount Marcy, and in the vicinity of little Lake Tear. Like the panther, it was also rabbit hunting, its foot-prints being superimposed upon those of its game, in the little paths which they had beaten in the snow. This large and apparently powerful animal, by some woodsmen erroneously called cat-a-mount, owes its imposing appearance to its heavy, dense covering of fur; and when deprived of its skin is so much reduced as to seem like another animal, the body looking much smaller, though the limbs and paws maintain the aspect of great strength. It is also entirely carnivorous, yet it is said by some to be good eating, its flesh resembling that of the rabbit. The flesh of any animal so purely carnivorous cannot, however, be considered fit food for man. Its usual residence is in the dense lowland swamps, and its presence at the altitude of over 4,300 feet in the gorges of the mountains indicates that it is not the swamps, but their inhabitants—the rabbit—that he desires. The trapping by a guide of two of these creatures near Elk lake, where the trail leaves it for Mount Marcy, seems to refute in some degree the opinion advanced by De Kay that it has no repugnance to water. The shallow and narrow outlet of the lake is nearly spanned at one point by a fallen tree which was selected by a pair of lynx as a bridge. A trap being set mid-way on the log, one of the creatures was captured, after which occurrence, unwarned by the fate of its companion, which could easily have been avoided if it had stepped through the shallow water, the other lynx, following the same path, planted its foot also in the trap. This is an animal which we might expect in a high, cold region, for to its general distribution throughout British America even to the shore of the Arctic sea, it owes its well earned title of *Canadian*. It is not recorded as having been met with in the State more than about one degree to the south of Mount Marcy.

One morning, this winter, as we ascended the steep slopes of Mount Skylight through the deep, freshly fallen snow, a dog belonging to one of the guides broke away fiercely upon a fresh trail, and filling the woods with his eager cry, combined into irregular echoing melody by the surrounding mountains, coursed his game to and fro, under the ledges and along the mountain sides to the steeper slopes of Marcy. An inspection of the trail showed the foot-prints of a black-cat—the *Mustela canadensis*, the animal often improperly known as the fisher—improperly because he is not a fisher, as it seldom eats other fish than those which it is able to steal from an angler. The foot-prints of this animal were frequently met with at different times and in different places upon Mount Marcy, the trail indicating animals different in size and age, so that it is probable that a number of these creatures make this vicinity their home. A carnivorous animal, agile and powerful withal, it was like its companion carnivora, hither come in search of rabbits, with (judging from the trail) an occasional diversion after mice, or other small game. Its inhabiting these mountain heights directly refutes the assertion that it does not frequent the same elevated regions as the martin. In one place, we observed where a black-cat at play had climbed to the summit of a huge rock, and doubling his forward paws beneath him, slid downward, ploughing up the snow. When pursued by the dog, they invariably took to their heels, and in long, easy leaps sped out upon the icy rocks fronting the precipitous sides of the mountain, and passed safely across the glary surface of the avalanche-swept slides. Constantly ranging, it seems to have no fixed habitation, and generally selects the night for its travel and its depredations.

The fourth of these mountain dwellers is the sable, of rich, rare fur and regal name; the *Mustella martes* of naturalists. This beautiful and rare animal, judging from the frequent tracks, is quite abundant in the forests on the side of Mount Marcy. It here occupies a region of country which owing to its elevation and coldness greatly resembles the semi-arctic portions of British America, and it is interesting to remark that no traces of it were found above the timber-line on the open, barren sub-Alpine portion of the mountain, in this respect maintaining the habits of their race, which—according to Hearne and Pennant, are never found in the barren lands near Behring's straits, either in America or Asia, though abundant in the scrubby forests margining the open. Thus this interesting little animal may be said to become a measure in climatology, and serves to give us as clear a conception of the relation of our mountain summits to the boreal regions of the continent, as does the better known arctic flora. Alas, for the poor rabbit, as though not sufficiently persecuted, he finds in the sable an insatiable foe. Hither and thither through the dwarf forest he pursues them; or, creeping stealthily, leaps upon one and opens its life blood upon the snow. Once this winter, I came upon a spot where a sable had killed a rabbit, evidently by seizing it by the throat and opening its veins. From the scene of slaughter a deep gouge-like depression in the snow, with foot-prints, showed where the sable had drawn away its quarry.

Tracks of the ermine, *Putoris noveboracensis* were recognized in one place, but it does not appear to be common; nor were the tracks of the other weasel distinctly recognized.

And now we come to the rabbit, as it is properly called, more properly known as the white or varying hare—*Lepus americanus.* Poor creature, it seems but created to be destroyed, yet is so abundant as to bear the inroads of its foes without apparent diminution. Timid and harmless, it seems to have the widest or most extensive range of any of the animals of north America, being found throughout nearly the whole of the British possessions from the Atlantic to the Pacific. As a true, varying hare, that is, annually changing its color, it seems to be confined to the districts of cold winters, and has everywhere the character of an inhabitant of boreal regions. The wonderful provision of nature, by which it is as well secured from observation in winter as in summer, is its most noticeable characteristic; and it is the more to be remarked, as with the exception of the ermine and weasel, it seems to be the only varying animal inhabiting the State. In 1872, in September, I captured a living specimen on the summit of Whiteface Mountain at an altitude of 4,900 feet. It was then of an even fawn-brown color and showed no sign of change. Early in November, in 1873, we met with many already turned entirely white, the snow having gained a depth of from a foot to eighteen inches. One or two glimpses of them this winter served to show that they were more like scudding snow than any animated thing. Their range upon Mount Marcy does not appear to extend above 5,000 feet, while upon the Rocky Mountains of our great west, I met with them at an altitude of 12,000 feet above the sea, associated with the ptarmigan and coney. Here, as among the snowy peaks of Colorado, I observed that while in the cold upper regions of ice and snow the hare had changed in color to its white winter coat, yet in the lowlands to which the snow had not yet reached they were still brown or mottled white and brown, indicating that they do not move from their localities with the coming of winter, and that climate controls the changing of their color. It may be possible that the polar hare, *Lepus glacialis* of Leach, has a home upon our high peaks, but this is as yet undetermined.

The common red squirrel, *Sciurus hudsonicus*, we found at an altitude of about 4,000 feet, increasing in abundance with decrease of altitude. The trails indicated that it was pursued and preyed upon by the sable. This squirrel here feeds on the seeds of the black spruce.

While engaged in trigonometrical work on the marsh, at the head of Lake Tear, from which during a thaw the snow had entirely disappeared, the guide's dog, which had been digging furiously for some time in the deep peat moss, suddenly drove from its burrow a good sized animal of the rat kind, resembling in size and color the star-nosed mole. Its rapid disappearance in some other hiding place prevented more than a brief glimpse of it. There was, however, a suggestion of resemblance to one of the geomys or sand rats. In color it was dark blue or gray-black, and its length was in the neighborhood of six inches. The soil in which it burrowed was (below the moss and peat) a coarse sand and fine gravel. The food of the animal is probably vegetable, the roots reached by its burrows.

Tracks of deer-mice were observed on the slopes of the mountain at all elevations not exceeding about 4,000 feet; and, occasionally the minute trail of a small shrew, supposed to be the *Sorex fosteri*, or Forster's shrew. I noticed it in many places where, as described by Richardson, it would leave the surface of the snow by descending some one of the little vertical tunnels left around some bough or branch or small sapling. This wonderful little animal inhabits even the desolate regions within the arctic circle, as far north as Latitude 67°. Richardson remarks that "The power of generating heat must be very great in this diminutive creature to preserve its slender limbs from freezing when the temperature sinks to 40 or 50 degrees below zero." If it is capable of enduring such a temperature, I am indeed surprised, as in 1872, early on a cold icy morning, on the summit of Mount Seward, the ground being covered with snow, I caught, alive, an active little specimen, which, to my surprise actually expired in my hands, apparently from cold. Nevertheless, it seems if not handled to be able to survive the most severe Adirondack winters.

Of birds, but three varieties have left their foot-prints on the snows of Mount Marcy, the raven, the partridge (ruffed grouse) and snow-birds. I never before met with a raven in the vicinity of Mount Marcy, but on my first ascent this winter as we mounted the ledges at the head of the great slide, a number of these huge birds arose, and uttering their peculiar hoarse croak, departed on slow, heavy-flapping pinions, regardless of revolver shots that followed them. The raven, therefore, is a winter habitant of Mount Marcy, leaving his foot-prints on the snowy ledges at 5,000 feet above the sea.

Early in last November, in one of our almost daily ascents of Mount Marcy, an eagle was noticed floating and circling with outstretched wings at about the height of the summit of the peak. It was apparently of the baldheaded variety. A large hawk—species unknown—was observed on another occasion, and one evening while we were descending from our labors, being still above the timber-line, a great owl sailed past, gazing upon us with huge eyes that appeared expressive of extreme wonder.

During the second or third day of survey work upon the summit of the mountain, late in the afternoon, a shout of surprise from one of the guides caused me to look quickly to the northward, where, judge my astonishment, not over 20 or 30 rods from us a flock of six wild geese flying with wonderful velocity, came towards us, passed over, and were gone. The faint, distant *honk* of the leader seeming to imply that they were bound for warmer latitudes. The wild goose is not an inhabitant of the Adirondacks, and these were evidently coming from more northern waters. This afforded, perhaps, the first opportunity of determining the height at which wild geese travel during their migrations. They seemed neither to ascend nor to descend, but kept a level course, and what is most remarkable, that course was as near the true astronomical meridian as it seems possible that a bird can fly! I would estimate the altitude of the flock in their flight at about 5,500 feet above the ocean level. It was the last place where I should have expected to have seen wild geese. A single discharge of a fowling-piece, had one been at hand, might have brought them all to the ground.

The Canada jay, *Garrulus canadensis*, was observed in the vicinity of little Lake Tear early in the winter, but with the increase of cold and snow seemed to leave the inhospitable heights, and descend to the depths of the Panther gorge. This might have been owing to the attractions of our camp, around which they fluttered in search of scraps.

A large, dark plumaged wood-pecker was noticed operating upon the spruce-trees at different points in the Panther gorge and on the slopes of the mountains, at an altitude of from 3,000 to 3,500 feet above tide. The species was not determined, but from its appearance it was supposed to be the *Picus villosus* or hairy wood-pecker.

Large flocks of the white snow-bird, *Plectrophanes nivalis*, were observed upon the snows, around the summit of Mount Marcy on different days; and once or twice two or three of a more plainly marked snow-bird, judged to be the Lapland (*P. Lapponicus*) were noticed. A small bird, not recognized, was seen feeding upon the cones of the spruce.

In entomology but few observations were made. Insects are the creatures of the summer. Bleak snows and freezing temperatures prohibit their appearance. During the latter portion of last October, the snows on Mount Marcy half disappeared from the open mountain in consequence of a thaw. This snow had been six inches deep in the valleys, a thousand feet below the summit. At this time, I noticed fluttering above the chilly rocks of the open summit, above the timber-line, a few solitary insects. A small moth which I caught proved entirely unknown to our accomplished State entomologist, and was forwarded by him to Dr. A. S. Packard, Jr., for examination. Dr. Packard recognizes it as the (*Cheimatobia*), *Operhoptera boreata* found in different portions of the country, and according to the doctor, "abundantly in Alaska." I also found a beetle during this thaw crawling upon the very summit of the peak.

In the spruce forest of the Panther gorge, at the foot of the mountain, many of the trees were observed to have been attacked by insects, probably the small beetles described by the State botanist in a recent paper before this Institute (*Hylurgus rufipennis* and *Apate rufipennis* Kirby). These trees were the resort of wood-peckers, who seemed to have a most active interest in the beetles or insects, piercing the bark everywhere, in search of them, and covering the snow at the foot of the trees with the fragments of bark.

Turning from the consideration of the animals which we have found in this cold upland region in winter, to those which, though their presence in such a locality might have been expected, are absent, we find the principal absentees to be:—

First. The moose, caraboo, deer, and the small or common gray rabbit. The marmot and the chipmunk or ground-squirrel are not to be expected, being winter sleepers, and seldom appearing during severe winters.

Second. The bear, porcupine, raccoon, wild cat or bay-lynx, wolf, fox, and the skunk—and, among birds the ptarmigan, blue-jay, and cedar-bird.

Early hunters and explorers assert that about half a century ago the moose was abundant and the caraboo or reindeer sometimes found on the upland barrens. They are not now found anywhere in this vicinity either in summer or winter. The absence of the deer is more remarkable, but this may be readily accounted for by the cold, barren, and sterile character of the country, and attractions of the more inviting lowlands, abounding in rich, juicy browse. Early in the winter the bear might have been expected, but not a single trail was seen, though within half a dozen miles in the lowlands their paw-writings in the snow were exceedingly abundant, and indeed hardly a week passed without the trapping and killing of one or more by guides, so that bear's meat, boiled, fried, or roast—in default of anything better—became in our camp a constant dish. To the skull of one of these bears, shot by a guide in the Round Mountain notch, I would call your attention, for a peculiarity in its dentition, as it lacks the exact number of teeth to which, according to classification it is properly entitled. This bear was killed at a spot elevated about 2,000 feet above tide. The porcupine (*urson*) can have no other excuse for its absence than the over abundance of the black-cat—its mortal enemy—who may possibly have exterminated it in this section. The absence of the wolf may be accounted for by his general scarcity; that of the fox by his being far too cunning to be found in any such cold country, and the raccoon also as a lover of the warmer lowlands could hardly be expected. The absence of the small gray rabbit or hare is a little surprising; perhaps it may yet be met with. The ptarmigan or white partridge is sought for in vain, and probably does not exist within the State. It would, undoubtedly, if introduced, find a livelihood upon the open or barren portion of Mount Marcy in summer, and secure sufficient support among the small dwarf timber in winter.

The blue-jay which I noticed frequently at this season at altitudes of from 1,000 to 2,500 feet did not show itself upon Mount Marcy, nor was a specimen of cedar-bird noticed anywhere, even in the valleys or lowlands.

But what a strange and wonderful winter habitation have these mountain dwellers. The peak's appearance at a distance is now that of a vast snow cone or dome uprearing itself against the dark-blue vault of heaven. Black ledges here and there show themselves in deep, sharp contrast with the spotless mantling around, and dark evergreen forests slope upward from the gloomy depths of the gorges; breaking, as the ledges are reached, into long, upward trending curves or belts of timber that struggle up the cliffs, diminishing and dwarfing till the timber-line is reached. From the icy summit we behold a very different view. We stand upon the highest land in New York, the centre of an icy citadel! Frozen clouds drift slowly and wearily below. Away to the south and west in billows and billows of dazzling silver, they extend to where the horizon joins with them in mingled brilliancy. The sun sinks slowly westward. Behind us on each mountain side the deepening shadows of other mountains climb. The gorges begin to fill with unutterable gloom; and now the sinking sun shakes from itself for one moment the haze and mist, and covers our mountain with a burst of glory that makes it seem transfigured. All the frost wreathed forest on the sun-side slopes, bursts into sparkling light, each tree a weird Christmas tree, adorned with wonderful and fantastic frost-work as though the frozen clouds had midst their limbs become entangled and, settling, enwrapped them all in silver fleece. The sun descends amidst the clouds; each white mountain peak beams with faintest crimson—then all is gray and chill and night.